COMPLETE BOOK OF
Grade 4

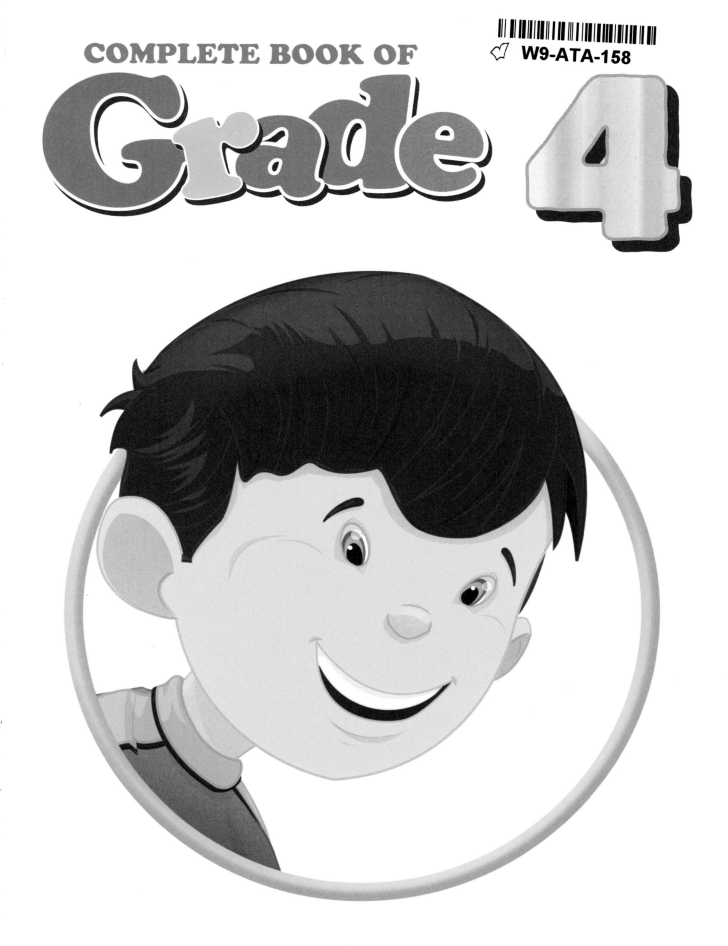

AMERICAN
EDUCATION
PUBLISHING™

An imprint of Carson-Dellosa Publishing LLC
Greensboro, North Carolina

American Education Publishing™
An imprint of Carson-Dellosa Publishing LLC
P.O. Box 35665
Greensboro, NC 27425 USA

06-174141120

Dear Parents, Caregivers, and Educators,

The *Complete Book* series provides young learners an exciting and dynamic way to learn the basic skills essential to learning success. This vivid workbook will guide your student step-by-step through a variety of engaging and developmentally appropriate activities in phonics, reading comprehension, math, problem solving, and writing.

The *Complete Book of Grade 4* is designed for learning reinforcement and can be used as a tool for independent study. This workbook includes:

- High-interest lessons.
- Easy-to-understand examples and directions.
- Challenging concepts presented in simple language.
- Review lessons to measure progress and reinforce skills.
- Expanded teaching suggestions to guide further learning.

To find other learning materials that will interest your young learner and encourage school success, visit www.carsondellosa.com

Reading

Say It Short

Vowels are the letters **a**, **e**, **i**, **o**, **u** and sometimes **y**. There are five short vowels: **ă** as in **a**pple, **ě** as in **e**gg and br**ea**th, **ĭ** as in s**i**ck, **ŏ** as in t**o**p and **ŭ** as in **u**p.

Directions: Complete the exercises using words from the box.

blend	insist	health	pump	crop
fact	pinch	pond	hatch	plug

1. Write each word under its vowel sound.

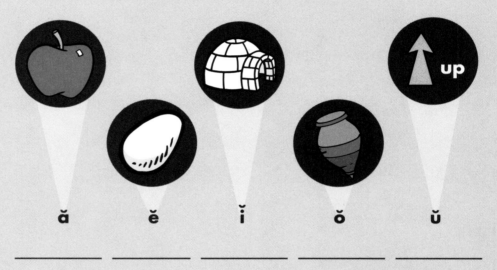

ă ⎮ ě ⎮ ĭ ⎮ ŏ ⎮ ŭ

_____ _____ _____ _____ _____

_____ _____ _____ _____ _____

2. Complete these sentences, using a word with the vowel sound given. Use each word from the box only once. Not all words will be used.

Here's an interesting (**ă**) _____ about your

(**ě**) _____ .

The boys enjoyed fishing in the (**ŏ**) _____ .

They (**ĭ**) _____ on watching the egg

(**ă**) _____ .

(**ě**) _____ in a (**ĭ**) _____ of salt.

Did you put the (**ŭ**) _____ in the bathtub this time?

Say It Long: a and e

Long **ā** can be spelled **a** as in **apron**, **ai** as in **pail**, **ay** as in **pay** or **a-e** as in **lake**. Long **ē** can be spelled **ea** as in **real** or **ee** as in **deer**.

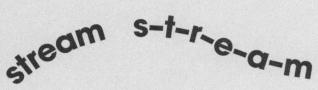

stream s-t-r-e-a-m stream

Directions: Complete the exercises with words from the box.

deal	clay	grade	weave	stream
pain	tape	sneeze	claim	treat

1. Write each word in the row with the matching vowel sound.

ā _____ _____ _____ _____ _____

ē _____ _____ _____ _____ _____

2. Complete each sentence, using a word with the vowel sound given. Use each word from the word box only once. Not all words will be used.

Everyone in (ā) _____ four ate an ice-cream

(ē) _____.

Every time I (ē) _____, I feel

(ā) _____ in my chest.

When I (ē) _____ with yarn, I put a piece of

(ā) _____ on the loose ends so they won't come undone.

You (ā) _____ you got a good

(ē) _____ on your new bike, but I still think you paid too much.

Say It Long: i and o

Long **ī** can be spelled **i** as in **wild**, **igh** as in **night**, **i-e** as in **wipe** or **y** as in **try**. Long **ō** can be spelled **o** as in **most**, **oa** as in **toast**, **ow** as in **throw** or **o-e** as in **hope**.

Directions: Complete the exercises with words from the box.

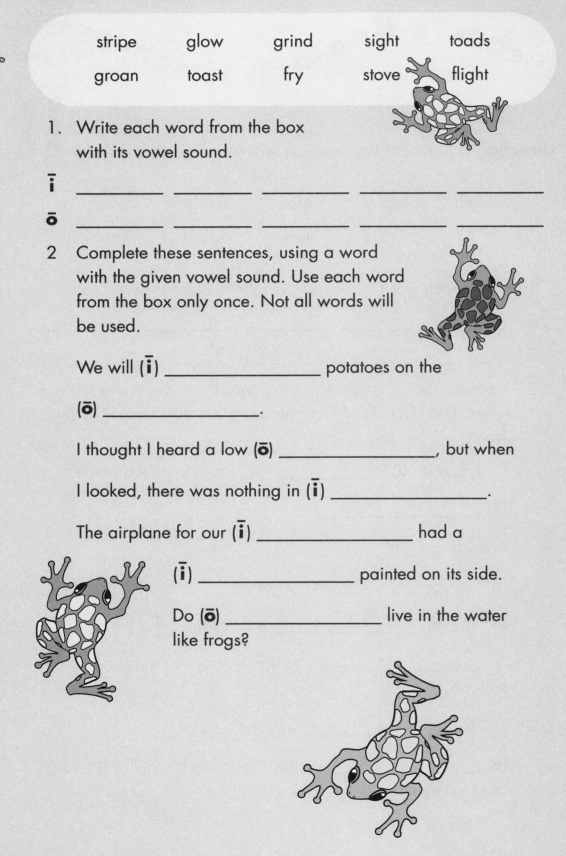

| stripe | glow | grind | sight | toads |
| groan | toast | fry | stove | flight |

1. Write each word from the box with its vowel sound.

   ī _____ _____ _____ _____ _____

   ō _____ _____ _____ _____ _____

2 Complete these sentences, using a word with the given vowel sound. Use each word from the box only once. Not all words will be used.

   We will (**ī**) _____ potatoes on the

   (**ō**) _____.

   I thought I heard a low (**ō**) _____, but when

   I looked, there was nothing in (**ī**) _____.

   The airplane for our (**ī**) _____ had a

   (**ī**) _____ painted on its side.

   Do (**ō**) _____ live in the water like frogs?

Say It Long: u

Long **ū** can be spelled, **u-e** as in **cube** or **ew** as in **few**. Some sounds are similar in sound to **u** but are not true **u** sounds, such as the **oo** in **tooth**, the **o-e** in **move** and the **ue** in **blue**.

Directions: Complete each sentence using a word from the box. Do not use the same word more than once.

| blew | tune | flute | cute | June | glue |

1. Yesterday, the wind _____ so hard it knocked down a tree on our street.

2. My favorite instrument is the _____.

3. The little puppy in the window is so _____.

4. I love _____ because it's so warm, and we get out of school.

5. For that project, you will need scissors, construction paper

   and _____.

6. I recognize that song because it has a

   familiar _____.

Get a Kick Out of k

The **k** sound can be spelled with **k** as in **peek**, **c** as in **cousin**, **ck** as in **sick**, **ch** as in **Chris** and **cc** as in **accuse**. In some words, however, one **c** may be pronounced **k** and the other **s** as in **accident**.

Directions: Answer the questions with words from the box.

Christmas	freckles	command	cork	jacket
accused	castle	stomach	rake	accident

1. Which two words spell **k** with a **k**?

   _____   _____

2. Which two words spell **k** with **ck**?

   _____   _____

3. Which two words spell **k** with **ch**?

   _____   _____

4. Which five words spell **k** with **c** or **cc**?

   _____   _____

   _____   _____

   _____

5. Complete these sentences, using a word with **k** spelled as shown. Use each word from the box only once. Not all words will be used.

   Dad gave Mom a garden (**k**) _____ for

   (**ch**) _____.

   There are (**ck**) _____ on my face and

   (**ch**) _____.

   The people (**cc**) _____ her of taking a

   (**ck**) _____.

   The police took (**c**) _____ after the

   (**cc**) _____.

Undercover f

The **f** sound can be spelled with **f** as in **fun**, **gh** as in **laugh** or **ph** as in **phone**.

Directions: Answer the questions with words from the box.

> fuss   paragraph   phone   friendship   freedom
> defend   flood   alphabet   rough   laughter

1. Which three words spell **f** with **ph**?

   _____   _____

   _____

2. Which two words spell **f** with **gh**?

   _____   _____

3. Which five words spell **f** with an **f**?

   _____   _____

   _____   _____

   _____

4. Complete these sentences, using a word with **f** spelled as shown. Use each word from the box only once. Not all words will be used.

   A **(f)** _____ can help you through

   (gh) _____ times.

   The soldiers will **(f)** _____ our

   (f) _____.

   Can you say the **(ph)** _____ backwards?

   When I answered the **(ph)** _____, all I

   could hear was **(gh)** _____.

   If it keeps raining, we'll have a **(f)** _____.

On the Scene with s

The **s** sound can be spelled with **s** as in **super** or **ss** as in **assign**, **c** as in **city**, **ce** as in **fence** or **sc** as in **scene**. In some words, though, **sc** is pronounced **sk**, as in **scare**.

exciting   medicine   lettuce   peace   scissors

slice   scientist   sauce   bracelet   distance

Directions: Answer the questions using words from the box.

1. Which five words spell **s** with an **s** or **ss**?

    _____   _____

    _____   _____

    _____

2. Which two words spell **s** with just a **c**?

    _____   _____

3. Which six words spell **s** with a **ce**?

    _____   _____

    _____   _____

    _____   _____

4. Which two words spell **s** with **sc**?

    _____   _____

5. Complete these sentences, using a word with **s** spelled as shown. Use each word from the box only once. Not all words will be used.

    My (**ce**) _____ fell off my wrist into the

    tomato _____ (**s and ce**).

    My salad was just a (**s and ce**) _____

    of (**ce**) _____.

    It was (**c**) _____ to see the lions, even though

    they were a long (**s and ce**) _____ away.

Give Me a Break

A **syllable** is a word—or part of a word—with only one vowel sound. Some words have just one syllable, such as **cat**, **dog**, and **house**. Some words have two syllables, such as **in-sist** and **be-fore**. Some words have three syllables, such as **re-mem-ber**; four syllables, such as **un-der-stand-ing**; or more. Often words are easier to spell if you know how many syllables they have.

Directions: Write the number of syllables in each word below.

Word	Syllables		Word	Syllables
1. amphibian	_____	11.	want	_____
2. liter	_____	12.	communication	_____
3. guild	_____	13.	pedestrian	_____
4. chili	_____	14.	kilo	_____
5. vegetarian	_____	15.	autumn	_____
6. comedian	_____	16.	dinosaur	_____
7. warm	_____	17.	grammar	_____
8. piano	_____	18.	dry	_____
9. barbarian	_____	19.	solar	_____
10. chef	_____	20.	wild	_____

Directions: Next to each number, write words with the same number of syllables. **syl-la-bles**

1 _____   _____

 _____   _____

2 _____   _____

 _____   _____

3 _____   _____

 _____

4 _____   _____

 _____

5 _____   _____

Say It with Synonyms

A **synonym** is a word that means the same, or nearly the same, as another word.

Example: quick and **fast**

Directions: Draw lines to match the words in Column A with their synonyms in Column B.

Column A	Column B
plain	unusual
career	vocation
rare	disappear
vanish	greedy
beautiful	finish
selfish	simple
complete	lovely

Directions: Choose a word from Column A or Column B to complete each sentence below.

1. Dad was very excited when he discovered the

   _____ coin for sale on the display counter.

2. My dog is a real magician; he can _____ into thin air when he sees me getting his bath ready!

3. Many of my classmates joined the discussion about

   _____ choices we had considered.

4. "You will need to _____ your report on ancient Greece before you sign up for computer time," said Mr. Rastetter.

5. Your _____ painting will be on display in the art show.

Madam, I'm Adam

Can you think forward and backward? If so, you should have no problem with palindromes. **Palindromes** are words or sentences that are spelled the same forward or backward.

Examples: noon, eve, mom, wow
a man, a plan, a canal, Panama

Directions: Read the definitions. Write the palindromes on the lines. If you get stuck, work with a partner.

1. Another name for a soft drink _____

2. What you typically call your father _____

3. Short for Nancy _____

4. What one does with one's eyes _____

5. Female sheep _____

6. An instrument used to locate airplanes _____

7. To choke _____

8. Boat used by Eskimos _____

Directions: Write as many palindromes as you can. A few have been done for you.

bib, Bob, did, dad _____

_____

_____

_____

12-7-15   Jon G

Hear! Here! Homophones!

Homophones are two words that sound the same, have different meanings and are usually spelled differently.

Example: write and **right**

Directions: Write the correct homophone in each sentence below.

weight — how heavy something is

wait — to be patient

threw — tossed

through — passing between

steal — to take something that doesn't belong to you

steel — a heavy metal

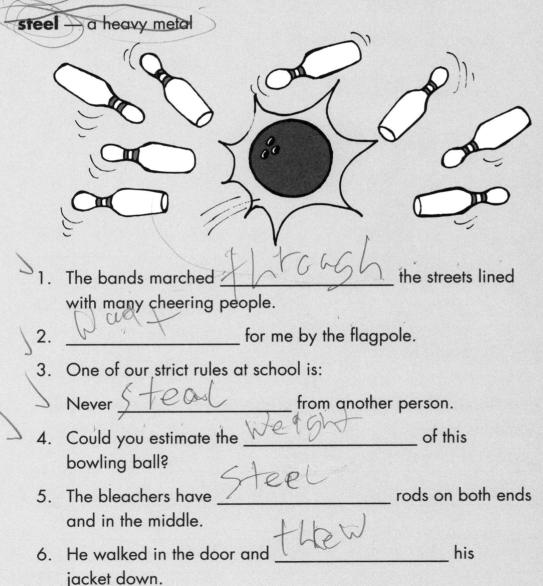

1. The bands marched _____through_____ the streets lined with many cheering people.

2. _____Wait_____ for me by the flagpole.

3. One of our strict rules at school is: Never _____steal_____ from another person.

4. Could you estimate the _____weight_____ of this bowling ball?

5. The bleachers have _____steel_____ rods on both ends and in the middle.

6. He walked in the door and _____threw_____ his jacket down.

Calling All Homophones

Directions: Choose the correct word in parentheses to complete each sentence. The first one is done for you.

1. Jimmy was so _____ **bored** _____ that he fell asleep. (board, bored)

2. We'll need a _____ and some nails to repair the fence. (board, bored)

3. Do you want _____ after dinner? (desert, dessert)

4. Did the soldier _____ his post? (desert, dessert)

5. The soldier had a _____ pinned to his uniform. (medal, meddle)

6. I told her not to _____ in other people's lives. (medal, meddle)

7. Jack had to repair the emergency _____ on his car. (brake, break)

8. Please be careful not to _____ my bicycle. (brake, break)

9. The race _____ was a very difficult one. (coarse, course)

10. We will need some _____ sandpaper to finish the job. (coarse, course)

Prefix Pros

A **prefix** is a syllable at the beginning of a word that changes its meaning.

Directions: Add a prefix to the beginning of each word in the box to make a word with the meaning given in each sentence below. The first one is done for you.

PREFIX	MEANING
bi	two or twice
en	to make
in	within
mis	wrong
non	not or without
pre	before
re	again
un	not

grown   write   information   large   cycle   sense

1. Antonio's foot hurt because his toenail was (growing within).

   ingrown

2. If you want to see what is in the background, you will have to (make bigger) the photograph.

   _____

3. I didn't do a very good job on my homework, so I will have to (write it again) it.

   _____

4. The newspaper article about the event has some (wrong facts).

   _____

5. I hope I get a (vehicle with two wheels) for my birthday.

   _____

6. The story he told was complete (words without meaning)!

   _____

Save the Best for Last

A **suffix** is a syllable at the end of a word that changes its meaning. In most cases, when adding a suffix that begins with a vowel, drop the final **e** of the root word. For example, **fame** becomes **famous**. Also, change a final **y** in the root word to **i** before adding any suffix except **ing**. For example, **silly** becomes **silliness**.

Directions: Add a suffix to the end of each word in the box to make a word with the meaning given (in parentheses) in each sentence below. The first one is done for you.

SUFFIX	MEANING
ful	full of
ity	quality or degree
ive	have or tend to be
less	without or lacking
able	able to be
ness	state of
ment	act of
or	person that does something
ward	in the direction of

like   thought   pay   thank   act   happy

1. Mike was (full of thanks) for a hot meal.

   thankful

2. I was (without thinking) for forgetting your birthday.

   _____

3. Tasha is such a (able to be liked) girl!

   _____

4. Jill's wedding day was one of great (the state of being happy).

   _____

5. The (person who performs) was very good in the play.

   _____

6. I have to make a (act of paying) for the stereo I bought.

   _____

Odd One Out

Classifying is placing similar things into categories.

Directions: Classify each group by crossing out the word that does not belong.

1. factory   hotel   lodge   pattern

2. Thursday   September   December   October

3. cottage   hut   carpenter   castle

4. cupboard   orchard   refrigerator stove

5. Christmas   Thanksgiving Easter   spring

6. brass   copper   coal   tin

7. stomach   breathe   liver   brain

8. teacher   mother   dentist   office

9. musket   faucet   bathtub   sink

10. basement   attic   kitchen   neighborhood

TV Time!

Directions: Read the title of each TV show. Write the correct number to tell what kind of show it is.

1 — Cooking	3 — Sports	5 — Humor
2 — Nature	4 — Mystery	6 — Famous People

_____   *The Secret of the Lost Locket*

_____   *Learn Tennis With the Pros*

_____   *Birds in the Wild*

_____   *The Life of George Washington*

_____   *Great Recipes From Around the World*

_____   *A Laugh a Minute*

Directions: Read the description of each TV show. Write the number of each show above in the blank.

_____   The years before he became the first president of the United States are examined.

_____   Featured: eagles and owls

_____   Clues lead Detective Logan to a cemetery in his search for the missing necklace.

_____   Famous players give tips on buying a racket.

_____   Six ways to cook chicken

_____   Cartoon characters in short stories

8 O'CLOCK MOVIE

Follow Me!

Directions: Follow the directions below to reach a "mystery" location on the map.

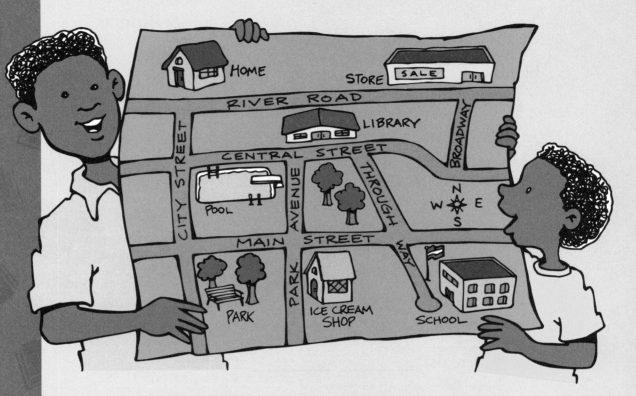

1. Begin at home.

2. Drive east on River Road.

3. Turn south on Broadway.

4. Drive to Central Street and turn west.

5. When you get to City Street, turn south.

6. Turn east on Main Street and drive one block to Park Avenue; turn north.

7. At Central Street turn east, then turn southeast on Through Way.

8. Drive to the end of Through Way. Your "mystery" location is to the east.

You are at the _____.

Can you write an easier way to get back home?

_____

_____

_____

Let's Get Cooking!

Sequencing is putting items or events in logical order.

Directions: Read the recipe. Then, number the steps in order for making brownies.

Preheat the oven to 350 degrees. Grease an 8-inch square baking dish.

In a mixing bowl, place two squares (2 ounces) of unsweetened chocolate and $\frac{1}{3}$ cup butter. Place the bowl in a pan of hot water and heat it to melt the chocolate and the butter.

When the chocolate is melted, remove the pan from the heat. Add 1 cup sugar and two eggs to the melted chocolate and beat it. Next, stir in $\frac{3}{4}$ cup sifted flour, $\frac{1}{2}$ teaspoon baking powder and $\frac{1}{2}$ teaspoon salt. Finally, mix in $\frac{1}{2}$ cup chopped nuts.

Spread the mixture in the greased baking dish. Bake for 30 to 35 minutes. The brownies are done when a toothpick stuck in the center comes out clean. Let the brownies cool. Cut them into squares.

_____ Stick a toothpick in the center of the brownies to make sure they are done.

_____ Mix in chopped nuts.

_____ Melt chocolate and butter in a mixing bowl over a pan of hot water.

_____ Cool brownies and cut into squares.

_____ Beat in sugar and eggs.

_____ Spread mixture in a baking dish.

_____ Stir in flour, baking powder and salt.

_____ Bake for 30 to 35 minutes.

_____ Turn oven to 350 degrees and grease pan.

Right on Track

Directions: Below is part of a schedule for trains leaving New York City for cities all around the country. Use the schedule to answer the questions.

Destination	Train Number	Departure Time	Arrival Time
Birmingham	958	9:00 a.m.	12:31 a.m.
Boston	611	7:15 a.m.	4:30 p.m.
Cambridge	398	8:15 a.m.	1:14 p.m.
Cincinnati	242	5:00 a.m.	7:25 p.m.
Detroit	415	1:45 p.m.	4:40 a.m.
Evansville	623	3:00 p.m.	8:28 a.m.

1. What is the number of the train that leaves latest in the day?

   _____

2. What city is the destination for train number 623?

   _____

3. What time does the train for Boston leave New York?

   _____

4. What time does train number 415 arrive in Detroit?

   _____

5. What is the destination of the train that leaves earliest in the day?

   _____

Label Lingo

Directions: You should never take any medicine without your parents' permission, but it is good to know how to read the label of a medicine bottle. Read the label to answer the questions.

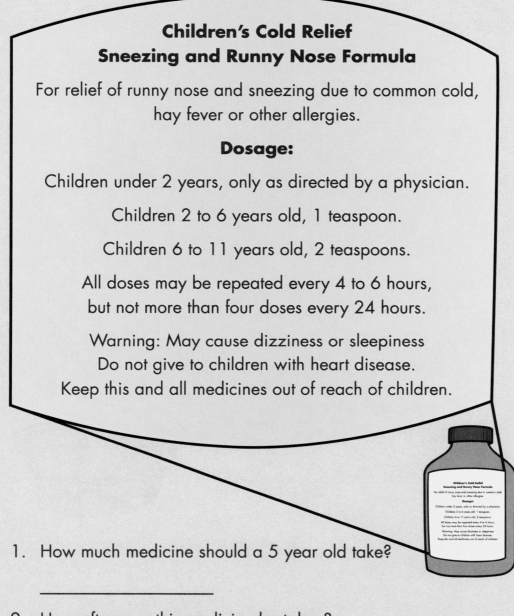

Children's Cold Relief
Sneezing and Runny Nose Formula

For relief of runny nose and sneezing due to common cold, hay fever or other allergies.

Dosage:

Children under 2 years, only as directed by a physician.

Children 2 to 6 years old, 1 teaspoon.

Children 6 to 11 years old, 2 teaspoons.

All doses may be repeated every 4 to 6 hours, but not more than four doses every 24 hours.

Warning: May cause dizziness or sleepiness
Do not give to children with heart disease.
Keep this and all medicines out of reach of children.

1. How much medicine should a 5 year old take?

_____

2. How often can this medicine be taken?

_____

3. How do you know how much medicine to give a 1 year old?

_____

4. Who should not take this medicine?

_____

Trees, Please

Directions: Use the following newspaper ad to answer the questions.

House of Plants
Colorful Flowering Trees

Flowering Crab Apple Trees
Sizes up to 10 ft.
Beautiful Colored Spring Flowers
Dark Green Foliage
Red, Pink, White Blossoms

25% OFF

Reg. $29.99 to $149.99
NOW $22.49 to $112.50

House of Plants
6280 River Road

1. How big are the biggest flowering crab apple trees for sale?

_____

2. What are the regular prices?

_____

3. What are the sale prices?

_____

That's a Fact!

Facts are statements or events that have happened and can be proven to be true.

Example: George Washington was the first president of the United States.

This statement is a fact. It can be proven to be true by researching the history of our country.

Opinions are statements that express how someone thinks or feels.

Example: George Washington was the greatest president the United States has ever had.

This statement is an opinion. Many people agree that George Washington was a great president, but not everyone agrees he was the greatest president. In some people's opinion, Abraham Lincoln was our greatest president.

Directions: Read each sentence. Write **F** for fact or **O** for opinion.

_____ 1. There is three feet of snow on the ground.

_____ 2. A lot of snow makes the winter enjoyable.

_____ 3. Chris has a better swing set than Mary.

_____ 4. Both Chris and Mary have swing sets.

_____ 5. California is a state.

_____ 6. California is the best state in the west.

Directions: Write three facts and three opinions.

Facts:

1) _____

2) _____

3) _____

Opinions:

1) _____

2) _____

3) _____

Catch a Clue

When you read, you may confuse words that look alike. You can tell when you read a word incorrectly because it doesn't make sense. You can tell from the **context** (the other words in the sentence or the sentences before or after) what the word should be. These **context clues** can help you figure out the meaning of a word by relating it to other words in the sentence.

Directions: Circle the correct word for each sentence below. Use the context to help you.

1. We knew we were in trouble as soon as we heard the crash.

   The baseball had gone (through, thought) the picture window!

2. She was not able to answer my question because her

   (month, mouth) was full of pizza.

3. Asia is the largest continent in the (world, word).

4. I'm not sure I heard the teacher correctly. Did he say what

   I (through, thought) he said?

5. I was not with them on vacation so I don't know a (think, thing) about what happened.

6. My favorite (month, mouth) of the year is July because I love fireworks and parades!

What Nonsense!

Directions: In each sentence below, circle the correct meaning for the nonsense word.

1. Be careful when you put that plate back on the shelf—
   it is **quibbable**.

   flexible   colorful   breakable

2. What is your favorite kind of **tonn**, pears or bananas?

   fruit   salad   purple

3. The **dinlay** outside this morning was very chilly; I needed
   my sweater.

   tree   vegetable   temperature

4. The whole class enjoyed the **weat**. They wanted to see it
   again next Friday.

   colorful   plant   video

5. Ashley's mother brought in a **zundy** she made by hand.

   temperature   quilt   plant

6. "Why don't you sit over here, Ronnie? That **sloey** is not very
   comfortable," said Mr. Gross.

   chair   car   cat

What's Next?

Directions: In each group below, one event in the sequence is missing. Write a sentence that makes sense in the sequence.

1. The clouds grew very dark and we could hear thunder.
2. All of a sudden, the wind started to blow very hard.
3. _____

1. The volleyball game was very boring at first.
2. _____
3. The home crowd cheered so loudly that I had to cover my ears.

1. _____
2. The boys gathered all the garden tools and put them in the wheelbarrow.
3. "Well, it was hard work, but we got it done, boys!" said Jim.

1. The teacher gave us our homework assignment early in the day.
2. Since the school assembly had to be cancelled, we had an extra study hall.
3. _____

Living a Double Life

Directions: Read about how a tadpole becomes a frog. Then, number the stages in order below.

Frogs and toads belong to a group of animals called *amphibians* (am-FIB-ee-ans). This means "living a double life." Frogs and toads live a "double life" because they live part of their lives in water and part on land. They are able to do this because their bodies change as they grow. This series of changes is called *metamorphosis* (met-a-MORE-fa-sis).

A mother frog lays her eggs in water and then leaves them on their own to grow. The eggs contain cells—the tiny "building blocks" of all living things—that multiply and grow. Soon the cells grow into a swimming tadpole. Tadpoles breathe through gills—small holes in their sides—like fish do. They spend all of their time in the water.

The tadpole changes as it grows. Back legs slowly form. Front legs begin inside the tadpole under the gill holes. They pop out when they are fully developed. At the same time, lungs, which a frog uses to breathe instead of gills, are almost ready to be used.

As the tadpole reaches the last days of its life in the water, its tail seems to disappear. When all of the tadpole's body parts are ready for life on land, it has become a frog.

_____ The front legs pop out. The lungs are ready to use for breathing.

_____ The cells in the egg multiply and grow.

_____ The tadpole has become a frog.

_____ Back legs slowly form.

_____ Soon the cells grow into a swimming tadpole.

_____ Front legs develop inside the tadpole.

_____ The tadpole's tail seems to disappear.

_____ A mother frog lays her eggs in water.

Get to the Point

The **main idea** is the most important idea, or main point, in a sentence, paragraph, or story.

Directions: Circle the main idea for each sentence.

1. Emily knew she would be late if she watched the end of the TV show.

   a. Emily likes watching TV.

   b. Emily is always running late.

   c. If Emily didn't leave, she would be late.

2. The dog was too strong and pulled Jason across the park on his leash.

   a. The dog is stronger than Jason.

   b. Jason is not very strong.

   c. Jason took the dog for a walk.

3. Jennifer took the book home so she could read it over and over.

   a. Jennifer loves to read.

   b. Jennifer loves the book.

   c. Jennifer is a good reader.

4. Jerome threw the baseball so hard it broke the window.

   a. Jerome throws baseballs very hard.

   b. Jerome was mad at the window.

   c. Jerome can't throw very straight.

5. Lori came home and decided to clean the kitchen for her parents.

   a. Lori is a very nice person.

   b. Lori did a favor for her parents.

   c. Lori likes to cook.

6. It was raining so hard that it was hard to see the road through the windshield.

   a. It always rains hard in April.

   b. The rain blurred our vision.

   c. It's hard to drive in the rain.

Winter Wonderland

The **main idea** of a story or report is a sentence that summarizes the most important point. If a story or report is only one paragraph in length, then the main idea is usually stated in the first sentence (topic sentence). If it is longer than one paragraph, then the main idea is a general sentence including all the important points of the story or report.

Directions: Read the story about snow fun. Then, draw an **X** in the blank for the main idea.

> After a big snowfall, my friends and I enjoy playing in the snow. We bundle up in snow clothes at our homes, then meet with sleds at the hill by my house.
>
> One by one, we take turns sledding down the hill to see who will go the farthest and the fastest. Sometimes we have a contest to see whose sled will reach the fence at the foot of the hill first.
>
> When we tire of sledding, we may build a snowman or snowforts. Sometimes we have a friendly snowball fight.
>
> The end of our snow fun comes too quickly, and we head home to warm houses, dry clothes and hot chocolate.

1. What is the main idea?

    _____ Playing in the snow with friends is an enjoyable activity.

    _____ Sledding in the snow is fast and fun.

If you selected the first option, you are correct. The paragraphs discuss the enjoyable things friends do on a snowy day.

The second option is not correct because the entire story is not about sledding. Only the second paragraph discusses sledding. The other paragraphs discuss the additional ways friends have fun in the snow.

2. Write a paragraph about what you like to do on snowy days. Remember to make the first sentence your main idea.

    _____

    _____

    _____

    _____

Taking a Trip

Directions: Read this story about a class field trip. Pay careful attention to the details. As you read, think about the beginning, middle and end of the story.

Megan was very excited on her way to school. This was the day her fourth-grade class was going on its field trip to the town historical museum. As she looked out the bus window, she noticed that the bus was stopping at her friend Emily's house. She watched as Emily and her little sister climbed aboard the bus.

"I see you remembered your sack lunch," said Megan as her friend plopped down into the seat next to her.

"Remember? How could I forget?" said Emily breathlessly. "That's all we've talked about in class for the last two days."

The girls knew everyone was looking forward to the trip. Some children in the class were looking forward to the trip because they usually didn't get to ride a bus to school. Others in the class had been enjoying the study of their town's history and learning about what early life had been like for their ancestors. The girls laughed as they remembered what their classmate Nico had said, "I can't wait for the field trip—a day out of school!"

Soon they were at school and joined the rest of the fourth graders in homeroom. Obviously, by the chatter around them, their classmates were just as excited as they were.

Taking a Trip

"Take your seats, class," said Miss Haynes. "No one gets on the bus for the trip until we take care of some business first. After I check attendance and all of you have your name tags, we can think about getting lined up. While I check attendance, Ms. Diehl and Mrs. Shaloub will collect your lunch sacks and put them in the cooler. Make sure your names are on your lunch sacks, please!"

All heads turned and looked at the back of the room as Nico let out a loud moan. "Oh, no! I left my lunch at home on the table by the door!"

Miss Haynes said, "Fortunately, the cafeteria will be able to put together a sack lunch for you." She wrote a note to the kitchen staff to explain the problem and sent a much happier Nico on his way down the hall. "Hurry, Nico, we load the bus for our trip in 10 minutes."

"Don't worry, Miss Haynes, I'll be there in time!" replied Nico as he hurried out the door.

True to his word, Nico returned, sack lunch in hand, with plenty of time to spare. Business was soon taken care of and the children and adults were on the bus, heading for their exciting day at the museum.

Taking a Trip

Directions: Reread the story, if necessary. Then, choose an important event from the beginning, middle and end of the story, and write it below.

Beginning: _____

_____

Middle: _____

_____

End: _____

_____

Directions: Number these story events in the order in which they happened.

_____ Nico moaned, "Oh, no! I left my lunch on the table at home!"

_____ Megan watched as the bus stopped at Emily's house to pick up Emily and her little sister.

_____ Miss Haynes sent Nico to the cafeteria with a note explaining the problem.

_____ The teacher said they had some business to take care of before they could leave on the trip.

_____ Nico quickly returned with a sack lunch packed by the cafeteria helpers.

_____ Megan told Emily, "I see you remembered your sack lunch."

_____ The fourth graders finally loaded onto the bus for the field trip.

Taking a Trip

Directions: Answer the questions below about the story.

1. Who were the two adult helpers that would be going on the trip with Miss Haynes' class?

   _____

2. The students in Miss Haynes' class were excited about the field trip for different reasons. What were the three different reasons mentioned in the story?

   a. _____

   b. _____

   c. _____

3. What business did Miss Haynes need to take care of before the class could leave on its trip?

   _____

Directions: Write the letter of the definition beside the word it defines. If you need help, use a dictionary or check the context of the story.

   _____ ancestors

   _____ fortunately

   _____ plopped

   _____ obviously

a. sat down, not very gently

b. easy to understand; without doubt

c. family members that lived in the past, such as grandparents

d. in a favorable way

The Princess and the Pea

Fairy tales are short stories written for children involving magical characters.

Directions: Read the story. Then, answer the questions.

Once there was a prince who wanted to get married. The catch was, he had to marry a real princess. The Prince knew that real princesses were few and far between. When they heard he was looking for a bride, many young women came to the palace. All claimed to be real princesses.

"Hmmm," thought the Prince. "I must think of a way to sort out the real princesses from the fake ones. I will ask the Queen for advice."

Luckily, since he was a prince, the Queen was also his mother. "A real princess is very delicate," said the Queen. "She must sleep on a mattress as soft as a cloud. If there is even a small lump, she will not be able to sleep."

"Why not?" asked the Prince. He was a nice man but not as smart as his mother.

"Because she is so delicate!" said the Queen impatiently. "Let me figure out a test. You go down and pick a girl to try out my plan."

The Prince went down to the lobby of the castle. A very pretty but humble-looking girl caught his eye. He brought her back to his mother, who welcomed her.

"Please be our guest at the castle tonight," said the Queen.

The girl was shown to her room. In it was a pile of five mattresses, all fluffy and clean. "A princess is delicate," said the Queen. "Sweet dreams!"

The girl climbed to the top of the pile and laid down, but she could not sleep. She tossed and turned and was quite cross the next morning. "I found this under the fourth mattress when I got up this morning," she said. She handed a small green pea to the Queen. "No wonder I couldn't sleep!"

The Queen clapped her hands. The Prince looked confused. "A real princess is delicate. If this pea I put under the mattress kept you awake, you are definitely a princess."

"Of course I am," said the Princess. "Now may I please take a nap?"

1. Why does the Prince worry about finding a bride?

   _____

2. According to the Queen, how can the Prince tell who is a real princess?

   _____

3. Who hides something under the girl's mattress? _____

The Princess and the Pea

Directions: Review the story "The Princess and the Pea." Then, answer the questions.

1. Why does the Prince need a test to see who is a real princess?

   _____

   _____

2. Why does the Princess have trouble sleeping?

   _____

   _____

3. In this story, the Queen puts a small pea under a pile of mattresses to see if the girl is delicate. What else could be done to test a princess for delicacy?

   _____

   _____

   _____

The story does not tell whether or not the Prince and Princess get married and live happily ever after, only that the Princess wants to take a nap.

Directions: Write a new ending to the story.

4. What do you think happens after the Princess wakes up?

   _____

   _____

   _____

   _____

   _____

The Frog Prince

Directions: Read the story "The Frog Prince." Then, answer the questions.

Once upon a time, there lived a beautiful princess who liked to play alone in the woods. One day, as she was playing with her golden ball, it rolled into a lake. The water was so deep she could not see the ball. The Princess was very sad. She cried out, "I would give anything to have my golden ball back!"

Suddenly, a large ugly frog popped out of the water. "Anything?" he croaked. The Princess looked at him with distaste. "Yes," she said, "I would give anything."

"I will get your golden ball," said the frog. "In return, you must take me back to the castle. You must let me live with you and eat from your golden plate."

"Whatever you want," said the Princess. She thought the frog was very ugly, but she wanted her golden ball.
The frog dove down and brought the ball to the Princess. She put the frog in her pocket and took him home. "He is ugly," the Princess said. "But a promise is a promise. And a princess always keeps her word."

The Princess changed her clothes and forgot all about the frog. That evening, she heard a tapping at her door. She ran to the door to open it and a handsome prince stepped in.

"Who are you?" asked the Princess, already half in love.

"I am the prince you rescued at the lake," said the handsome Prince. "I was turned into a frog one hundred years ago today by a wicked lady. Because they always keep their promises, only a beautiful princess could break the spell. You are a little forgetful, but you did keep your word!"

Can you guess what happened next? Of course, they were married and lived happily ever after.

1. What does the frog ask the Princess to promise?

   _____

   _____

2. Where does the Princess put the frog when she leaves the lake?

   _____

3. Why could only a princess break the spell?

   _____

   _____

The Frog Prince

Directions: Review the story "The Frog Prince." Then, answer the questions.

1. What does the Princess lose in the lake? _____

2. How does she get it back? _____

   _____

   _____

3. How does the frog turn back into a prince?_____

   _____

4. What phrases are used to begin and end this story? _____

   _____

5. Are these words used frequently to begin and end fairy tales?

   _____

There is more than one version of most fairy tales. In another version of this story, the Princess has to kiss the frog in order for him to change back into a prince.

Directions: Write your answers.

6. What do you think would happen in a story where the Princess kisses the frog, but he remains a frog?

   _____

   _____

   _____

7. Rewrite the ending to "The Frog Prince" so that the frog remains a frog and does not turn into a handsome prince. Continue your story on another sheet of paper.

Review

Directions: Think of fairy tales you know from books or videos, like "Cinderella," "Snow White," "Sleeping Beauty," "Rapunzel" and "Beauty and the Beast." Then, answer the questions.

1. What are some common elements in all fairy tales?_____

_____

_____

2. How do fairy tales usually begin?_____

3. How do fairy tales usually end? _____

_____

Directions: Locate and read several different versions of the same fairy tale. For example, "Cinderella," "Princess Furball," "Cinderlad" and "Yah Shen." Then, answer the questions.

4. How are the stories alike? _____

_____

_____

_____

5. How are they different?_____

_____

_____

_____

6. Which story is best developed by the author?

_____

7. Which story did you like best? Why?_____

_____

_____

Review

Most of us have read many fairy tales and have seen them in movies. Fairy tales have a certain style and format they usually follow.

Directions: Use another sheet of paper to write another fairy tale. Use the following questions to help you brainstorm ideas.

1. What is the name of the kingdom? _____

2. What is the size of the kingdom, its climate, trees, plants, animals, etc.?

   _____

   _____

3. What kind of magic happens there? _____

   _____

4. Who are the characters?

   Good guys   Bad guys

   _____   _____

   _____   _____

5. What does each character look like? _____

   _____

6. What kind of spell is cast on a particular character and why?

   _____

   _____

   _____

   _____

7. What happens to the good characters and the bad characters in the end?

   _____

   _____

   _____

Kanati's Son

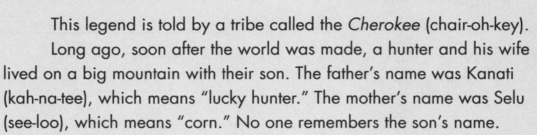

A legend is a story or group of stories handed down through generations. Legends are usually about an actual person.

Directions: Read about Kanati's son. Then, number the events in order.

This legend is told by a tribe called the *Cherokee* (chair-oh-key).

Long ago, soon after the world was made, a hunter and his wife lived on a big mountain with their son. The father's name was Kanati (kah-na-tee), which means "lucky hunter." The mother's name was Selu (see-loo), which means "corn." No one remembers the son's name.

The little boy used to play alone by the river each day. One day, elders of the tribe told the boy's parents they had heard two children playing. Since their boy was the only child around, the parents were puzzled. They told their son what the elders had said.

"I do have a playmate," the boy said. "He comes out of the water. He says he is the brother that mother threw in the river."

Then, Selu knew what had happened.

"He is formed from the blood of the animals I washed in the river," she told Kanati. "After you kill them, I wash them in the river before I cook them."

Here is what Kanati told his boy: "Tomorrow when the other boy comes, wrestle with him. Hold him to the ground and call for us."

The boy did as his parents told him. When he called, they came running and grabbed the wild boy. They took him home and tried to tame him. The boy grew up with magic powers. The Cherokee called this "adawehi" (ad-da-we-hi). He was always getting into mischief! But he saved himself with his magic.

_____ Selu and Kanati try to tame the boy from the river.

_____ The little boy tells Selu and Kanati about the other boy.

_____ The little boy's parents are puzzled.

_____ The new boy grows up with magic powers.

_____ The elders tell Selu and Kanati they heard two children playing.

_____ The little boy wrestles his new playmate to the ground.

Why Bear Has a Short Tail

Some stories try to explain the reasons why certain things occur in nature.

Directions: Read the legend "Why Bear Has a Short Tail." Then, answer the questions.

Long ago, Bear had a long tail like Fox. One winter day, Bear met Fox coming out of the woods. Fox was carrying a long string of fish. He had stolen the fish, but that is not what he told Bear.

"Where did you get those fish?" asked Bear, rubbing his paws together. Bear loved fish. It was his favorite food.

"I was out fishing and caught them," replied Fox.

Bear did not know how to fish. He had only tasted fish that others gave him. He was eager to learn to catch his own.

"Please Fox, will you tell me how to fish?" asked Bear.

So, the mean old Fox said to Bear, "Cut a hole in the ice and stick your tail in the hole. It will get cold, but soon the fish will begin to bite. When you can stand it no longer, pull your tail out. It will be covered with fish!"

"Will it hurt?" asked Bear, patting his tail.

"It will hurt some," admitted Fox. "But the longer you leave your tail in the water, the more fish you will catch."

Bear did as Fox told him. He loved fish, so he left his tail in the icy water a very, very long time. The ice froze around Bear's tail. When he pulled free, his tail remained stuck in the ice. That is why bears today have short tails.

1. How does Fox get his string of fish? _____

_____

2. What does he tell Bear to do? _____

_____

3. Why does Bear do as Fox told him?_____

_____

4. How many fish does Bear catch? _____

5. What happens when Bear tries to pull his tail out?

_____

Why Bear Has a Short Tail

Directions: Review the legend "Why Bear Has a Short Tail." Then, answer the questions.

1. When Bear asks Fox where he got his fish, is Fox truthful in his response? Why or why not?

   _____

   _____

2. Why does Bear want to know how to fish? _____

   _____

3. In reality, are bears able to catch their own fish? How? _____

   _____

4. Is Bear very smart to believe Fox? Why or why not? _____

   _____

5. How would you have told Bear to catch his own fish? _____

   _____

6. What is one word you would use to describe Fox? _____

   Explain your answer. _____

   _____

7. What is one word you would use to describe Bear? _____

   Explain your answer. _____

   _____

8. Is this story realistic? _____

9. Could it have really happened? Explain your answer. _____

   _____

How the Donkey Got Long Ears

Directions: Write your predictions to answer these questions.

1. How do you think animals got their names? _____

    _____

2. Why would it be confusing if animals did not have names?

    _____

Directions: Read the legend "How the Donkey Got Long Ears."
Then, answer the questions.

In the beginning, when the world was young, animals had no names. It
was very confusing! A woman would say, "Tell the thingamajig to bring in the
paper." The man would say, "What thingamajig?" She was talking about the dog,
of course, but the man didn't know that.

Together, they decided to name the animals on their farm. First, they named
their pet thingamajig Dog. They named the pink thingamajig that oinked Pig. They
named the red thingamajig that crowed Rooster. They named the white
thingamajig that laid eggs Hen. They named the little yellow thingamajigs that
cheeped Chicks. They named the big brown thingamajig they rode Horse.

Then, they came to another thingamajig. It looked like Horse, but was
smaller. It would be confusing to call the smaller thingamajig Horse, they decided.

"Let's name it Donkey," said the woman. So they did.

Soon all the animals knew their names. All but Donkey, that is. Donkey
kept forgetting.

"What kind of a thingamajig am I again?" he would ask the man.

"You are Donkey!" the man would answer. Each time Donkey forgot,
the man tugged on Donkey's ears to help him remember.
Soon, however, Donkey would forget his name again.

"Uh, what's my name?" he would ask the woman.

She would answer, "Donkey! Donkey! Donkey!" and pull his
ears each time. She was a clever woman but not very patient.

At first, the man and woman did not notice that Donkey's
ears grew longer each time they were pulled. Donkey was patient
but not very clever. It took him a long time to learn his name. By the time he
remembered his name was Donkey, his ears were much longer than Horse's ears.
That is why donkeys have long ears.

3. What words could you use to describe Donkey? _____

    _____

How the Donkey Got Long Ears

Directions: Review the legend "How the Donkey Got Long Ears." Then, answer the questions.

1. What do the man and woman call the animals before they have names?

    _____

2. Why do they decide to name the animals? _____

    _____

3. What is the first animal they name? _____

4. Besides being impatient, what else is the woman? _____

5. What did the people do each time they reminded Donkey of his name?

    _____

6. Which thingamajigs are yellow? _____

7. Which thingamajig is pink? _____

8. What is the thingamajig they ride? _____

9. Why don't they call the donkey Horse? _____

Directions: Imagine that you are the one who gets to name the animals. Write names for these new "animals."

10. A thingamajig with yellow spots that swims _____

11. A thingamajig with large ears, a short tail and six legs

    _____

12. A thingamajig with purple wings that flies and sings sweet melodies

    _____

13. A thingamajig that gives chocolate milk _____

    _____

Mr. Nobody

Directions: After reading the poem "Mr. Nobody," number in order the things people blame him for.

I know a funny little man
As quiet as a mouse,
Who does the mischief that is done
In everybody's house!
No one ever sees his face.
And yet we all agree
That every plate we break was cracked
By Mr. Nobody.
It's he who always tears out books,
Who leaves the door ajar,
He pulls the buttons from our shirts,
And scatters pins afar;
That squeaking door will always squeak,
The reason is, you see,
We leave the oiling to be done
By Mr. Nobody.
The finger marks upon the wall
By none of us are made;
We never leave the blinds unclosed
To let the carpet fade.
The bowl of soup we do not spill,
It's not our fault, you see
These mishaps—every one is caused
By Mr. Nobody.

_____ Putting finger marks on walls   _____ Scattering pins

_____ Leaving the door ajar   _____ Breaking plates

_____ Spilling soup   _____ Tearing out books

_____ Squeaking doors   _____ Pulling buttons
                                           off shirts

_____ Leaving the blinds open

Over the Hills and Far Away

Directions: Read "Over the Hills and Far Away." Then, answer the questions.

Tom, Tom the piper's son,
Learned to play when he was one,
But the only tune that he could play
Was "Over the Hills and Far Away."

Now Tom with his pipe made such a noise
That he pleased the girls and he pleased the boys,
And they all danced when they heard him play
"Over the Hills and Far Away."

Tom played his pipe with such great skill,
Even pigs and dogs could not keep still.
The dogs would wag their tails and dance,
The pigs would oink and grunt and prance.

Yes, Tom could play, his music soared—
But soon the pigs and dogs got bored.
The children, too, thought it was wrong,
For Tom to play just one dull song.

1. How old is Tom when he learns to play? _____

2. What tune does Tom play? _____
_____

3. What do the dogs do when Tom plays? _____
_____

4. Why does everyone get tired of Tom's music? _____
_____

5. What do the pigs do when Tom plays? _____
_____

6. What instrument does Tom play? _____

A California Tribe

Directions: Read about the Yuma. Then, answer the questions.

California was home to many Native Americans. The weather was warm, and food was plentiful. California was an ideal place to live.

One California tribe that made good use of the land was the Yuma. The Yuma farmed and gathered roots and berries. They harvested dozens of wild plants. They gathered acorns, ground them up and used them in cooking. The Yuma mixed acorns with flour and water to make a kind of oatmeal. They fished in California's rich waters. They hunted deer and small game. The Yuma made the most of what Mother Nature offered.

The Yuma lived in huts. The roofs were made of dirt. The walls were made of grass. Some Yuma lived together in big round buildings made with poles and woven grasses. As many as 50 people lived in these large homes.

Like other tribes, the Yuma made crafts. Their woven baskets were especially beautiful. The women also wove cradles, hats, bowls and other useful items for the tribe.

When it was time to marry, a boy's parents chose a 15-year-old girl for him. The girl was a Yuma, too, but from another village. Except for the chief, each man took only one wife.

When a Yuma died, a big ceremony was held. The Yumas had great respect for death. After someone died, his or her name was never spoken again.

1. What were two reasons why California was an ideal place to live?

   _____

   _____

2. What did the Yuma use acorns for? _____

   _____

3. What was a beautiful craft made by the Yuma? _____

4. How old was a Yuma bride? _____

5. What types of homes did the Yuma live in? _____

6. How did the Yuma feel about death? _____

   _____

A California Tribe

Directions: Review what you read about the Yuma.
Write the answers.

1. How did the Yuma make good use of the land? _____

   _____

   _____

2. How were the Yuma like the Pueblo people? _____

   _____

   _____

3. How were they different? _____

   _____

   _____

   _____

4. Why did the Yuma have homes different than those of the
   Pueblo tribes?

   _____

   _____

5. When it was time for a young Yuma man to marry, his parents
   selected a fifteen-year-old bride for him from another tribe. Do
   you think this is a good idea? Why or why not?

   _____

   _____

6. Why do you suppose the Yuma never spoke a person's name
   after he/she died?

   _____

   _____

7. Do you think this would be an easy thing to do? Explain
   your answer.

   _____

   _____

Setting Sail

Directions: Read about the Sailor Native Americans of Puget Sound. Then, work the puzzle.

     Three tribes lived on Puget (pew-jit) Sound in Washington state. They made their living from the sea. People later called them the "Sailor" Indians.

     These Native Americans fished for salmon. They trapped the salmon in large baskets. Sometimes they used large nets. The sea was filled with fish. Their nets rarely came up empty.

     The Sailor Native Americans also gathered roots and berries. They hunted deer, black bear and ducks.

     Their homes were amazing! They built big wooden buildings without nails. They did not use saws to cut the wood. The walls and roofs were tied together. Each building had different homes inside. As many as 50 families lived in each big building.

Across:

1. The three tribes on Puget Sound were called the "_____" Native Americans.

2. The _____ and roofs of their buildings were tied together.

4. Because their buildings were tied together, they did not need _____.

Down:

1. Type of fish the "Sailor" Native Americans caught

3. As many as _____ families could live in their big buildings.

5. The buildings were put together without using _____ to cut the wood.

Setting Sail

Directions: Review what you read about the Sailor Native Americans. Write your answers.

1. How were the housing arrangements of the Puget Sound Native Americans similar to those of the Yuma?

   _____

2. How was the diet of the Sailor Native Americans like those of the Yuma and Pueblo?

   _____

3. How was it different? _____

   _____

4. The Sailor Native Americans made a living from the sea, and their nets were rarely empty. What type of transportation do you think these Native Americans used to get their nets to the sea?

   _____

5. Where could you find more information on this group of Native Americans to check your answer? _____

   _____

6. Verify your answer. Were you correct? _____

7. Who do you think performed the many tasks in the Sailor village? Write men, women, boys and/or girls for your answers.

   Built homes?   _____

   Made fishing baskets?   _____

   Fished?   _____

   Gathered roots and berries?   _____

   Hunted game?   _____

   Made fishing nets?   _____

Review

Review what you read about Native Americans.
Then, answer the questions.

1. Of the tribes discussed, which one would you most like to have been a member of? Explain your answer.

   _____

   _____

2. Why did each of the tribes have a different lifestyle?

   _____

   _____

3. How did their location influence how each of the tribes functioned?

   _____

   _____

Directions: Select two of the Native American tribes you read about. Compare and contrast their homes, clothing and lifestyle in the Venn diagram. Write words and phrases that were unique to one group or the other in the correct parts of the circle. Write words and phrases that are common to both groups in the section where the circles intersect.

Wild and Free

Directions: Read about wild horses. Then, answer the questions.

Have you ever heard of a car called a *Mustang*? It is named after a type of wild horse.

In the 1600s, the Spanish explorers who came to North America brought horses with them. Some of these horses escaped onto the prairies and plains. With no one to feed them or ride them, they became wild. Their numbers quickly grew, and they roamed in herds. They ran free and ate grass on the prairie.

Later, when the West was settled, people needed horses. They captured wild ones. This was not easy to do. Wild horses could run very fast. They did not want to be captured!

Some men made their living by capturing wild horses, taming them and selling them. These men were called *mustangers*. Can you guess why?

After cars were invented, people did not need as many horses. Not as many mustangers were needed to catch them. More and more wild horses roamed the western prairies. In 1925, about a million mustangs were running loose.

The government was worried that the herds would eat too much grass. Ranchers who owned big herds of cattle complained that their animals didn't have enough to eat because the mustangs ate all the grass. Permission was given to ranchers and others to kill many of the horses. Thousands were killed and sold to companies that made them into pet food.

Now, wild horses live in only 12 states. The largest herds are in California, New Mexico, Oregon, Wyoming, and Nevada. Most people who live in these states never see wild horses. The herds live away from people in the distant plains and mountains. They are safer there.

1. What is one type of wild horse called? _____

2. What were men called who captured wild horses? _____

3. About how many wild horses were running free in the U.S. in 1925? _____

4. The wild mustangs were killed and turned into

   ❏ cars.   ❏ pet food.   ❏ lunch meat.

5. The largest herds of wild horses are now in

   ❏ Oregon.   ❏ Ohio.   ❏ New Mexico.   ❏ Wyoming.

   ❏ California.   ❏ Nevada.   ❏ Kansas.   ❏ Arkansas.

Suffixes

SUFFIXES	MEANING
ful	full of
ity	quality or degree
ive	have or tend
to	be
less	without or lacking
able	able to be
ness	state of
ment	act of
or	person that does something
ward	in the direction of

Prefixes &

PREFIXES	MEANING
bi	two or twice
en	to make
in	within
mis	wrong
non	not or without
pre	before
re	again
un	not

UNITED STATE

1st state	2nd state	3rd state	4th state	5th state	6th state	7th state	8th state	9th state	10th state	11th state	12th state	13th s
DELAWARE	PENNSYLVANIA	NEW JERSEY	GEORGIA	CONNECTICUT	MASSACHUSETTS	MARYLAND	SOUTH CAROLINA	NEW HAMPSHIRE	VIRGINIA	NEW YORK	NORTH CAROLINA	RHODE IS
Dec 7, 1787	Dec 12, 1787	Dec 18, 1787	Jan 2, 1788	Jan 9, 1788	Feb 6, 1788	April 28, 1788	May 23, 1788	June 21, 1788	June 26, 1788	July 26, 1788	Nov 21, 1789	May 29,

th state	27th state	28th state	29th state	30th state	31st state	32nd state	33rd state	34th state	35th state	36th state	37th state	38th st
ICHIGAN	FLORIDA	TEXAS	IOWA	WISCONSIN	CALIFORNIA	MINNESOTA	OREGON	KANSAS	WEST VIRGINIA	NEVADA	NEBRASKA	COLORA
6, 1837	March 3, 1845	Dec 29, 1845	Dec 28, 1846	May 29, 1848	Sept 9, 1850	May 11, 1858	Feb 14, 1859	Jan 29, 1861	June 20, 1863	Oct 31, 1864	March 1, 1867	Aug 1, 1

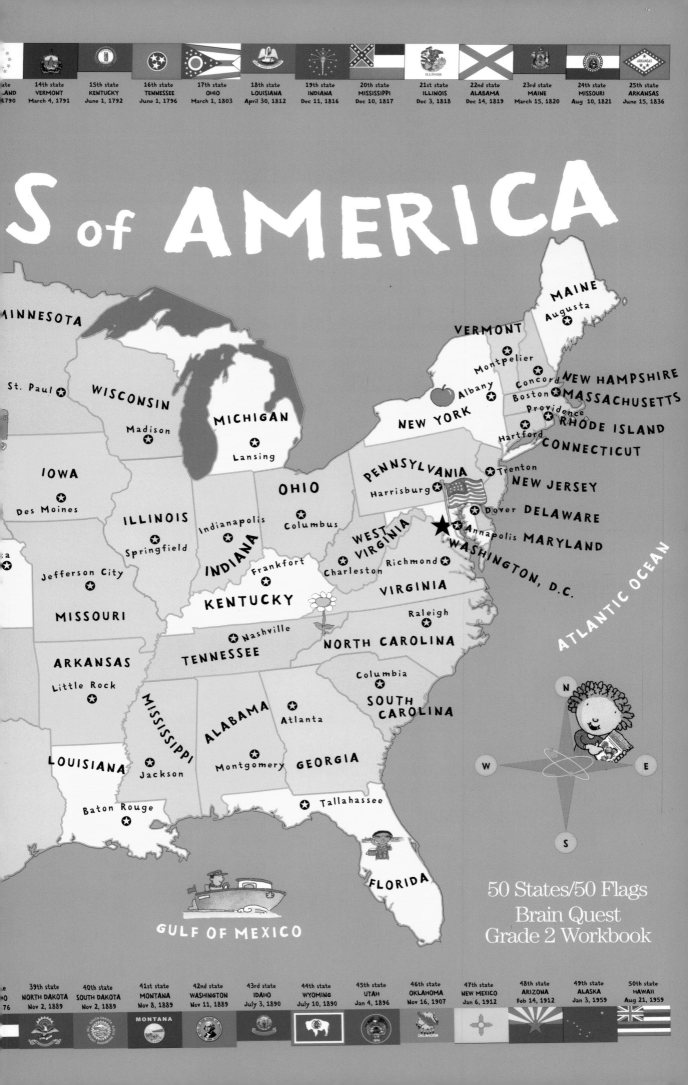

Wild and Free

Directions: Read more about wild horses.
Then, answer the questions.

Have you noticed that in any large group, one person seems to be the leader? This is true for wild horses, too. The leader of a band of wild horses is a stallion. Stallions are adult male horses.

The stallion's job is important. He watches out for danger. If a bear or other animal comes close, he lets out a warning cry. This helps keep the other horses safe. Sometimes they all run away together. Other times, the stallion protects the other horses. He shows his teeth. He rears up on his back legs. Often, he scares the other animal away. Then, the horses can safely continue eating grass.

Much of the grass on the prairies is gone now. Wild horses must move around a lot to find new grass. They spend about half their time eating and looking for food. If they cannot find prairie grass, wild horses will eat tree bark. They will eat flowers. If they can't find these either, wild horses will eat anything that grows!

Wild horses also need plenty of water. It is often hot in the places where they roam. At least twice a day, they find streams and take long, long drinks. Like people, wild horses lose water when they sweat. They run and sweat a lot in hot weather. To survive, they need as much water as they can get.

Wild horses also use water another way. When they find deep water, they wade into it. It feels good! It cools their skin.

1. What is the main idea? (Check one.)

   _____ Wild horses need plenty of water.

   _____ Wild horses move in bands protected by a stallion.

   _____ Wild horses eat grass.

2. What are two reasons why wild horses need water? _____

   _____

3. Why do wild horses move around so much? _____

   _____

4. What do wild horses most like to eat? _____

5. What do wild horses spend half their time doing?

   _____

Wild and Free

Directions: Review what you read about wild horses. Then, answer the questions.

1. How did horses come to North America and become wild?

   _____

   _____

2. Why is it so difficult to capture, tame and train wild horses?

   _____

   _____

3. Do you think it was right of the government to allow the killing of wild horses? _____

   Explain your answer. _____

   _____

4. Do you think the remaining wild horses should be protected?

   _____

   Explain your answer._____

   _____

5. What is the role of the lead stallion in a wild horse herd?

   _____

6. What are some things wild horses have in common with giraffes?

   _____

   _____

   _____

7. What do you think will happen to wild horses as the prairie lands continue to disappear as a result of developments for homes and businesses?

   _____

   _____

   _____

Space Pioneer

Neil Armstrong is one of the great pioneers of space. On July 20, 1969, Armstrong was commander of Apollo 11, the first manned American spacecraft to land on the Moon. He was the first person to walk on the Moon.

Armstrong was born in Ohio in 1930. He took his first airplane ride when he was 6 years old. As he grew older, he did jobs to earn money to learn to fly. On his 16th birthday, he received his student pilot's license.

Armstrong served as a Navy fighter pilot during the Korean War. He received three medals. Later, he was a test pilot. He was known as one of the best pilots in the world. He was also an engineer. He contributed much to the development of new methods of flying. In 1962, he was accepted into an astronaut training program.

Armstrong had much experience when he was named to command the historic flight to the Moon. It took four days to fly to the Moon. As he climbed down the ladder to be the first person to step onto the Moon, he said these now famous words: "That's one small step for (a) man, one giant leap for mankind."

Directions: Answer these questions about Neil Armstrong.

1. What did Neil Armstrong do before any other person in the world?

   _____

2. How old was Neil Armstrong when he got his student pilot's license?

   _____

3. What did Armstrong do during the Korean War?

   _____

4. On what date did a person first walk on the Moon?

   _____

A Ride in Space

Directions: Read about Sally Ride. Then, answer the questions.

Sally Ride was the first American woman in space. She was only 31 years old when she went into space in 1982. Besides being the first American woman, she was also the youngest person ever to go into space!

Many people wanted to be astronauts. When Sally Ride was chosen, there were 8,000 people who wanted to be in the class. Only 35 were selected. Six of those people were women.

Sally Ride rode in the spaceship *Challenger*. She was called a *Mission Specialist*. Like any astronaut, Sally Ride had to study for several years before she went into space. She spent 6 days on her journey. She has even written a book for children about her adventure! It is called *To Space and Back*.

1. What was significant about Sally Ride's journey into space?

   _____

   _____

2. How old was Sally ride when she went into space? _____

3. What was the name of her spaceship? _____

4. What was her title on the trip into space? _____

5. How long did Sally Ride's journey last? _____

6. What was the name of the book she wrote?

   _____

7. Why do you think many people want to be astronauts? _____

   _____

   _____

   _____

Floating Free

Directions: Read about life in space. Then, answer the questions.

Life in space is very different from life on Earth. There is no gravity in space. Gravity is what holds us to the ground. In space, everything floats around.

Astronauts wear suction cups on their shoes to hold them to the floor of their spaceships. At night, they do not crawl into bed like you do. Instead, they climb into sleeping bags that hang on the wall and then they zip themselves in.

If an astronaut is thirsty, he or she cannot simply pour a glass of water. The water would form little balls that would float around the spaceship! Instead, water has to be squirted into the astronauts' mouths from bottles or containers.

When astronauts are in space, they do a lot of floating around outside their spaceship. Astronauts always have special jobs to do in space. One astronaut is the pilot of the spaceship. The other astronauts do experiments, make repairs and gather information about their trip.

1. What is the main idea?

    _____ Life in space is much different than it is on Earth.

    _____ Without gravity, people on Earth would float around.

    _____ Gravity makes life on Earth much different
    than life in space.

2. What does gravity do? _____

    _____

3. How do astronauts sleep? _____

    _____

4. What do astronauts do in space? _____

    _____

    _____

5. How do astronauts drink water? _____

6. Would you like to be an astronaut? Why or why not? _____

    _____

Review

Directions: Read about early ideas for space travel. Then, answer the questions.

People have dreamed about going into space for thousands of years. There are legends that tell about inventors who wanted to get birds to fly to the Moon. In 1864, a French author named Jules Verne wrote a book called *From the Earth to the Moon*. In the book, he wrote about men being shot into space from a huge cannon.

Jules Verne made up that story. Other writers also made up stories about going to the Moon. During the 1920s, several scientists wrote about sending rockets into space. They decided that liquid fuel was needed. Since then, space exploration has come a long way!

A Russian named Yuri A. Gagarin was the first person in space. An American, Alan B. Shepard, Jr., went into space next. Both men did experiments that later helped other astronauts in their trips to outer space!

1. What is the main idea?

    _____ People have thought about going into space since 1920.

    _____ People have thought about going into space for many years.

    _____ People like Jules Verne had many ideas about how to get to the Moon.

2. Who wrote a book called *From the Earth to the Moon*?

    _____

3. What did he write about?

    _____

4. When was that book written? _____

5. In what country did Jules Verne live? _____

6. What did scientists in the 1920s think we needed to go to space?

    _____

7. How did Yuri Gagarin and Alan Shepard help future astronauts?

    _____

English

highest

higher

high

Ask It, State It

A **statement** tells some kind of information.
It is followed by a period (.).

Examples: It is a rainy day. We are
going to the beach next summer.

A question asks for a specific
piece of information.
It is followed by a question mark (?).

Examples: What is the weather like today? When are you going to
the beach?

Directions: Write whether each sentence is a statement or question.
The first one has been done for you.

1. Jamie went for a walk at the zoo. <u>statement</u>

2. The leaves turn bright colors in the fall. _____

3. When does the Easter Bunny arrive? _____

4. Madeleine went to the new art school. _____

5. Is school over at 3:30? _____

6. Grandma and Grandpa are moving. _____

7. Anthony went home. _____

8. Did Malia go to Amy's house? _____

9. Who went to work late? _____

10. Ms. Gomez is a good teacher. _____

Directions: Write two statements and two questions below.

Statements:

_____

_____

Questions:

_____

_____

Taking Command

A **command** tells someone to do something.
It is followed by a period (.).

Examples: Get your math book.
Do your homework.

An exclamation shows strong
feeling or excitement.
It is followed by an exclamation mark (!).

Examples: Watch out for that car! Oh, no! There's a snake!

Directions: Write whether each sentence is a command or
exclamation. The first one has been done for you.

1. Please clean your room.   **command**

2. Wow! Those fireworks are beautiful!   _____

3. Come to dinner now.   _____

4. Color the sky and water blue.   _____

5. Trim the paper carefully.   _____

6. Hurry, here comes the bus!   _____

7. Isn't that a lovely picture!   _____

8. Time to stop playing and clean up.   _____

9. Brush your teeth before bedtime.   _____

10. Wash your hands before you eat!   _____

Directions: Write two commands and two exclamations below.

Commands:

_____

_____

Exclamations:

_____

_____

Subject Matters

The **subject** of a sentence tells you who or what the sentence is about. A subject is either a common noun, a proper noun or a pronoun.

Examples: Li went to the store.
Li is the subject of the sentence.

The tired boys and girls walked home slowly.
The tired boys and girls is the subject of the sentence.

Directions: Underline the subject of each sentence. The first one has been done for you.

1. The birthday cake was pink and white.

2. Anthony celebrated his fourth birthday.

3. The tower of building blocks fell over.

4. On Saturday, our family will go to a movie.

5. The busy editor was writing sentences.

6. Seven children painted pictures.

7. Two happy dolphins played cheerfully on the surf.

8. A sand crab buried itself in the dunes.

Directions: Write a subject for each sentence.

1. <u>Chocolate-chip ice cream</u> was melting in the heat.

2. _____ ran down the steep hill.

3. _____ are full of colors.

4. _____ sang a cheerful tune.

5. _____ made her a beautiful dress.

6. _____ hopped, skipped and jumped all the way home.

Find the Action

The **predicate** of a sentence tells what the subject is doing. The predicate contains the action, linking and/or helping verb.

Examples: Li went to the store.

Went to the store is the predicate.

The tired boys and girls walked home slowly.

Walked home slowly is the predicate.

Hint: When identifying the predicate, look for the verb. The verb is usually the first word of the predicate.

Directions: Underline the predicate in each sentence with two lines. The first one has been done for you.

1. The choir <u>sang joyfully</u>.

2. Their song had both high and low notes.

3. Sal played the piano while they sang.

4. This Sunday the orchestra will have a concert in the park.

5. John is working hard on his homework.

6. He will write a report on electricity.

7. The report will tell about Ben Franklin's kite experiment.

8. Elena, Lily, and Amy played on the swings.

Directions: Write a predicate for each sentence.

1. Sam and Libby

   _____.

2. At school, the children

   _____.

3. The football team

   _____.

4. Seven silly serpents

   _____.

Sentence Superstars

The **subject** tells who or what the sentence is about. The **predicate** tells what the subject does, did, is doing, or will do. A complete sentence must have a subject and a predicate.

Examples:

Subject	Predicate
Sharon	writes to her grandmother every week.
The horse	ran around the track quickly.
My mom's car	is bright green.
Bella	will be here after lunch.

Directions: Circle the subject of each sentence. Underline the predicate.

1. My sister is a very happy person.

2. I wish we had more holidays in the year.

3. Laura is one of the nicest girls in our class.

4. Samir is fun to have as a friend.

5. The rain nearly ruined our picnic!

6. My birthday present was exactly what I wanted.

7. Your bicycle is parked beside my skateboard.

8. The printer will need to be filled with paper before you use it.

9. Six dogs chased my cat home yesterday!

Sentence Starters

Directions: Write subjects to complete the following sentences.

1. _____ went to school last Wednesday.

2. _____ did not understand the joke.

3. _____ barked so loudly that no one could sleep a wink.

4. _____ felt unhappy when the ball game was rained out.

5. _____ wonder what happened at the end of the book.

6. _____ jumped for joy when she won the contest.

Directions: Write predicates to complete the following sentences.

7. Everyone

_____.

8. Dogs

_____.

9. I

_____.

10. Justin

_____.

11. Jokes

_____.

12. Twelve people

_____.

Double Duty

A **compound subject** is a subject with two parts joined by the word **and** or another conjunction. Compound subjects share the same predicate.

Example:

Her shoes were covered with mud. Her ankles were covered with mud, too.

Compound subject:

Her shoes and ankles were covered with mud.

The predicate in both sentences is **were covered with mud**.

Directions: Combine each pair of sentences into one sentence with a compound subject.

1. Bill ~~sneezed.~~ *and* Kassie sneezed.

   Bill and Kassie sneezed

2. Carmen ~~made cookies.~~ *and* Joey made cookies.

   Carmen and Joey made cookies

3. Fruit flies are insects. Ladybugs are insects.

   _____

4. The girls are planning a dance. The boys are planning a dance.

   The girls and boys are planning a dance

5. Our dog ran after the ducks. Our cat ran after the ducks.

   Our dog and cat ran after ducks

6. Joshua got lost in the parking lot. DeShaun got lost in the parking lot.

   _____

It's Fine to Combine

A **compound predicate** is a predicate with two parts joined by the word **and** or another conjunction. Compound predicates share the same subject.

Example:

The baby grabbed the ball. The baby threw the ball.

Compound predicate:
The baby grabbed the ball and threw it.

The subject in both sentences is **the baby**.

Directions: Combine each pair of sentences into one sentence to make a compound predicate.

1. Leah jumped on her bike. Leah rode around the block.

   _____

2. Father rolled out the pie crust. Father put the pie crust in the pan.

   _____

3. Colin slipped on the snow. Colin nearly fell down.

   _____

4. My friend lives in a green house. My friend rides a red bicycle.

   _____

5. I opened the magazine. I began to read it quietly.

   _____

6. My father bought a new plaid shirt. My father wore his new red tie.

   _____

   _____

Review

Directions: Circle the subjects.

1. Everyone felt the day had been a great success.

2. No one really understood why he was crying.

3. Mr. Winston, Ms. Fuller, and Ms. Rosenberg took us on a field trip.

Directions: Underline the predicates.

4. Who can tell what will happen tomorrow?

5. Mark was a carpenter by trade and a talented painter, too.

6. The animals yelped and whined in their cages.

Directions: Combine the sentences to make one sentence with a compound subject.

9. Elizabeth ate everything in sight. George ate everything in sight.

   _____

10. Wishing something will happen won't make it so. Dreaming something will happen won't make it so.

   _____

Directions: Combine the sentences to make one sentence with a compound predicate.

11. I jumped for joy. I hugged all my friends.

   _____

12. She ran around the track before the race. She warmed up before the race.

   _____

Nouns All Around

Common nouns name general people, places and things.

Examples: boy, girl, cat, dog, park, city, building

Proper nouns name specific persons, places and things.

Examples: Owen, Mary, Fluffy, Rover, Central Park, Chicago, Empire State Building

Proper nouns begin with capital letters.

Directions: Read the following nouns. On the blanks, indicate whether the nouns are common or proper. The first two have been done for you.

1. New York City _____ _proper_
2. house _____ _common_
3. car _____
4. Ohio _____
5. river _____
6. Rocky Mountains _____
7. Dr. DiCarlo _____
8. man _____
9. Rock River _____
10. building _____
11. lawyer _____
12. Grand Canyon _____

On another sheet of paper, write proper nouns for the above common nouns.

Directions: Read the following sentences. Underline the common nouns. Circle the proper nouns.

1. Addy's birthday is Friday, October 7.

2. She likes having her birthday in a fall month.

3. Her friends will meet her at the Video Arcade for a party.

4. Ms. McCarthy and Mr. Landry will help with the birthday party games.

5. Addy's friends will play video games all afternoon.

A Capital Idea

Proper nouns always begin with a capital letter.

Examples:

Monday

Texas

Karen

Mr. Antonelli

Hamburger Avenue

Rover

Directions: Cross out the lower-case letters at the beginning of the proper nouns. Write capital letters above them. The first one has been done for you.

1. My teddy bear's name is C̶ocoa.

2. ms. bernhard does an excellent job at crestview elementary school.

3. anh, elizabeth, and megan live on main street.

4. I am sure our teacher said the book report is due on monday.

5. I believe you can find lake street if you turn left at the next light.

6. Will your family be able join our family for dinner at burger barn?

7. The weather forecasters think the storm will hit the coast of

   louisiana friday afternoon.

8. My family went to washington, d.c. this summer.

Plural Power

Nouns come in two forms: singular and plural. When a noun is **singular**, it means there is only one person, place, or thing.

Examples: car, swing, box, truck, slide, bus

When a noun is **plural**, it means there is more than one person, place, or thing.

Examples: two cars, four trucks, three swings, five slides, six boxes, three buses

Usually an **s** is added to most nouns to make them plural. However, if the noun ends in **s**, **x**, **ch** or **sh**, then **es** is added to make it plural.

Directions: Write the singular or plural form of each word.

	Singular	Plural		Singular	Plural
1.	car	_____	7.	_____	tricks
2.	bush	_____	8.	mess	_____
3.	wish	_____	9.	box	_____
4.	_____	foxes	10.	dish	_____
5.	_____	rules	11.	_____	boats
6.	stitch	_____	12.	path	_____

Directions: Rewrite the following sentences and change the bold nouns from singular to plural or from plural to singular. The first one has been done for you.

1. She took a **book** to school.

   <u>She took books to school.</u>

2. Tommy made **wishes** at his birthday party.

   _____

3. The **fox** ran away from the **hunters**.

   _____

4. The **houses** were painted white.

   _____

Plural Power

When a word ends with a consonant before **y**, to make it plural, drop the **y** and add **ies**.

Examples: party   parties

cherry   cherries

daisy   daisies

However, if the word ends with a vowel before **y**, just add **s**.

Examples: boy   boys

toy   toys

monkey   monkeys

Directions: Write the singular or plural form of each word.

	Singular	Plural		Singular	Plural
1.	fly	_____	7.	_____	decoys
2.	_____	boys	8.	candy	_____
3.	_____	joys	9.	toy	_____
4.	spy	_____	10.	_____	cries
5.	_____	keys	11.	monkey	_____
6.	_____	dries	12.	daisy	_____

Directions: Write six sentences of your own using any of the plurals above.

_____

_____

_____

_____

_____

_____

Breaking the Rules

Some words in the English language do not follow any of the plural rules discussed earlier. These words may not change at all from singular to plural, or they may completely change spellings.

No Change	Examples:	Complete Change	Examples:
Singular	**Plural**	**Singular**	**Plural**
deer	deer	goose	geese
pants	pants	ox	oxen
scissors	scissors	man	men
moose	moose	child	children
sheep	sheep	leaf	leaves

Directions: Write the singular or plural form of each word. Use a dictionary to help if necessary.

	Singular	Plural		Singular	Plural
1.	moose	_____	6.	leaf	_____
2.	woman	_____	7.	_____	sheep
3.	_____	deer	8.	scissors	_____
4.	_____	children	9.	tooth	_____
5.	_____	hooves	10.	wharf	_____

Directions: Write four sentences of your own using two singular and two plural words from above.

_____

_____

_____

_____

Pronoun Lowdown

A **pronoun** is a word that takes the place of a noun in a sentence.

Examples:

> I, my, mine, me
>
> we, our, ours, us
>
> you, your, yours
>
> he, his, him
>
> she, her, hers
>
> it, its
>
> they, their, theirs, them

Directions: Underline the pronouns in each sentence.

1. Bring them to us as soon as you are finished.

2. She has been my best friend for many years.

3. They should be here soon.

4. We enjoyed our trip to the Mustard Museum.

5. Would you be able to help us with the project on Saturday?

6. Our homeroom teacher will not be here tomorrow.

7. My uncle said that he will be leaving soon for Australia.

8. Hurry! Could you please open the door for him?

Verb Alert

Verbs are the action words in a sentence. There are three kinds of verbs: action verbs, linking verbs, and helping verbs.

An **action verb** tells the action of a sentence.

Examples: run, hop, skip, sleep, jump, talk, snore

Michael **ran** to the store. **Ran** is the action verb.

A **linking verb** joins the subject and predicate of a sentence.

Examples: am, is, are, was, were

Michael **was** at the store. **Was** is the linking verb.

A **helping verb** is used with an action verb to "help" the action of the sentence.

Examples: am, is, are, was, were

Matthew **was** helping Michael. **Was** helps the action verb **helping**.

action

linking

helping

Directions: Read the following sentences. Underline the verbs. Above each, write **A** for action verb, **L** for linking verb and **H** for helping verb. The first one has been done for you.

1. Amy ⟨A⟩ <u>jumps</u> rope.

2. Kahlil was jumping rope, too.

3. They were working on their homework.

4. The math problem requires a lot of thinking.

5. Addition problems are fun to do.

6. The baby sleeps in the afternoon.

7. Grandma is napping also.

8. Sam is going to bed.

9. Jackson paints a lovely picture of the sea.

10. The colors in the picture are soft and pale.

Tense Tips

Not only do verbs tell the action of a sentence but they also tell when the action takes place. This is called the **verb tense**. There are three verb tenses: past, present and future tense.

Present-tense verbs tell what is happening now.

Example: Jane **spells** words with long vowel sounds.

Past-tense verbs tell about action that has already happened. Past-tense verbs are usually formed by adding **ed** to the verb.

Example: stay — stayed
Vidas **stayed** home yesterday.

Past-tense verbs can also be made by adding helping verbs **was** or **were** before the verb and adding **ing** to the verb.

Example: talk — was talking
Sally **was talking** to her mom.

Future-tense verbs tell what will happen in the future. Future-tense verbs are made by putting the word **will** before the verb.

Example: paint — will paint
Amelia and Ana-Maria **will paint** the house.

Directions: Read the following verbs. Write whether the verb tense is past, present or future.

Verb	Tense		Verb	Tense
1. watches	present	8.	writes	_____
2. wanted	_____	9.	vaulted	_____
3. will eat	_____	10.	were sleeping	_____
4. was squawking	_____	11.	will sing	_____
5. yawns	_____	12.	is speaking	_____
6. crawled	_____	13.	will cook	_____
7. will hunt	_____	14.	likes	_____

Writing with "ing"

Remember, use **is** and **are** when describing something happening right now. Use **was** and **were** when describing something that already happened.

Directions: Use the verb in bold to complete each sentence. Add **ing** to the verb and use **is**, **are**, **was**, or **were**.

Examples:

When it started to rain,

we ___**were raking**___ the leaves.   **rake**

When the soldiers marched up that hill,

Captain Stevens **was commanding** them.   **command**

1. Now, the police _____   **accuse**
   them of stealing the money.

2. Look! The eggs _____.   **hatch**

3. A minute ago, the sky _____.   **glow**

4. My dad says he _____   **treat**
   us to ice cream!

5. She _____ the whole time   **sneeze**
   we were at the mall.

6. While we were playing outside at recess, he   **grade**
   _____ our tests.

Put It in the Past

To make many verbs past tense, add **ed**.

Examples:

cook + ed = cooked   wish + ed = wished   play + ed = played

When a verb ends in a **silent e**, drop the **e** and add **ed**.

Examples:

hope + ed = hoped   hate + ed = hated

When a verb ends in **y** after a consonant, change the **y** to **i** and add **ed**.

Examples:

hurry + ed = hurried   marry + ed = married

When a verb ends in a single consonant after a single short vowel, double the final consonant before adding **ed**.

Examples:

stop + ed = stopped   hop + ed = hopped

Directions: Write the past tense of the verb correctly. The first one has been done for you.

1. call   <u>called</u>   9. reply   _____

2. copy   _____   10. top   _____

3. frown   _____   11. clean   _____

4. smile   _____   12. scream   _____

5. live   _____   13. clap   _____

6. talk   _____   14. mop   _____

7. name   _____   15. soap   _____

8. list   _____   16. choke   _____

That's History!

Irregular verbs change completely in the past tense. Unlike regular verbs, past-tense forms of irregular verbs are not formed by adding **ed**.

Example: The past tense of **go** is **went**.

Other verbs change some letters to form the past tense.

Example: The past tense of **break** is **broke**.

A **helping verb** helps to tell about the past. **Has**, **have** and **had** are helping verbs used with action verbs to show the action occurred in the past. The past-tense form of the irregular verb sometimes changes when a helping verb is added.

Present Tense Irregular Verb	Past Tense Irregular Verb	Past Tense Irregular Verb With Helper
go	went	have/has/had gone
see	saw	have/has/had seen
do	did	have/has/had done
bring	brought	have/has/had brought
sing	sang	have/has/had sung
drive	drove	have/has/had driven
swim	swam	have/has/had swum
sleep	slept	have/has/had slept

Directions: Choose four words from the chart. Write one sentence using the past-tense form of the verb without a helping verb. Write another sentence using the past-tense form with a helping verb.

1. _____

   _____

2. _____

   _____

3. _____

   _____

4. _____

   _____

It's Meant to Be!

Be is an irregular verb. The present-tense forms of **be** are **be**, **am**, **is** and **are**. The past-tense forms of **be** are **was** and **were**.

Directions: Write the correct form of **be** in the blanks. The first one has been done for you.

1. I _____**am**_____ so happy for you!

2. Jared _____ unfriendly yesterday.

3. English can _____ a lot of fun to learn.

4. They _____ among the nicest people I know.

5. They _____ late yesterday.

6. She promises she _____ going to arrive on time.

7. I _____ nervous right now about the test.

8. If you _____ satisfied now, so am I.

9. He _____ as nice to me last week as I had hoped.

10. He can _____ very gracious.

11. Would you _____ offended if I moved your desk?

12. He _____ watching at the window for me yesterday.

Prescription for Description

Adjectives tell more about nouns. Adjectives are describing words.

Examples: scary animals   **bright** glow   **wet** frog

Directions: Add at least two adjectives to each sentence below. Use your own words or words from the box.

> pale   soft   sticky   burning   furry   glistening   peaceful
>
> faint   shivering   slippery   gleaming   gentle   foggy   tangled

Example: The stripe was blue.

The wide stripe was light blue.

1. The frog had eyes.

   _____

2. The house was a sight.

   _____

3. A boy heard a noise.

   _____

4. The girl tripped over a toad.

   _____

5. A tiger ran through the room.

   _____

6. They saw a glow in the window.

   _____

From Smarter to Smartest

Directions: Circle the correct adjective for each sentence. The first one has been done for you.

1. Of all the students in the gym, her voice was (louder, (loudest)).

2. "I can tell you are (busier, busiest) than I am," he said to the librarian.

3. If you and Carl stand back to back, I can see which one is (taller, tallest).

4. She is the (kinder, kindest) teacher in the whole building.

5. Wow! That is the (bigger, biggest) pumpkin I have ever seen!

6. I believe your flashlight is (brighter, brightest) than mine.

7. "This is the (cleaner, cleanest) your room has been in a long time," Mother said.

Bigger, Better, and Much More Fun

Directions: Add the word or words needed in each sentence. The first one has been done for you.

1. I thought the book was **more interesting** than the movie. (interesting)

2. Do you want to carry this box? It is _____ than the one you have now. (light)

3. I noticed you are moving _____ this morning. Does your ankle still bother you? (slow)

4. Thomas Edison is probably _____ for his invention of the electric light bulb than of the phonograph. (famous)

5. She stuck out her lower lip and whined, "Your ice-cream cone is _____ than mine!" (big)

6. Mom said my room was _____ than it has been in a long time. (clean)

Making the Most of It

Most adjectives of two or more syllables are preceded by the word most as a way to show comparison between more than two things.

Examples:

Correct: intelligent, most intelligent
Incorrect: intelligentest
Correct: famous, most famous
Incorrect: famousest

Directions: Read the following groups of sentences. In the last sentence for each group, write the adjective preceded by **most**. The first one has been done for you.

1. My uncle is intelligent.
    My aunt is more intelligent.

    My cousin is the _____ most intelligent _____.

2. I am thankful.
    My brother is more thankful.

    My parents are the _____.

3. Your sister is polite.
    Your brother is more polite.

    You are the _____.

4. The blouse was expensive.
    The sweater was more expensive.

    The coat was the _____.

5. The class was fortunate.
    The teacher was more fortunate.

    The principal was the _____.

6. The cookies were delicious.
    The cake was even more delicious.

    The brownies were the _____.

Absolutely Adverbs

Like adjectives, **adverbs** are describing words. They describe verbs. Adverbs tell how, when or where action takes place.

Examples:

How	When	Where
slowly	yesterday	here
gracefully	today	there
swiftly	tomorrow	everywhere
quickly	soon	

How?

When?

Where?

Hint: To identify an adverb, locate the verb, then ask yourself if there are any words that tell how, when or where action takes place.

Directions: Read the following sentences. Underline the adverbs, then write whether they tell how, when or where. The first one has been done for you.

1. At the end of the day, the children ran <u>quickly</u> home from school. _____how_____

2. They will have a spelling test tomorrow. _____

3. Slowly, the children filed to their seats. _____

4. The teacher sat here at her desk. _____

5. She will pass the tests back later. _____

6. The students received their grades happily. _____

Directions: Write four sentences of your own using any of the adverbs above.

_____

_____

_____

_____

Adverb Adventure

Adverbs are words that tell when, where, or how.

Adverbs of time tell when.

Example:

The train left yesterday.
Yesterday is an adverb of time. It tells when the train left.

Adverbs of place tell where.

Example:

The girl walked away.
Away is an adverb of place. It tells where the girl walked.

Adverbs of manner tell how.

Example:

The boy walked quickly.
Quickly is an adverb of manner. It tells how the boy walked.

Directions: Write the adverb for each sentence in the first blank. In the second blank, write whether it is an adverb of time, place or manner. The first one has been done for you.

1. The family ate downstairs.

    <u>downstairs</u>   <u>place</u>

2. The relatives laughed loudly.

    _____   _____

3. We will finish tomorrow.

    _____   _____

4. The snowstorm will stop soon.

    _____   _____

5. She sings beautifully!

    _____   _____

6. The baby slept soundly.

    _____   _____

7. She ran outside.

    _____   _____

Tell Me More

Directions: Write **ADJ** on the line if the bold word is an adjective. Write **ADV** if the bold word is an adverb. The first one has been done for you.

_____ 1. That road leads **nowhere**.

_____ 2. The squirrel was **nearby**.

_____ 3. Her **delicious** cookies were all eaten.

_____ 4. Everyone rushed **indoors**.

_____ 5. He **quickly** zipped his jacket.

_____ 6. She hummed a **popular** tune.

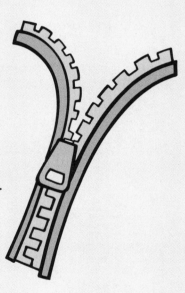

_____ 7. Her **sunny** smile warmed my heart.

_____ 8. I hung your coat **there**.

_____ 9. Bring that **here** this minute!

_____10. We all walked **back** to school.

_____11. The **skinniest** boy ate the most food!

_____12. She acts like a **famous** person.

_____13. The **silliest** jokes always make me laugh.

Review

Directions: Write the correct words to complete the sentences. Use the words on the presents at the bottom of the page.

1. The suffix _____ and the word

   _____ are used when comparing two things.

2. One example of an adverb of time is _____.

3. When an adjective ends with _____, you change the **y** to **i** before adding er or est.

4. An _____ is a word that tells when, where or how.

5. An example of an adverb of place is _____.

6. The suffix _____ and the word

   _____ are used when comparing more that two things.

7. An _____ is a word that describes a noun.

8. An example of an adverb of manner is _____.

adjective   est   softly

adverb   er

y   most   there

more   tomorrow

Join the Fun

Conjunctions are joining words that can be used to combine sentences. Words such as **and**, **but**, **or**, **when** and **after** are conjunctions.

Examples:

Kaitlyn went to the mall. She went to the movies.
Kaitlyn went to the mall, and she went to the movies.

We can have our vacation at home. We can vacation at the beach.
We can have our vacation at home, or we can vacation at the beach.

Jada fell on the playground. She did not hurt herself.
Jada fell on the playground, but she did not hurt herself.

Note: The conjunctions **after** or **when** are usually placed at the beginning of the sentence.

Example: Amrita went to the store. She went to the gas station.
After Amrita went to the store, she went to the gas station.

Directions: Combine the following sentences using a conjunction.

1. Peter fell down the steps. He broke his foot. (and)

   _____

2. I visited New York. I would like to see Chicago. (but)

   _____

3. Rosie can edit books. She can write stories. (or)

   _____

4. He played in the barn. John started to sneeze. (when)

   _____

5. The team won the playoffs. They went to the championships. (after)

   _____

Directions: Write three sentences of your own using the conjunctions **and**, **but**, **or**, **when** and **after**.

_____

_____

_____

Conjunction Function

Directions: Choose the best conjunction from the box to combine the pairs of sentences. Then, rewrite the sentences.

and   but   or   because   when   after   so

1. I like Leah. I like Ben.

    _____

2. Should I eat the orange? Should I eat the apple?

    _____

3. You will get a reward. You turned in the lost item.

    _____

4. I really mean what I say! You had better listen!

    _____

5. I like you. You're nice, friendly, helpful and kind.

    _____

6. You can have dessert. You ate all your peas.

    _____

7. I like your shirt better. You should decide for yourself.

    _____

Writing

Common Commas

Use a comma to separate the number of the day of a month and the year. Do not use a comma to separate the month and year if no day is given.

Examples:

June 14, 2010

June 2009

Use a comma after _____ the first word in a sentence.

Examples:

Yes, I wi_____

No,_____

**Directi_____ ctly. Draw an
X if the se_____ one has been
done for you.**

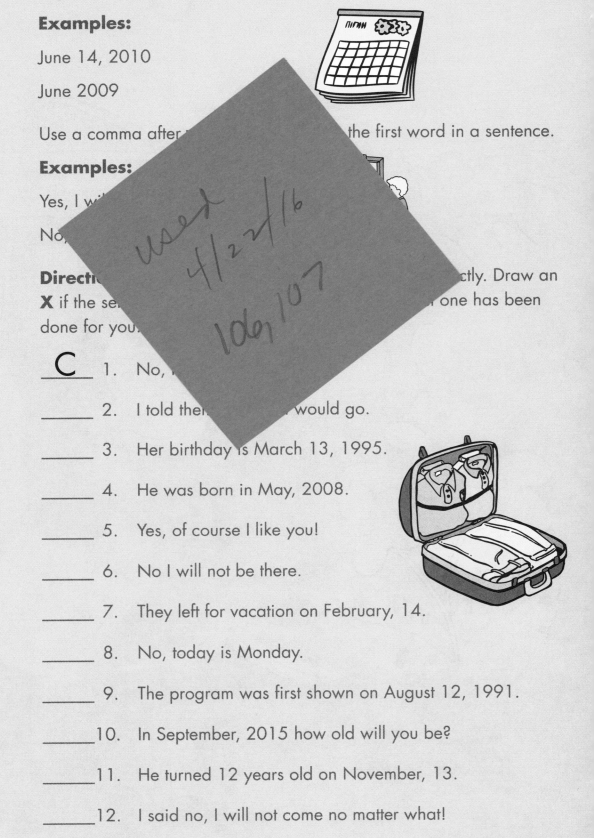

(handwritten note: used 4/22/16 106, 107)

___C___ 1. No, _____

_____ 2. I told the_____ would go.

_____ 3. Her birthday is March 13, 1995.

_____ 4. He was born in May, 2008.

_____ 5. Yes, of course I like you!

_____ 6. No I will not be there.

_____ 7. They left for vacation on February, 14.

_____ 8. No, today is Monday.

_____ 9. The program was first shown on August 12, 1991.

_____10. In September, 2015 how old will you be?

_____11. He turned 12 years old on November, 13.

_____12. I said no, I will not come no matter what!

The Comma Connection

Use a comma to separate words in a series. A comma is used after each word in a series but is not needed before the last word. Both ways are correct. In your own writing, be consistent about which style you use.

Examples:

We ate apples, oranges, and pears.
We ate apples, oranges and pears.

Always use a comma between the name of a city and a state.

Example:

She lives in Fresno, California.
He lives in Wilmington, Delaware.

Directions: Write **C** if the sentence is punctuated correctly. Draw an **X** if the sentence is not punctuated correctly. The first one has been done for you.

_X_ 1. She ordered shoes, dresses and shirts to be sent to her home in Oakland California.

_____ 2. No one knew her pets' names were Fido, Spot and Tiger.

_____ 3. He likes green beans lima beans, and corn on the cob.

_____ 4. Typing paper, pens and pencils are all needed for school.

_____ 5. Send your letters to her in College Park, Maryland.

_____ 6. Orlando Florida is the home of Disney World.

_____ 7. Mickey, Minnie, Goofy and Daisy are all favorites of mine.

_____ 8. Send your letter to her in Reno, Nevada.

_____ 9. Before he lived in New York, City he lived in San Diego, California.

_____10. She mailed postcards, and letters to him in Lexington, Kentucky.

_____11. Teacups, saucers, napkins, and silverware were piled high.

Good Reads

All words in the title of a book are underlined. Underlined words also mean italics.

Examples:

<u>The Hunt for Red October</u> was a best-seller!
(*The Hunt for Red October*)

Have you read <u>Lost in Space</u>?
(*Lost in Space*)

Directions: Underline the book titles in these sentences. The first one has been done for you.

1. <u>The Dinosaur Poster Book</u> is for eight year olds.

2. Have you read Lion Dancer by Kate Waters?

3. Baby Dinosaurs and Giant Dinosaurs were both written by Peter Dodson.

4. Have you heard of the book That's What Friends Are For by Carol Adorjan?

5. J.B. Stamper wrote a book called The Totally Terrific Valentine Party Book.

6. The teacher read Almost Ten and a Half aloud to our class.

7. Marrying Off Mom is about a girl who tries to get her widowed mother to start dating.

8. The Snow and The Fire are the second and third books by author Caroline Cooney.

9. The title sounds silly, but Goofbang Value Daze really is the name of a book!

10. A book about space exploration is The Day We Walked on the Moon by George Sullivan.

11. Alice and the Birthday Giant tells about a giant who came to a girl's birthday party.

Hooked on Books

Capitalize the first and last word of book titles. Capitalize all other words of book titles except short prepositions, such as **of**, **at** and **in**; conjunctions, such as **and**, **or** and **but**; and articles, such as **a**, **an** and **the**.

Examples:

Have you read <u>War and Peace</u>?

Pippi Longstocking in Moscow is her favorite book.

Directions: Underline the book titles. Circle the words that should be capitalized. The first one has been done for you.

1. (murder) in the (blue room) by Elliot Roosevelt

2. growing up in a divided society by Sandra Burnham

3. the corn king and the spring queen by Naomi Mitchison

4. new kids on the block by Grace Catalano

5. best friends don't tell lies by Linda Barr

6. turn your kid into a computer genius by Carole Gerber

7. 50 simple things you can do to save the earth by Earth Works Press

8. garfield goes to waist by Jim Davis

9. the hunt for red october by Tom Clancy

10. fall into darkness by Christopher Pike

11. oh the places you'll go! by Dr. Seuss

12. amy the dancing bear by Carly Simon

You Said It!

Use quotation marks (" ") before and after the exact words of a speaker.

Examples:

> I asked Aunt Martha, "How do you feel?"
> "I feel awful," Aunt Martha replied.

Do not put quotation marks around words that report what the speaker said.

Examples:

> Aunt Martha said she felt awful.
> I asked Aunt Martha how she felt.

Directions: Write **C** if the sentence is punctuated correctly. Draw an **X** if the sentence is not punctuated correctly. The first one has been done for you.

__C__ 1. "I want it right now!" she demanded angrily.

_____ 2 "Do you want it now? I asked."

_____ 3. She said "she felt better" now.

_____ 4. Her exact words were, "I feel much better now!"

_____ 5. "I am so thrilled to be here!" he shouted.

_____ 6. "Yes, I will attend," she replied.

_____ 7. Elizabeth said "she was unhappy."

_____ 8. "I'm unhappy," Elizabeth reported.

_____ 9. "Did you know her mother?" I asked.

_____ 10. I asked "whether you knew her mother."

_____ 11. I wondered, "What will dessert be?"

_____ 12. "Which will it be, salt or pepper?" the waiter asked.

Sing Me a Song

Use quotation marks around the titles of songs and poems.

Examples:

Have you heard "Still Cruising" by the Beach Boys?

"Ode To a Nightingale" is a famous poem.

Directions. Write **C** if the sentence is punctuated correctly. Draw an **X** if the sentence is not punctuated correctly. The first one has been done for you.

__C__ 1. Do you know "My Bonnie Lies Over the Ocean"?

_____ 2. We sang The Stars and Stripes Forever" at school.

_____ 3. Her favorite song is "The Eensy Weensy Spider."

_____ 4. Turn the music up when "A Hard Day's "Night comes on!

_____ 5. "Yesterday" was one of Paul McCartney's most famous songs.

_____ 6. "Mary Had a Little Lamb" is a very silly poem!

_____ 7. A song everyone knows is "Happy Birthday."

_____ 8. "Swing Low, Sweet Chariot" was first sung by slaves.

_____ 9. Do you know the words to Home on "the Range"?

_____10. "Hiawatha" is a poem many older people had to memorize.

_____11. "Happy Days Are Here Again! is an upbeat tune.

_____12. Frankie Valli and the Four Seasons sang "Sherry."

Review

Directions: The following sentences have errors in punctuation, capitalization or both. The number in parentheses **( )** at the end of each sentence tells you how many errors it contains. Correct the errors by rewriting each sentence.

1. I saw mr. Johnson reading War And Peace to his class. (3)

   _____

2. Do you like to sing "Take me Out to The Ballgame"? (2)

   _____

3. He recited Hiawatha to Miss. Simpson's class. (2)

   _____

4. Bananas, and oranges are among Dr patel's favorite fruits. (3)

   _____

5. "Daisy, daisy is a song about a bicycle built for two. (2)

   _____

6. Good Morning, Granny Rose is about a woman and her dog. (1)

   _____

7. Garfield goes to waist is a very funny book! (3)

   _____

8. Peanut butter, jelly, and bread are miss. Lee's favorite treats. (1)

   _____

Proof It!

Proofreading means searching for and correcting errors by carefully reading and rereading what has been written. Use the proofreading marks below when correcting your writing or someone else's.

To insert a word or a punctuation mark that has been left out, use this mark: ∧. It is called a *caret*.

Example: We ∧to the dance together.
               went

To show that a letter should be capitalized, put three lines under it.

Example: Mrs. jones drove us to school.
                  ≡

To show a capital letter should be small or lowercase, draw a diagonal line through it.

Example: Mrs. Jones D̸rove us to school.

To show that a word is spelled incorrectly, draw a horizontal line through it and write the correct spelling above it.

Example: The ~~wolros~~ is an amazing animal. walrus
                   walrus

Directions: Proofread the two paragraphs using proofreading marks you learned. The author's last name, Towne, is spelled correctly.

The Modern ark

My book report is on the modern ark by Cecilia Fitzsimmons. The book tells abut 80 of worlds endangered animals. The book also an arc and animals inside for kids put together.

Their House

there house is a Great book! The arthur's name is Mary Towne. they're house tells about a girl name Molly. Molly's Family bys an old house from some people named warren. Then, there big problems begin!

Key Facts

Directions: Proofread the sentences. Write **C** if the sentence has no errors. Draw an **X** if the sentence contains missing words or other errors. The first one has been done for you.

____**C**____ 1.   The new Ship Wreck Museum in Key West is exciting!

_____ 2.   Another thing I liked was the litehouse.

_____ 3.   Do you remember Hemingway's address in Key West?

_____ 4.   The Key West semetery is on 21 acres of ground.

_____ 5.   Ponce de eon discovered Key West.

_____ 6.   The cemetery in Key West is on Francis Street.

_____ 7.   My favorete tombstone was the sailor's.

_____ 8.   His wife wrote the words on it. Remember?

_____ 9.   The words said, "at least I know where to find him now!"

_____10.   That sailor must have been away at sea all the time.

_____11.   The troley ride around Key West is very interesting.

_____12.   Do you why it is called Key West?

A Tropical Paradise

Directions: Proofread the paragraphs, using the proofreading marks you learned. There are seven capitalization errors, three missing words and eleven errors in spelling or word usage.

Key West

key West has been tropical paradise ever since Ponce de Leon first saw the set of islands called the keys in 1513. Two famus streets in Key West are named duval and whitehead. You will find the city semetery on Francis Street. The tombstones are funny!

The message on one is, "I told you I was sick!" On sailor's tombston is this mesage his widow: "At lease I no where to find him now."

The cemetery is on 21 akres in the midle of town. The most famous home in key west is that of the authur, Ernest Hemingway. Heminway's home was at 907 whitehead Street. He lived their for 30 years.

On the Run

A **run-on sentence** occurs when two or more sentences are joined together without punctuation.

Examples:

Run-on sentence:
I lost my way once did you?

Two sentences with correct punctuation:
I lost my way once. Did you?

Run-on sentence:
I found the recipe it was not hard to follow.

Two sentences with correct punctuation:
I found the recipe. It was not hard to follow.

Directions: Rewrite the run-on sentences correctly with periods, exclamation points, and question marks. The first one has been done for you.

1. Did you take my umbrella I can't find it anywhere!

   <u>Did you take my umbrella? I can't find it anywhere!</u>

2. How can you stand that noise I can't!

   _____

3. The cookies are gone I see only crumbs.

   _____

4. The dogs were barking they were hungry.

   _____

5. She is quite ill please call a doctor immediately!

   _____

6. The clouds came up we knew the storm would hit soon.

   _____

7. You weren't home he stopped by this morning.

   _____

Putting It Together

Directions: Make each pair of sentences into one sentence. (You may have to change the verbs for some sentences—from **is** to **are**, for example.)

Example:

Our house was flooded. Our car was flooded.

Our house and car were flooded.

1. Dmitry sees a glow.   Carrie sees a glow.

    _____

2. Our new stove came today.   Our new refrigerator came today.

    _____

3. The pond is full of toads.   The field is full of toads.

    _____

4. Stripes are on the flag.   Stars are on the flag.

    _____

5. The ducks took flight.   The geese took flight.

    _____

6. Joe reads stories.   Dana reads stories.

    _____

Frosty Fun

A **paragraph** is a group of sentences that share the same idea.

Directions: Rewrite the paragraph by combining the simple sentences into larger sentences.

Jason awoke early. He threw off his covers. He ran to his window. He looked outside. He saw snow. It was white and fluffy. Jason thought of something. He thought of his sled. His sled was in the garage. He quickly ate breakfast. He dressed warmly. He got his sled. He went outside. He went to play in the snow.

_____

_____

_____

_____

_____

_____

_____

_____

_____

_____

_____

_____

_____

Friends to the End

A **paragraph** is a group of sentences that tells about one main idea. A **topic sentence** tells the main idea of a paragraph.

Many topic sentences come first in the paragraph. The topic sentence in the paragraph below is underlined. Do you see how it tells the reader what the whole paragraph is about?

<u>Friendships can make you happy or make you sad.</u> You feel happy to do things and go places with your friends. You get to know each other so well that you can almost read each others' minds. But friendships can be sad when your friend moves away—or decides to be best friends with someone else.

Directions: Underline the topic sentence in the paragraph below.

We have two rules about using the phone at our house. Our whole family agreed on them. The first rule is not to talk longer than 10 minutes. The second rule is to take good messages if you answer the phone for someone else.

Directions: After you read the paragraph below, write a topic sentence for it.

_____

_____

_____

For one thing, you could ask your neighbors if they need any help. They might be willing to pay you for walking their dog or mowing their grass or weeding their garden. Maybe your older brothers or sisters would pay you to do some of their chores. You also could ask your parents if there's an extra job you could do around the house to make money.

Directions: Write a topic sentence for a paragraph on each of these subjects.

Homework: _____

_____

Television: _____

_____

Rain, Rain, Go Away

Supporting sentences provide details about the topic sentence of a paragraph.

Directions: In the paragraph below, underline the topic sentence. Then, cross out the supporting sentence that does not belong in the paragraph.

One spring it started to rain and didn't stop for 2 weeks. All the rivers flooded. Some people living near the rivers had to leave their homes. Farmers couldn't plant their crops because the fields were so wet. Plants need water to grow. The sky was dark and gloomy all the time.

Directions: Write three supporting sentences to go with each topic sentence below. Make sure each supporting sentence stays on the same subject as the topic sentence.

Not everyone should have a pet.

_____

_____

_____

I like to go on field trips with my class.

_____

_____

_____

I've been thinking about what I want to be when I get older.

_____

_____

_____

Thanks for Your Support!

Directions: For each topic below, write a topic sentence and four supporting details.

Example:

Playing with friends:

(topic sentence)
Playing with my friends can be lots of fun.

(details)

1.   We like to ride our bikes together.

2.   We play fun games like "dress up" and "animal hospital."

3.   Sometimes, we swing on the swings or slide down the slides on our swingsets.

4.   We like to pretend we are having tea with our stuffed animals.

Recess at school:

_____

_____

_____

_____

Summer vacation:

_____

_____

_____

_____

Brothers or sisters: _____

_____

_____

_____

_____

Paragraph Perfection

When you have many good ideas about a subject, you need to organize your writing into more than one paragraph. It is easy to organize your thoughts about a topic if you use a "cluster of ideas" chart.

Example:

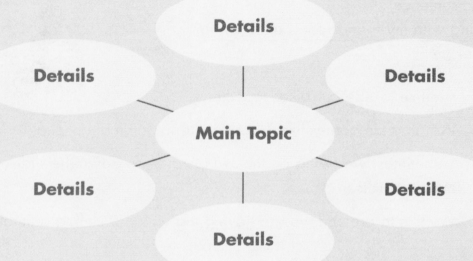

The main topic of your story is stated in the middle circle. Details about the main topic are listed in the outer circles.

Study the following "cluster of ideas" and note how the thoughts are organized in paragraph form on the following page.

Dressed for the Day

Once your ideas are "clustered," go back and decide which ideas should be the first, second, third, and so on. These numbers will be the order of the paragraph in the finished story.

Directions: Read the story paragraphs below.

Clothes for Saturday

This Saturday, my family and I will be working in the yard. We will be mowing grass, raking leaves and pulling weeds. When I get up that day, I know I will need to wear clothes that will keep me warm in the autumn air. My clothes will also need to be ones that will not be ruined if they get muddy or dirty.

The best choice of pants for our busy day will be my jeans. They are nicely faded and well worn, which means they are quite comfortable. They will be good for yard work since mud and grass stains wash out of them easily.

My shirt will be my yellow golf shirt. It will match the blue of my jeans. Also, its short sleeves will be fine if the weather is warm.

For warmth on Saturday, if the day is cool, will be my yellow and red sweater. It is made from cotton and has long sleeves and high buttons to keep out frosty air.

Yard work means lots of walking, so I will need comfortable shoes. The best choice will be my white sneakers. They aren't too tight or too loose and keep my feet strong. Saturday will be a busy day, but I'll be ready!

When "Clothes for Saturday" was written, the author added both an introductory and concluding paragraph. This helps the reader with the flow of the story.

Directions: Now, it's your turn. Select a topic from the list below or choose one of your own. Create a "cluster of ideas" chart on a blank sheet of paper and write a brief story.

Topics:

chores	holidays	all about me	sports
homework	family	pets	vacation

Note It!

Taking notes effectively can help you in many ways with schoolwork. It will help you better understand and remember what you read and hear. It will also help you keep track of important facts needed for reports, essays and tests.

Each person develops his/her own way of taking notes. While developing your style, keep in mind the following:

- Write notes in short phrases instead of whole sentences.
- Abbreviate words to save time.
  Examples: pres for president or **&** for and
- If you use the same name often in your notes, use initials.
  Examples: GW for George Washington
  AL for Abraham Lincoln.
- Be brief, but make sure you understand what you write.
- Number your notes, so you can understand where each note starts and stops.
- When taking notes from a long article or book, write down one or two important points per paragraph or chapter.

Directions: Reread the article "Floating Free"on page 71. As you read the first three paragraphs, fill in the note-taking format below with your notes.

Title of Article or Story _____

Important Points

Paragraph 1 _____

_____

_____

Paragraph 2 _____

_____

_____

Paragraph 3 _____

_____

_____

Notable Notes

Directions: Use this guide for taking notes on the articles in the next two pages. Set up your own paper in a similar way, or make several photocopies, for note-taking on future pages.

Penguins Are Unusual Birds
(Title)

Paragraph or
Chapter numbers   Important Points

1 _____

_____

_____

2 _____

_____

_____

3 _____

_____

_____

From Grapes to Raisins
(Title)

Paragraph or
Chapter numbers   Important Points

1 _____

_____

_____

2 _____

_____

_____

3 _____

_____

_____

A Most Unusual Bird

Directions: Use a sheet of paper to cover up the story about penguins. Then, read the questions.

1. Why are penguins unusual?

2. Do penguins swim?

3. Where do penguins live?

4. Do penguins lay eggs like other birds?

Directions: Read about penguins. While reading, make notes on the note-taking sheet on the previous page.

Penguins may be the most unusual birds. They cannot fly, but they can swim very fast through ice-cold water. They can dive deep into the water, and they can jump high out of it. Sometimes they make their nests out of rocks instead of twigs and grass. Some penguins live in very cold parts of the world. Others live in warmer climates. All penguins live south of the equator.

Unlike other birds, penguins lay only one egg at a time. Right after a mother penguin lays her egg, she waddles back to the ocean. The father penguin holds the egg on his feet, covering it with part of his stomach to keep it warm. When the egg is ready to hatch, the mother penguin returns. Then, the father penguin takes a turn looking for food.

When a penguin swims, its white belly and dark back help it hide from enemies. From under the water, predators cannot see it. From on top of the water, large birds cannot see it either. This is how the penguin stays safe!

Directions: Use your notes to complete these sentences.

1. Penguins cannot fly, but _____.

2. Penguins can dive deep and _____.

3. Penguins lay only _____.

4. Father penguins keep the egg _____.

5. Mother penguins return when the egg _____

m Grapes to Raisins

tions: Use a piece of paper to cover up the story about how
es become raisins. Then, read the questions.

1. How do grapes become raisins?

2. What happens after the grapes become raisins?

3. Why are raisins brown?

4. In what countries do grapes grow?

Directions: Read about how grapes become raisins. While reading,
make notes on the note-taking sheet on page 125.

Grapes grow well in places that have lots of sun. In the United
States, California is a big producer of grapes and raisins. When
grapes are plump and round, they can be picked from their vines to
be made into raisins. After the grapes are picked, they are put on big
wooden or paper trays. They sit in the sun for many days.

Slowly, the grapes begin to dry and turn into wrinkled raisins.
The sun causes them to change colors. Grapes turn brown as they
become raisins. Machines take off the stems. Then, the raisins are
washed. After being dried again, they are put into boxes.

Some places use machines to make raisins dry faster. The
grapes are put into ovens that have hot air blowing around inside.
These ovens make the grapes shrivel and dry.

Raisins are made in many countries that grow grapes. Besides
the United States, countries such as Greece, Turkey, Iran, Spain and
Australia produce a lot of raisins.

Directions: Use your notes to answer the four questions at the top of
the page. Write your answers on the lines below.

1. _____

   _____

2. _____

   _____

   _____

3. _____

4. _____

Garden Growing

Outlines are plans that help you organize your thou[ghts]
writing an essay, an outline helps you decide what to w[rite]
should look similar to this:

I.   First main idea
   A.   A smaller idea
      1.   An example
      2.   An example
II. Second main idea
   A.   A smaller idea
   B.   Another smaller idea
III. Third main idea

I.   Planting a garde[n]
   A.   Choosing see[ds]
      1.   Tomatoes
      2.   Lettuce
II. Taking care of the garden
   A.   Pulling the weeds
   B.   Watering the garden
III. Harvesting
   A.   Are they ripe?
   B.   How to pick them
      1.   Pick only the
         tomato off the
         vine

Done 5/13/16

2. What are the two smaller ideas listed under "Taking care of the garden"?

   1) _____

   2) _____

3. What are the smaller ideas listed under "Harvesting"?

   1) _____

   2) _____

4. What is listed under the smaller idea "How to pick them"?

   _____

All About Me

When you summarize an article, book or speech, you are simply writing a shorter article that contains only the main points. This shorter article of main points is called a summary.

To prepare for writing a summary of your life, you would begin with an outline. Since a summary is a brief account of main points, you will not be able to include every detail of your life. Your summary should include only basic facts.

I. Yourself
   A. Name
   B. Age and grade in school
       1. Subjects you like in school
       2. Subjects you do not like in school
   C. Looks
       1. Eye color
       2. Hair color
       3. Other features
II. Your family
   A. Parents
   B. Brothers/sisters
   C. Pets
III. Hobbies and interests
   A. Sports
   B. Clubs

Directions: Follow the format above to write an outline about your life. Feel free to add more main ideas, smaller ideas, or examples.

_____

_____

_____

_____

_____

_____

_____

Busy Kids

Directions: Read about settler children. Then, complete the list of main points at the end of the article.

In the 1700s and 1800s, many children from other countries came with their parents to America. In the beginning, they had no time to go to school. They had to help their families work in the fields, care for the animals and clean the house. They also helped care for their younger brothers and sisters.

Sometimes settler children helped build houses and schools. Usually, these early school buildings were just one room. There was only one teacher for all the children. Settler children were very happy when they could attend school.

Because settler children worked so much, they had little time to play. There were not many things settler children could do just for fun. One pastime was gardening. Weeding their gardens taught them how to be orderly. Children sometimes made gifts out of the things they grew.

The settlers also encouraged their children to sing. Each one was expected to play at least one musical instrument. Parents wanted their children to walk, ride horses, visit friends and relatives and read nonfiction books.

Most settler children did not have many toys. The toys they owned were made by their parents and grandparents. They were usually made of cloth or carved from wood. The children made up games with string, like "cat's cradle." They also made things out of wood, such as seesaws. Settler children did not have all the toys we have today, but they managed to have fun anyway!

The main points of this article are:

1. Settler children worked hard.

2. Settler children had many jobs.

3. _____

4. _____

5. _____

Directions: Use the main points to write a summary of this article on a separate sheet of paper.

Out of This World

The history of the American space program is a very fascinating topic. The articles presented earlier in this book (pages 69–72) provided many interesting facts about some of the astronauts, what their jobs were and what space travel was like.

Besides books and encyclopedias, magazine articles and the Internet are other good reference sources you can use to learn more about a topic.

Directions: Neil Armstrong was the first man to walk on the Moon in July 1969. Use reference sources to answer these questions.

1. What two other astronauts were with him?

   _____

2. What was the name of the Apollo mission that went

   to the Moon? _____

3. What was the exact date of the first Moon landing?

   _____

4. Why was the U.S. racing Russia to the Moon?

   _____

Directions: John Glenn first orbited Earth in 1962. Use reference sources to answer these questions.

5. How old was he then? _____

6. When did John Glenn return to space? _____

7. How old was he on this second trip? _____

8. Why did he return to space?

   _____

Directions: Compare and contrast Glenn's two trips.

9. _____

Simply Cinquains

Another form of unrhymed poetry that can express many ideas in only a few words is the **cinquain**. A cinquain is a simple five-line verse.

In a cinquain, the number of syllables does not matter. What is important is the number of words in each line and the specific type of words used.

Cinquain pattern:

Line 1 — A noun
Line 2 — 2 adjectives describing the noun in line 1
Line 3 — 3 ing verbs describing the noun in line 1
Line 4 — A 4-word phrase
Line 5 — A noun that is a synonym for the word in line 1

Example cinquains:

Apple
Shiny, smooth
Crunching, munching, slurping
Healthy snack to eat
Fruit

Grace
Young, active
Trying, discovering, learning
Anxious to grow up
Daughter

Directions: Think of someone you know well. Write a cinquain about that person. Prewrite words and phrases to get started. Write your final draft on the lines.

_____

_____

_____

_____

Directions: Select your favorite holiday and write a cinquain about it.

_____

_____

_____

_____

Math

Finding Your Place

Place value is the value of a digit, or numeral, shown by where it is in the number. For example, in 1,234, 1 has the place value of thousands, 2 is hundreds, 3 is tens, and 4 is ones.

Directions: Write the numbers in the correct boxes to find how far the car has traveled.

one thousand

six hundreds

eight ones

nine ten thousands

four tens

two millions

five hundred thousands

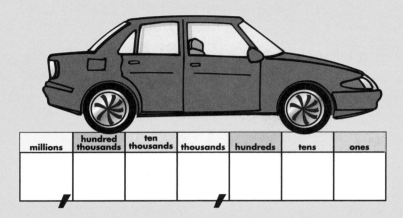

millions	hundred thousands	ten thousands	thousands	hundreds	tens	ones

How many miles has the car traveled? _____

Directions: In the number . . .

2,386 _____ is in the ones place.

4,957 _____ is in the hundreds place.

102,432 _____ is in the ten thousands place.

1,743,998 _____ is in the millions place.

9,301,671 _____ is in the hundred thousands place.

Going in Circles

Directions: Where the circles meet, write the sum of the numbers from the circles on the right and left and above and below. The first row shows you what to do.

7 16 9 21 12 20 8

4   6   5   1

0   3   2   10

11   15   20   12

13   16   14   17

Adding On

When adding two-, three- and four-digit numbers, add the ones first, then tens, hundreds, thousands, and so on.

Example:

Tens	Ones
5	4
+2	5
	9

Tens	Ones
5	4
+2	5
7	9

Directions: Add the following numbers.

$$
\begin{array}{r} 81 \\ +23 \\ \hline \end{array}
\qquad
\begin{array}{r} 67 \\ +22 \\ \hline \end{array}
\qquad
\begin{array}{r} 34 \\ +82 \\ \hline \end{array}
\qquad
\begin{array}{r} 730 \\ +265 \\ \hline \end{array}
$$

$$
\begin{array}{r} 76 \\ +73 \\ \hline \end{array}
\qquad
\begin{array}{r} 1{,}803 \\ +1{,}104 \\ \hline \end{array}
\qquad
\begin{array}{r} 523 \\ +476 \\ \hline \end{array}
\qquad
\begin{array}{r} 267 \\ +\ 12 \\ \hline \end{array}
$$

$$
\begin{array}{r} 4{,}254 \\ +\ 545 \\ \hline \end{array}
\qquad
\begin{array}{r} 111 \\ +\ 82 \\ \hline \end{array}
$$

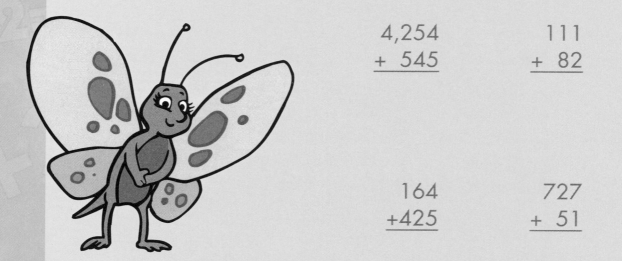

$$
\begin{array}{r} 164 \\ +425 \\ \hline \end{array}
\qquad
\begin{array}{r} 727 \\ +\ 51 \\ \hline \end{array}
$$

In the Doghouse

Regrouping uses 10 ones to form one 10, 10 tens to form one hundred, one 10 and 5 ones to form 15, and so on.

Directions: Add using regrouping. Color in all the boxes with a 5 in the answer to help the dog find its way home.

		5,268			
	63 +22	4,910 +1,683	248 +463	291 +543	2,934 + 112
1,736 +5,367	2,946 +7,384	3,245 1,239 + 981	738 +692	896 +728	594 +738
2,603 +5,004	4,507 + 289	1,483 +6,753	1,258 +6,301	27 469 +6,002	4,637 +7,531
782 + 65	485 +276	3,421 +8,064			
48 93 +26	90 263 +864	362 453 +800			

Subtraction Action

Subtraction is "taking away" or subtracting one number from another.

Directions: Complete the following problems as quickly and as accurately as you can.

18 − 9	13 − 6	12 − 5	17 − 8	16 − 8

12 − 5	10 − 4	5 −3	14 − 6	15 − 9

9 −5	8 −3	6 −2	5 −4	10 − 7

11 − 4	12 − 8	16 − 9	11 − 8	10 −10

How quickly did you complete this page? _____

Take It Away!

When you subtract larger numbers, subtract the ones first, then the tens, hundreds, thousands, and so on.

Example:

Tens	Ones
9	4
−2	1
3	

Tens	Ones
9	4
−2	1
7	3

Directions: Solve these subtraction problems.

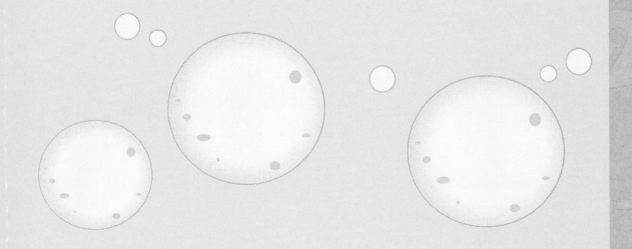

$$\begin{array}{r} 29 \\ -26 \\ \hline \end{array}$$

$$\begin{array}{r} 99 \\ -58 \\ \hline \end{array}$$

$$\begin{array}{r} 359 \\ -\ 55 \\ \hline \end{array}$$

$$\begin{array}{r} 735 \\ -734 \\ \hline \end{array}$$

$$\begin{array}{r} 849 \\ -726 \\ \hline \end{array}$$

$$\begin{array}{r} 7,678 \\ -4,321 \\ \hline \end{array}$$

$$\begin{array}{r} 865 \\ -731 \\ \hline \end{array}$$

$$\begin{array}{r} 55 \\ -25 \\ \hline \end{array}$$

$$\begin{array}{r} 9,876 \\ -1,234 \\ \hline \end{array}$$

Regrouping Roundup

Directions: Subtract using regrouping.

Examples:

23	1	243	113
−18	~~23~~	− 96	~~243~~
	−18		− 96
	5		147

81	76	94	156	341
−53	−49	−38	− 77	− 83

568	806	743	903	647
−173	−738	−550	−336	−289

730	961	573	604	265
−518	−846	− 76	− 55	− 19

111	358	147
− 82	− 99	− 49

180	325	873
−106	− 68	− 35

Pond Play

Directions: Add or subtract, using regrouping when needed.

```
   38      1,269               629
   43      2,453     5,792     491      4,697
  +21     +8,219    -4,814    +308     -2,988
```

```
                     68       197
 5,280       27      436      7,321     456
-3,147      +42     +213     -2,789    +974
```

```
             492
 3,932       863    9,873     4,978     6,235
+4,681      + 57   +5,483    +2,131    +2,986
```

Elena stocked her pond with 263 bass
and 187 trout. 97 fish swam away in a
flood. How many fish are left?   _____

Turtles All A-Round

Rounding a number means expressing it to the nearest ten, hundred, thousand, and so on. Knowing how to round numbers makes estimating sums, differences and products easier. When rounding to the nearest ten, the key number is in the ones place. If the ones digit is 5 or larger, round up to the next highest ten. If the ones digit is 4 or less, round down to the nearest ten.

Examples:

- Round 81 to the nearest ten.
- 1 is the key digit.
- If it is less than 5, round down.
- **Answer:** 80

- Round 246 to the nearest ten.
- 6 is the key digit.
- If it is more than 5, round up.
- **Answer:** 250

Directions: Round these numbers to the nearest ten.

41 ____

32 ____

75 ____

481 ____

165 ____

29 ____

89 ____

17 ____

38 ____

68 ____

52 ____

87 ____

573 ____

98 ____

43 ____

12 ____

Round Up, Round Down

When rounding to the nearest hundred, the key number is in the tens place. If the tens digit is 5 or larger, round up to the nearest hundred. If the tens digit is 4 or less, round down to the nearest hundred.

Examples:

Round 871 to the nearest hundred.

7 is the key digit.

If it is more than 5, round up.

Answer: 900

Round 421 to the nearest hundred.

2 is the key digit.

If it is less than 4, round down.

Answer: 400

Directions: Round these numbers to the nearest hundred.

255 _____   368 _____   443 _____

562 _____   698 _____   99 _____

812 _____   592 _____   124 _____

When rounding to the nearest thousand, the key number is in the hundreds place. If the hundreds digit is 5 or larger, round up to the nearest thousand. If the hundreds digit is 4 or less, round down to the nearest thousand.

Examples:

Round 7,932 to the nearest thousand.

9 is the key digit.

If it is more than 5, round up.

Answer: 8,000

Round 1,368 to the nearest thousand.

3 is the key digit.

If it is less than 4, round down.

Answer: 1,000

Directions: Round these numbers to the nearest thousand.

8,631 _____   1,248 _____   798 _____

999 _____   6,229 _____   8,461 _____

9,654 _____   4,963 _____   99,923 _____

Can't Wait to Estimate!

Estimating is used for certain mathematical calculations. For example, to figure the cost of several items, round their prices to the nearest  dollar, then add up the approximate cost. A store clerk, on the other hand, needs to know the exact prices in order to charge the correct amount. To estimate to the nearest hundred, round up numbers over 50. **Example:** 251 is rounded up to 300. Round down numbers less than 50. **Example:** 128 is rounded down to 100.

Directions: In the following situations, write whether an exact or estimated answer should be used.

Example:

You make a deposit in your bank account.
Do you want an estimated total or an exact total? _____**Exact**_____

1. Your family just ate dinner at a restaurant. Your parents are trying to calculate the tip for your server. Should they estimate by rounding or use exact numbers?

   _____

2. You are at the store buying candy, and you want to know if you have enough money to pay for it. Should you estimate or use exact numbers?

   _____

3. Some friends are planning a trip from New York City to Washington, D.C. They need to know about how far they will travel in miles. Should they estimate or use exact numbers?

   _____

4. You plan a trip to the zoo. Beforehand, you call the zoo for the price of admission. Should the person at the zoo tell you an estimated or exact price?

   _____

5. The teacher is grading your papers. Should your scores be exact or estimated?

   _____

Game On!

Directions: Round the numbers to the nearest hundred. Then, solve the problems.

Example:

Jack and Alex were playing a computer game. Jack scored 428 points. Alex scored 132. About how many more points did Jack score than Alex?

Round Jack's 428 points down to the nearest hundred, 400.

Round Alex's 132 points down to 100. Subtract.

$$
\begin{array}{r}
400 \\
-100 \\
\hline
\textbf{300}
\end{array}
$$

estimate

258 ⟶ 300 +117 ⟶ +100 **375** **400**	493 ⟶ +114 ⟶
837 ⟶ −252 ⟶	928 ⟶ −437 ⟶
700 ⟶ −491 ⟶	319 ⟶ +630 ⟶
493 ⟶ −162 ⟶	1,356 ⟶ +2,941 ⟶

Missing Multiples

A multiple is the product of a specific number and any other number. For example, the multiples of 2 are 2 (2 x 1), 4 (2 x 2), 6, 8, 10, 12, and so on.

Directions: Write the missing multiples.

Example: Count by 5's.

5, 10, 15, 20, 25, 30, 35. These are multiples of 5.

Fact Factory

Factors are the numbers multiplied together in a multiplication problem. The product is the answer.

Directions: Write the missing factors or products.

×5		×9		×7		×3		×1		×8	
1	5	8	72	2	14	7		1		9	
5		3		5		4		12		8	
4	20	4			42	6		10		4	
6		9		8		1		3	3	5	
3		6	54	7		3		5		6	
2	10	7		4		2		7		7	
7		2			21	5		6		3	
9	45	1	9	0		8		4		2	

×2		×4		×6		×10		×11		×12	
	24	2		7			20	4		1	
	2	4		6		3		7		2	24
	22	6		5			40	9		3	
	4	8		4		5		10		4	48
	20		4	3			60	3		5	
	6		12	2		7		5		6	
	18		20	1			80	6		7	
	8		28	0		9		8		8	

Multiplication Mania

Multiplication is a short way to find the sum of adding the same number a certain amount of times, such as 7 x 4 = 28 instead of 7 + 7 + 7 + 7 = 28.

Directions: Multiply as quickly and as accurately as you can.

4 x7	7 x6	0 x8	7 x2	9 x5	1 x5
8 x3	7 x1	4 x2	9 x6	8 x5	6 x7
3 x5	7 x8	3 x9	5 x6	9 x9	7 x5

	3 x6	2 x8	8 x6
	0 x7	3 x3	

How quickly did you complete this page? _____

At the Pumpkin Patch

Directions: Multiply. Regroup when needed.

Example:

```
     563
   x 248
   4,504
  22,520
+112,600
 139,624
```

Hint: When Multiplying by the tens, start writing the number in the tens place. When multiplying by the hundreds, start in the hundreds place.

842	932	759	531
x167	x272	x468	x556

383	523	229	738
x476	x349	x189	x513

James grows pumpkins on his farm. He has 362 rows of pumpkins. There are 593 pumpkins in each row. How many pumpkins does James grow? _____

Caterpillar Crawl

Division is a way to find out how many times one number is contained in another number. For example, $28 \div 7 = 4$ means that there are 4 groups of 7 in 28.

Division problems can be written two ways: $36 \div 6 = 6$ or $6\overline{)36}$

These are the parts of a division problem:

dividend → $36 \div 6 = 6$ ← quotient
divisor

6 ← quotient
divisor → $6\overline{)36}$ ← dividend

Directions: Divide.

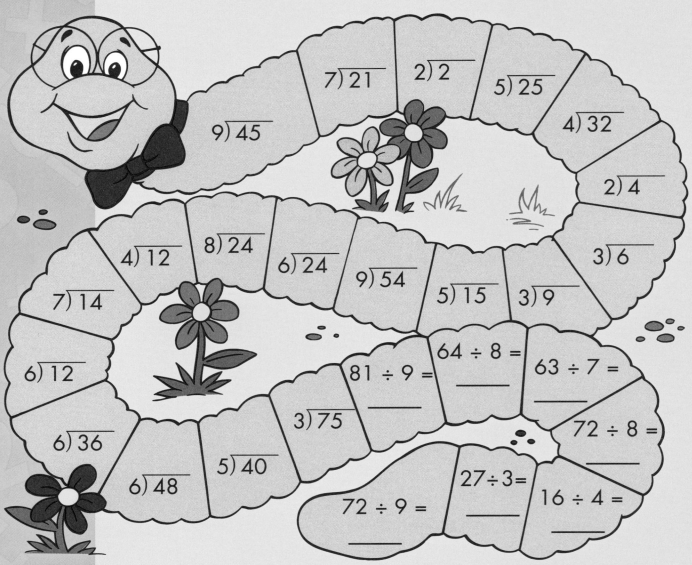

$9\overline{)45}$ $7\overline{)21}$ $2\overline{)2}$ $5\overline{)25}$ $4\overline{)32}$ $2\overline{)4}$ $3\overline{)6}$

$4\overline{)12}$ $8\overline{)24}$ $6\overline{)24}$ $9\overline{)54}$ $5\overline{)15}$ $3\overline{)9}$

$7\overline{)14}$ $6\overline{)12}$ $6\overline{)36}$ $6\overline{)48}$ $5\overline{)40}$ $3\overline{)75}$

$81 \div 9 =$ ____ $64 \div 8 =$ ____ $63 \div 7 =$ ____

$72 \div 8 =$ ____

$72 \div 9 =$ ____ $27 \div 3 =$ ____ $16 \div 4 =$ ____

Leftovers

Sometimes groups of objects or numbers cannot be divided into equal groups. The **remainder** is the number left over in the quotient of a division problem. The remainder must be smaller than the divisor.

Example:

Divide 18 butterflies into groups of 5.
You have 3 equal groups,
with 3 butterflies left over.

$18 \div 5 = 3 \text{ R}3$

or

$$\begin{array}{r} 3 \text{ R}3 \\ 5\overline{)18} \\ -15 \\ \hline 3 \end{array}$$

Directions: Divide. Some problems may have remainders.

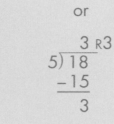

$9\overline{)84}$ $7\overline{)65}$ $8\overline{)25}$ $5\overline{)35}$ $5\overline{)34}$

$4\overline{)25}$ $6\overline{)56}$ $4\overline{)7}$ $4\overline{)16}$ $8\overline{)37}$

$7\overline{)27}$ $2\overline{)5}$ $2\overline{)4}$ $8\overline{)73}$ $4\overline{)9}$

$9\overline{)46}$ $5\overline{)17}$ $2\overline{)3}$ $4\overline{)13}$ $5\overline{)25}$

Check It Out!

To check a division problem, multiply the quotient by the divisor. Add the remainder. The answer will be the dividend.

Example:

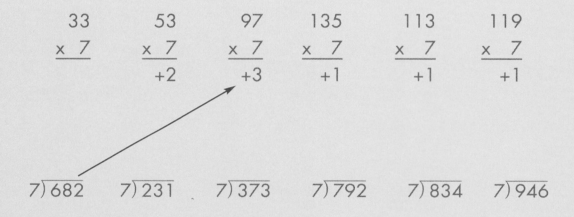

$$\begin{array}{r} \text{quotient} \\ 58 \text{ R}1 \\ \text{divisor} \rightarrow 3\overline{)175} \\ -15 \\ \hline 25 \\ -24 \\ \hline \text{remainder} \longrightarrow 1 \end{array}$$

$$\begin{array}{r} 58 \leftarrow \text{quotient} \\ \times\ 3 \leftarrow \text{divisor} \\ \hline 174 \\ +\ 1 \leftarrow \text{remainder} \\ \hline 175 \leftarrow \text{dividend} \end{array}$$

Directions: Divide each problem, then draw a line from the division problem to the correct checking problem.

33	53	97	135	113	119
x 7	x 7	x 7	x 7	x 7	x 7
	+2	+3	+1	+1	+1

7)682   7)231   7)373   7)792   7)834   7)946

The toy factory puts 7 robot dogs in each box. The factory has 256 robot dogs. How many boxes will they need? _____

Above Average

Directions: Find the averages.

Dominic went bowling.
He had scores of 112, 124 and 100.
What was his average?

_____

Abby ran 3 races.
Her times were 9 seconds,
10 seconds and 8 seconds.
What was her average?

_____

The baseball team played 6 games.
They had 12 hits, 6 hits, 18 hits,
36 hits, 11 hits and 7 hits.
What is the average number of hits in a game?

_____

In 3 games of football,
Chris gained 156, 268 and 176 yards running.
How many yards did he average in a game?

_____

Destiny scored 18, 15, 26 and
21 points in 4 basketball games.
How many points did she average?

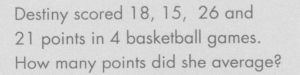

_____

A Piece of the Pie

A **fraction** is a number that names part of a whole, such as $\frac{1}{2}$ or $\frac{1}{3}$.

A fraction is made up of two numbers—the **numerator** (top number) and the **denominator** (bottom number). The larger the denominator, the smaller each of the equal parts: $\frac{1}{16}$ is smaller than $\frac{1}{2}$.

Directions: Study the fractions below.

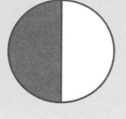

1 whole.

2 equal parts or halves
One-half of the circle is shaded. $\frac{1}{2}$

3 equal parts or thirds
One-third of the circle is shaded. $\frac{1}{3}$

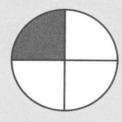

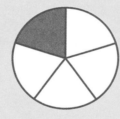

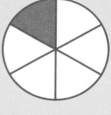

4 equal parts or fourths
One-fourth of the circle is shaded. $\frac{1}{4}$

5 equal parts or fifths
One-fifth of the circle is shaded. $\frac{1}{5}$

6 equal parts or sixths
One-sixth of the circle is shaded. $\frac{1}{6}$

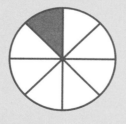

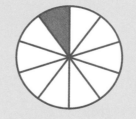

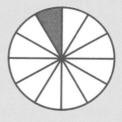

8 equal parts or eighths
One-eighth of the circle is shaded. $\frac{1}{8}$

10 equal parts or tenths
One-tenth of the circle is shaded. $\frac{1}{10}$

12 equal parts or twelfths
One-twelfth of the circle is shaded. $\frac{1}{12}$

Cut It Out!

Directions: Cut apart the fraction pieces below. Use them to help you work with fractions. Store the fraction sets in separate plastic bags.

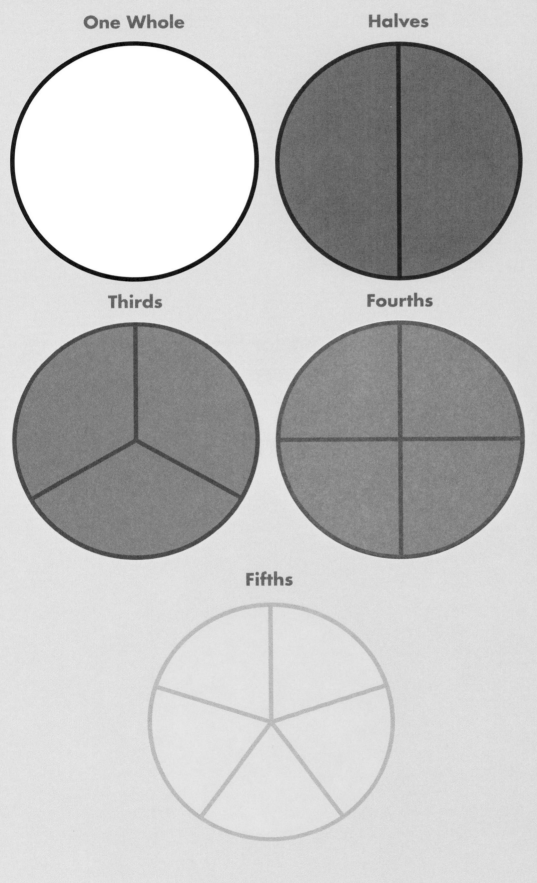

One Whole

Halves

Thirds

Fourths

Fifths

This page is blank for the cutting activity
on the opposite side.

Cut It Out!

Directions: Cut apart the fraction pieces below. Use them to help you work with fractions. Store the fraction sets in separate plastic bags.

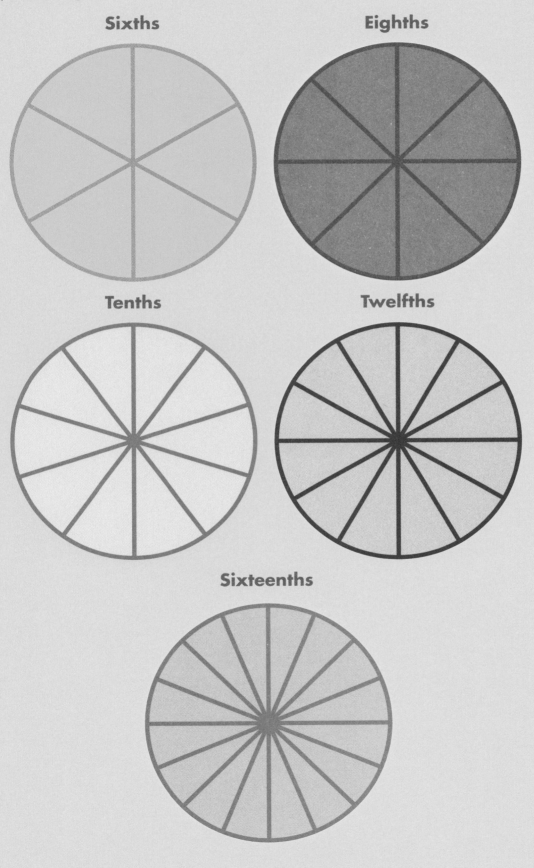

Sixths

Eighths

Tenths

Twelfths

Sixteenths

This page is blank for the cutting activity on the opposite side.

Made in the Shade

Directions: Name the fraction that is shaded.

Examples:

3 of 4 equal parts are shaded.   12 of 16 equal parts are shaded.

$$\frac{3}{4}$$

$$\frac{12}{16}$$

Flower Power

When adding fractions with the same denominator, the denominator stays the same. Add only the numerators.

Example: numerator $\frac{1}{8} + \frac{2}{8} = \frac{3}{8}$
denominator

Directions: Add the fractions on the flowers. Begin in the center of each flower and add each petal. The first one is done for you.

Example:

Fraction Subtraction

When subtracting fractions with the same denominator, the denominator stays the same. Subtract only the numerators.

Directions: Solve the problems, working from left to right. As you find each answer, copy the letter from the key into the numbered blanks. The answer is the name of a famous American. The first one is done for you.

T $\frac{1}{8}$ F $\frac{4}{12}$ E $\frac{3}{9}$ R $\frac{7}{16}$ Q $\frac{1}{32}$ A $\frac{1}{12}$ N $\frac{2}{6}$

P $\frac{5}{24}$ E $\frac{2}{7}$ O $\frac{2}{9}$ O $\frac{2}{8}$ M $\frac{1}{3}$ R $\frac{12}{15}$ O $\frac{11}{15}$

H $\frac{1}{4}$ J $\frac{3}{12}$ F $\frac{4}{8}$ Y $\frac{8}{20}$ S $\frac{5}{20}$ S $\frac{3}{5}$

1. $\frac{3}{8} - \frac{2}{8} = \underline{\frac{1}{8}}$

2. $\frac{2}{4} - \frac{1}{4} = \underline{\hspace{1cm}}$

3. $\frac{5}{9} - \frac{3}{9} = \underline{\hspace{1cm}}$

4. $\frac{2}{3} - \frac{1}{3} = \underline{\hspace{1cm}}$

5. $\frac{8}{12} - \frac{7}{12} = \underline{\hspace{1cm}}$

6. $\frac{4}{5} - \frac{1}{5} = \underline{\hspace{1cm}}$

7. $\frac{6}{12} - \frac{3}{12} = \underline{\hspace{1cm}}$

8. $\frac{4}{9} - \frac{1}{9} = \underline{\hspace{1cm}}$

9. $\frac{11}{12} - \frac{7}{12} = \underline{\hspace{1cm}}$

10. $\frac{7}{8} - \frac{3}{8} = \underline{\hspace{1cm}}$

11. $\frac{4}{7} - \frac{2}{7} = \underline{\hspace{1cm}}$

12. $\frac{14}{16} - \frac{7}{16} = \underline{\hspace{1cm}}$

13. $\frac{18}{20} - \frac{13}{20} = \underline{\hspace{1cm}}$

14. $\frac{13}{15} - \frac{2}{15} = \underline{\hspace{1cm}}$

15. $\frac{5}{6} - \frac{3}{6} = \underline{\hspace{1cm}}$

Who helped write the Declaration of Independence?

$\frac{T}{1} \frac{}{2} \frac{}{3} \frac{}{4} \frac{}{5} \frac{}{6} \quad \frac{}{7} \frac{}{8} \frac{}{9} \frac{}{10} \frac{}{11} \frac{}{12} \frac{}{13} \frac{}{14} \frac{}{15}$

Any Way You Slice It

Equivalent fractions are two different fractions that represent the same number.

Example:

$\frac{1}{2}$ = $\frac{3}{6}$

Directions: Complete these equivalent fractions. Use your fraction pieces from pages 167 and 169.

$$\frac{1}{3} = \frac{}{6} \qquad \frac{1}{2} = \frac{}{4} \qquad \frac{3}{4} = \frac{}{8} \qquad \frac{1}{3} = \frac{}{9}$$

Directions: Circle the figures that show a fraction equivalent to figure a. Write the fraction for the shaded area under each figure.

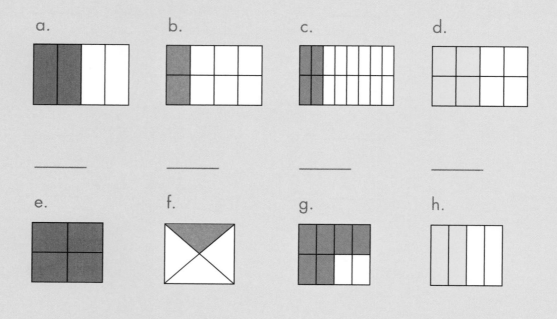

a. _____   b. _____   c. _____   d. _____

e. _____   f. _____   g. _____   h. _____

To find an equivalent fraction, multiply both parts of the fraction by the same number.

Example: $\frac{2}{3} \times \frac{3}{3} = \frac{6}{9}$

Directions: Find an equivalent fraction.

$$\frac{1}{4} = \frac{}{8} \qquad \frac{3}{4} = \frac{}{16} \qquad \frac{4}{5} = \frac{8}{} \qquad \frac{3}{8} = \frac{}{24}$$

Finding Home

Reducing a fraction means to find the greatest common factor and divide.

Example: $\dfrac{5}{15}$ factors of 5: 1, 5
factors of 15: 1, 3, 5, 15

5 is the greatest common factor. Divide both the numerator and denominator by 5.

$$5 \div 5 = \dfrac{1}{3}$$
$$15 \div 5 = 3$$

Directions: Reduce each fraction. Circle the correct answer.

$\dfrac{2}{4} = \dfrac{1}{2}, \dfrac{1}{6}, \dfrac{1}{8}$ 　　$\dfrac{3}{9} = \dfrac{1}{6}, \dfrac{1}{3}, \dfrac{3}{6}$ 　　$\dfrac{5}{10} = \dfrac{1}{5}, \dfrac{1}{2}, \dfrac{5}{6}$

$\dfrac{4}{12} = \dfrac{1}{4}, \dfrac{1}{3}, \dfrac{2}{3}$ 　　$\dfrac{10}{15} = \dfrac{2}{3}, \dfrac{2}{5}, \dfrac{2}{7}$ 　　$\dfrac{12}{14} = \dfrac{1}{8}, \dfrac{6}{7}, \dfrac{3}{5}$

Directions: Find the way home. Color the boxes with fractions equivalent to $\dfrac{1}{8}$ and $\dfrac{1}{3}$.

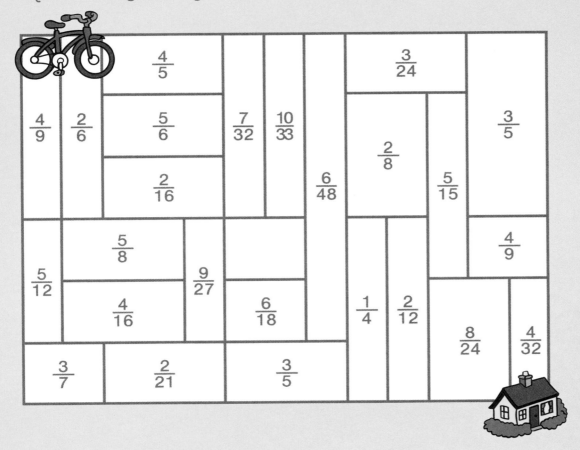

Mix It up!

A mixed number is a number written as a whole number and a fraction, such as $6\frac{5}{8}$.

To change a fraction into a mixed number, divide the denominator (bottom number) into the numerator (top number). Write the remainder over the denominator.

Example: $\frac{14}{6} = 2\frac{2}{6}$

$$6\overline{)14} \quad \begin{array}{r} 2\ R2 \\ -12 \\ \hline 2 \end{array}$$

Example: $3\frac{1}{7} = \frac{22}{7}$ $(7 \times 3) + 1 = \frac{22}{7}$

To change a mixed number into a fraction, multiply the denominator by the whole number, add the numerator and write it on top of the denominator.

Directions: Write each fraction as a mixed number. Write each mixed number as a fraction.

$\frac{21}{6} = $ _____ $\frac{24}{5} = $ _____ $\frac{10}{3} = $ _____ $\frac{21}{4} = $ _____

$\frac{11}{6} = $ _____ $\frac{13}{4} = $ _____ $\frac{12}{5} = $ _____ $\frac{10}{9} = $ _____

$4\frac{3}{8} = \frac{}{8}$ $2\frac{1}{3} = \frac{}{3}$ $4\frac{3}{5} = \frac{}{5}$ $3\frac{4}{6} = \frac{}{6}$

$7\frac{1}{4} = \frac{}{4}$ $2\frac{3}{5} = \frac{}{5}$ $7\frac{1}{2} = \frac{}{2}$ $6\frac{5}{7} = \frac{}{7}$

$\frac{11}{8} = $ _____ $\frac{21}{4} = $ _____ $\frac{33}{5} = $ _____ $\frac{13}{6} = $ _____

Mix and Match

When adding mixed numbers, add the fractions first, then the whole numbers.

Examples:

$$9\frac{1}{3}$$
$$+3\frac{1}{3}$$
$$\overline{12\frac{2}{3}}$$

$$2\frac{3}{6}$$
$$+1\frac{1}{6}$$
$$\overline{3\frac{4}{6}}$$

Directions: Add the number in the center to the number in each surrounding section.

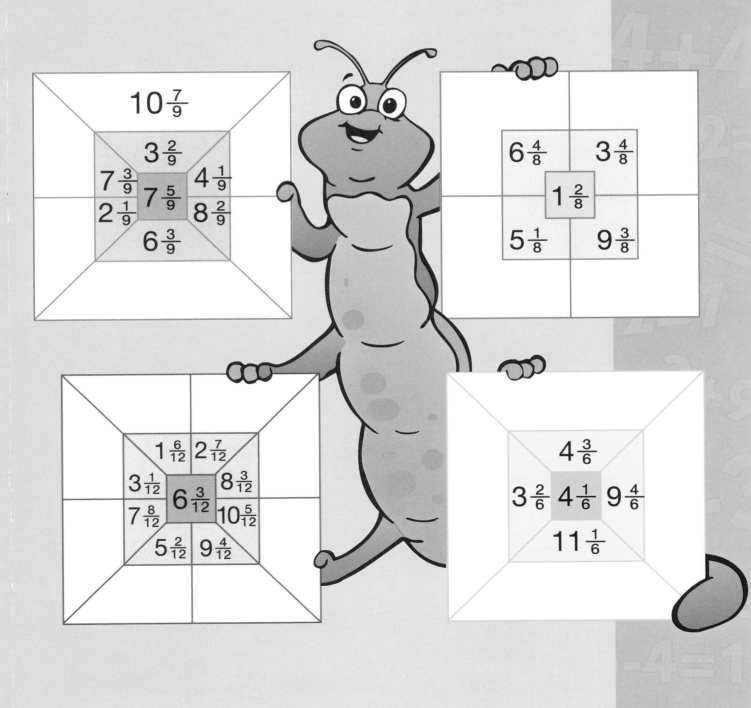

Mixed Up Math

When subtracting mixed numbers, subtract the fractions first, then the whole numbers.

Directions: Subtract the mixed numbers. The first one is done for you.

$$
\begin{array}{ccccc}
7\frac{3}{8} & 4\frac{5}{6} & 4\frac{1}{2} & 7\frac{5}{8} & 6\frac{6}{8} \\
-4\frac{2}{8} & -3\frac{1}{6} & -3\phantom{\frac{1}{2}} & -6\frac{3}{8} & -1\frac{1}{8} \\
\hline
3\frac{1}{8} & & & &
\end{array}
$$

$$
\begin{array}{ccccc}
5\frac{2}{3} & 4\frac{8}{10} & 9\frac{8}{9} & 7\frac{2}{3} & 7\frac{2}{3} \\
-3\frac{1}{3} & -3\frac{3}{10} & -4\frac{3}{9} & -6\frac{1}{3} & -5\phantom{\frac{1}{3}} \\
\hline
\end{array}
$$

$$
\begin{array}{ccccc}
4\frac{7}{9} & 6\frac{7}{8} & 6\frac{3}{4} & 5\frac{6}{7} & 7\frac{6}{7} \\
-2\phantom{\frac{7}{9}} & -5\frac{3}{8} & -3\frac{1}{4} & -3\frac{1}{7} & -2\frac{4}{7} \\
\hline
\end{array}
$$

Tessa needs $1\frac{3}{8}$ yards of cloth to make a dress. She has $4\frac{5}{8}$ yards. How much cloth will be left over?

_____

Talking about Tenths

When a figure is divided into 10 equal parts, the parts are called *tenths*. Tenths can be written two ways—as a fraction or a decimal. A decimal is a number with one or more places to the right of a decimal point, such as 6.5 or 2.25. A decimal point is the dot between the ones place and the tenths place.

0.3 or $\frac{3}{10}$ = 2 ways to write BUT mean the same thing

Examples:

ones	tenths
0	3

out of this 10 — 3 are red? = ok

10 — right 3

$\frac{3}{10}$ or 0.3 of the square is shaded.

$\frac{6}{10}$ 0.6

0.3 = $\frac{3}{10}$ twins! good

Directions: Write the decimal and fraction for the shaded parts of the following figures.

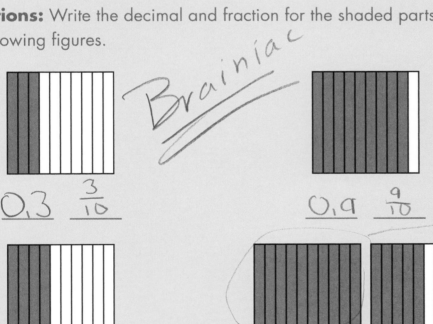

Brainiac

0.3 $\frac{3}{10}$

0.9 $\frac{9}{10}$

try to trick you here

0.4 $\frac{2}{5}$

1.5 $1\frac{1}{2}$

1.8 $1\frac{4}{5}$

0.8 $\frac{4}{5}$

Fill It Up!

Directions: Add or subtract. Remember to include the decimal point in your answers.

Example:

$1\frac{3}{10}$ = 1.3

$1\frac{6}{10}$ = 1.6

$$\begin{array}{r} 1.3 \\ +1.6 \\ \hline 2.9 \end{array}$$

8.1 +1.7	4.1 +6.2	0.5 +1.6	7.6 −6.5	7.2 −2.6
		7.8 −6.8	16.5 − 7.3	6.4 +5.3
		0.42 +0.35	0.98 −0.87	0.78 −0.13
		0.95 −0.14	3.23 +2.48	4.68 −2.65
		6.98 +1.40	3.27 +1.82	4.65 −1.32

Mr. Martin went on a car trip with his family.
Mr. Martin purchased gas 3 times. He bought
6.7 gallons, 7.3 gallons, then 5.8 gallons
of gas. How much gas did he purchase in all? _____

Get on Track

Directions: Add or subtract the problems. Then, fill in the circle next to the correct answer.

Example: 2.4   ○ 2.5
               +1.7   ○ 3.1
                      ● 4.1

2.8 +3.4	○ 5.2 ○ 7.4 ○ 6.2	5.7 −3.8	○ 1.9 ○ 2.5 ○ 2.9
7.6 +8.9	○ 15.9 ○ 16.5 ○ 17.3	16.3 + 9.8	○ 25.11 ○ 26.1 ○ 26.01
28.6 +43.9	○ 73.6 ○ 72.5 ○ 71.9	43.9 +56.5	○ 100.4 ○ 107.4 ○ 101.4
12.87 − 3.45	○ 16.32 ○ 10.31 ○ 9.42	47.56 −33.95	○ 13.61 ○ 80.41 ○ 14.61
93.6 −79.8	○ 14.8 ○ 15.3 ○ 13.8	11.57 +10.64	○ 22.21 ○ 1.93 ○ 21.12
27.83 −14.94	○ 14.09 ○ 12.89 ○ 11.97	106.935 − 95.824	○ 111.1 ○ 111.11 ○ 11.111

The high-speed train traveled 87.90 miles on day one, 127.86 miles on day two and 113.41 miles on day three. How many miles did it travel in all?

_____

Inching Along

An **inch** is a unit of length in the standard system equal to $\frac{1}{12}$ of a foot. A ruler is used to measure inches.

This illustration shows a ruler measuring a 4-inch pencil, which can be written as 4" or 4 in.

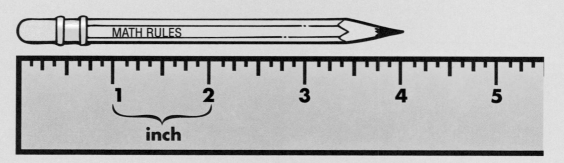

Directions: Use a ruler to measure each object to the nearest inch.

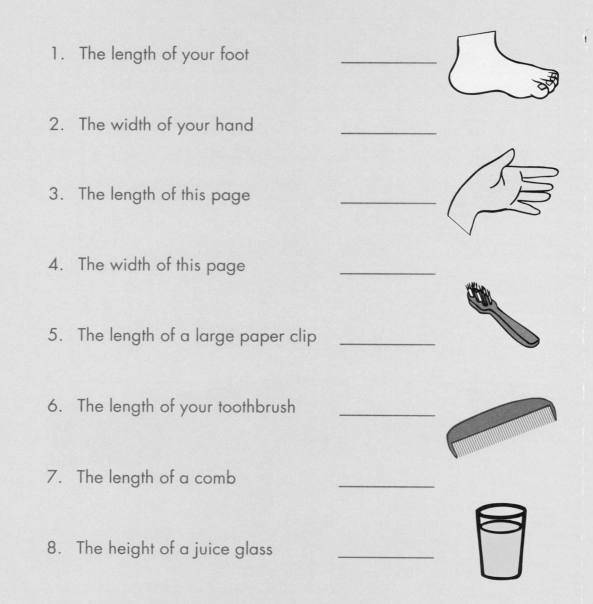

1. The length of your foot　　＿＿＿＿＿

2. The width of your hand　　＿＿＿＿＿

3. The length of this page　　＿＿＿＿＿

4. The width of this page　　＿＿＿＿＿

5. The length of a large paper clip　＿＿＿＿＿

6. The length of your toothbrush　　＿＿＿＿＿

7. The length of a comb　　＿＿＿＿＿

8. The height of a juice glass　　＿＿＿＿＿

Rulers Rule

An inch is divided into smaller units, or fractions of an inch.

Example: This stick of gum is $2\frac{3}{4}$ inches long.

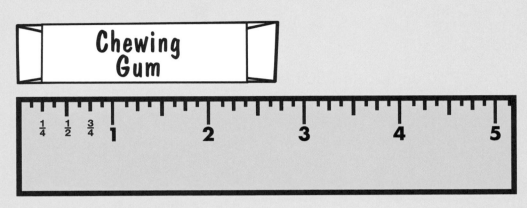

Directions: Use a ruler to measure each line to the nearest quarter of an inch. The first one is done for you.

1. $\frac{3}{4}$ inch _____

2. _____ _____

3. _____ _____

4. _____ _____

5. _____ _____

6. _____ _____

7. _____ _____

How Do You Measure Up?

Directions: Choose the measure of distance you would use for each object.

1 foot = 12 inches

1 yard = 3 feet

1 mile = 1,760 yards or 5,280 feet

 inches

Make It Metric

In the metric system, there are three units of linear measurement: centimeter (cm), meter (m), and kilometer (km).

Centimeters (cm) are used to measure the lengths of small to medium-sized objects. **Meters (m)** measure the lengths of longer objects, such as the width of a swimming pool or height of a tree (100 cm = 1 meter). **Kilometers (km)** measure long distances, such as the distance from Cleveland to Cincinnati or the width of the Atlantic Ocean (1,000 m = 1 km).

Directions: Write whether you would use cm, m, or km to measure each object.

cm.

ft./m

Chicago

New York City

Km.

inch/km

m.

Km.

in/cm

m.

m.

Figure It Out

Perimeter is the distance around a figure. It is found by adding the lengths of the sides. **Area** is the number of square units needed to cover a region. The area is found by adding the number of square units. A unit can be any unit of measure. Most often, inches, feet, or yards are used.

Directions: Find the perimeter and area for each figure. The first one is done for you.

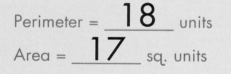 = 1 square unit

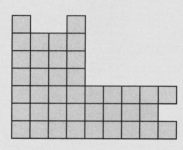

Perimeter = **18** units

Area = **17** sq. units

Perimeter = _____ units

Area = _____ sq. units

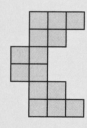

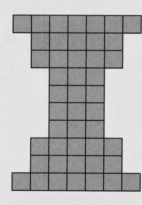

Perimeter = _____ units

Area = _____ sq. units

Perimeter = _____ units

Area = _____ sq. units

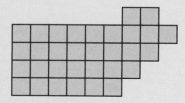

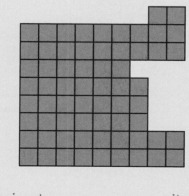

Perimeter = _____ units

Area = _____ sq. units

Perimeter = _____ units

Area = _____ sq. units

Inside, Outside, All Around

Area is also calculated by multiplying the length times the width of a square or rectangular figure. Use the formula: A = l x w.

Directions: Calculate the perimeter of each figure.

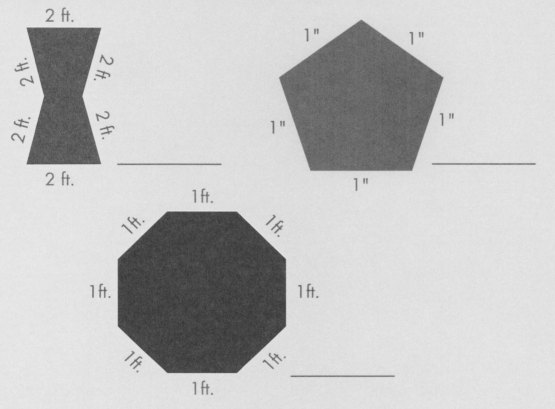

2 ft.

2 ft.

2 ft.

2 ft.

2 ft.

2 ft.

_____

1" 1"

1" 1"

1"

_____

1 ft.

1 ft.   1 ft.

1 ft.   1 ft.

1 ft.   1 ft.

1 ft.

_____

Directions: Calculate the area of each figure.

5 ft.

3 ft.

_____

1 yd.

4 yd.

_____

24 ft.

20 ft.

_____

Turn Up the Volume!

Volume is the number of cubic units that fit inside a figure.

Directions: Find the volume of each figure. The first one is done for you.

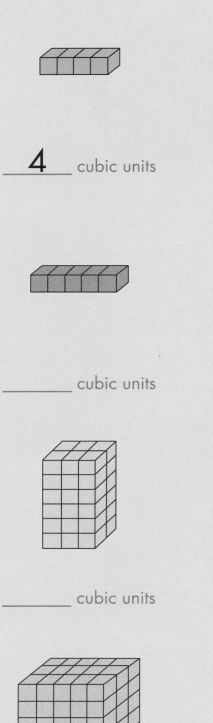

_____**4**_____ cubic units

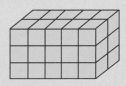

_____ cubic units

_____ cubic units

_____ cubic units

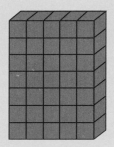

_____ cubic units

_____ cubic units

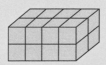

_____ cubic units

_____ cubic units

Taking Up Space

The volume of a figure can also be calculated by multiplying the length times the width times the height.

Use the formula: V= l x w x h.

Example:

3 x 5 x 2 = 30 cubic feet

Directions: Find the volume of the following figures. Label your answers in cubic feet, inches or yards. The first one is done for you.

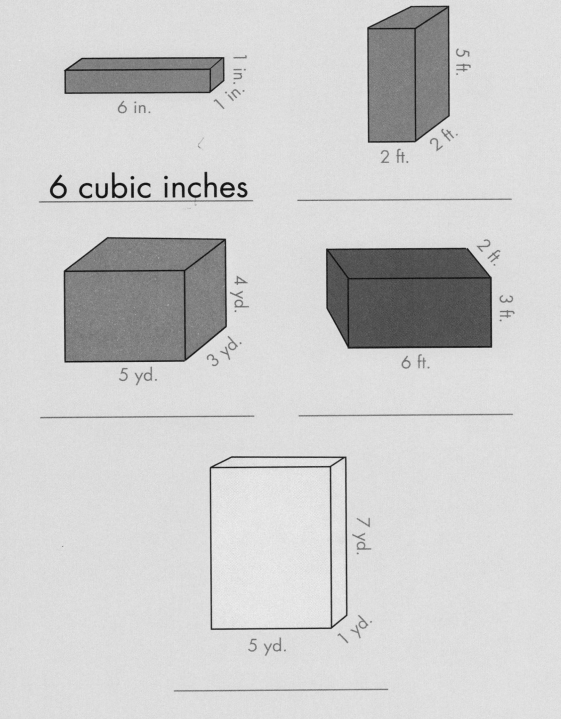

3 ft.

2 ft.

5 ft.

6 in.

1 in.

1 in.

5 ft.

2 ft.

2 ft.

6 cubic inches

4 yd.

3 yd.

5 yd.

2 ft.

3 ft.

6 ft.

7 yd.

1 yd.

5 yd.

Weight for Me!

The **ounce**, **pound** and **ton** are units in the standard system for measuring weight.

Directions: Choose the measure of weight you would use for each object.

16 ounces = 1 pound

2,000 pounds = 1 ton

ounce   **pound**   **ton**

Example:

 ounces

 ton

 pound

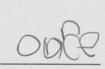 ouce

pound

ton

 ton

 oues

Gram by Gram

review

Grams and **kilograms** are measurements of weight in the metric system. A gram (g) weighs about $\frac{1}{28}$ of an ounce. A grape or paper clip weighs about one gram. There are 1,000 grams in a kilogram. A kilogram (kg) weighs about 2.2 pounds. A brick weighs about 1 kilogram.

Directions: Choose grams or kilograms to measure the following.

Example:

grams

kilo

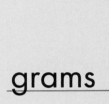

kilo

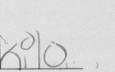

kilo

kilo

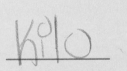

grams

kilo

kilo

kilo

kilo

Counting Quarts

The **cup**, **pint**, **quart** and **gallon** are units in the standard system for measuring liquids.

Directions: Gather the following materials: 2 dish tubs, one filled with water, sand or rice; measuring cups; pint container; quart container; gallon container. Then, answer the questions and complete the chart.

1. Use the cup measure to pour water, sand or rice into the pint container. How many cups did it take?

    _____ cups = 1 pint

2. Use the cup measure to find out how many cups are in a quart and a gallon.

    _____ cups = 1 quart

    _____ cups = 1 gallon

3. Use the pint container to pour water, sand or rice into the quart container. How many pints are in a quart?

    _____ pints = 1 quart

4. How many pints does it take to fill a gallon?

    _____ pints = 1 gallon

5. Use the quart measure to find out how many quarts are in a gallon.

    _____ quarts = 1 gallon

Measurement Chart

_____ cups = 1 pint

_____ cups = 1 quart

_____ cups = 1 gallon

_____ pints = 1 quart

_____ pints = 1 gallon

_____ quarts = 1 gallon

The Same Game

Directions: Circle the number of objects to the right that equal the objects on the left. The first one is done for you.

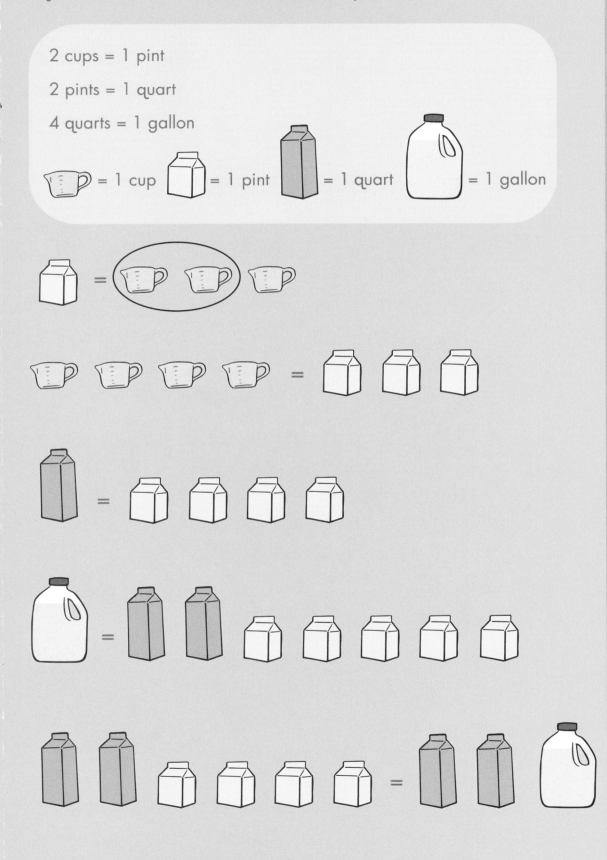

2 cups = 1 pint

2 pints = 1 quart

4 quarts = 1 gallon

= 1 cup   = 1 pint   = 1 quart   = 1 gallon

Liter Reader

Liters and **milliliters** are measurements of liquid in the metric system. A milliliter (mL) equals 0.001 liter or 0.03 fluid ounces. A drop of water equals about 1 milliliter. Liters (L) measure large amounts of liquid. There are 1,000 milliliters in a liter. One liter measures 1.06 quarts. Soft drinks are often sold in 2-liter bottles.

Directions: Choose milliliters or liters to measure these liquids.

Example:

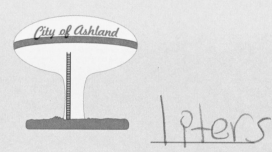 milliliters

 mililiters

 Liters

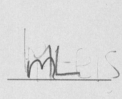 MLeis

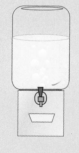 mL

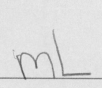 liter

 L

 L

review

_Do_ ☺

Weigh In

Directions: Choose grams (g) or kilograms (kg) to weigh the following objects. The first one is done for you.

rhinoceros <u>kg</u>   person _____

dime _____   airplane _____

bucket of wet sand _____   spider _____

eyeglasses _____   pair of scissors _____

Directions: Choose milliliters (mL) or liters (L) to measure the liquids in the following containers. The first one is done for you.

swimming pool <u>L</u>   baby bottle _____

small juice glass _____   teapot _____

gasoline tank _____   outdoor fountain _____

test tube _____   ink pen _____

review

Focus on Fahrenheit

Fahrenheit is used to measure temperature in the standard system.
°F stands for degrees Fahrenheit.

28°F   72°F

Directions: Use the thermometer to answer these questions.

Do

At what temperature does
water boil? $210°F$

At what temperature does
water freeze? $32°F$

What is normal
body temperature? $98.6°F$

Is a 100°F day warm,
hot or cold?   hot

Is a 0°F day warm,
hot or cold?   cold

Which temperature best
describes room temperature? $70°$
58°F   70°F   80°F

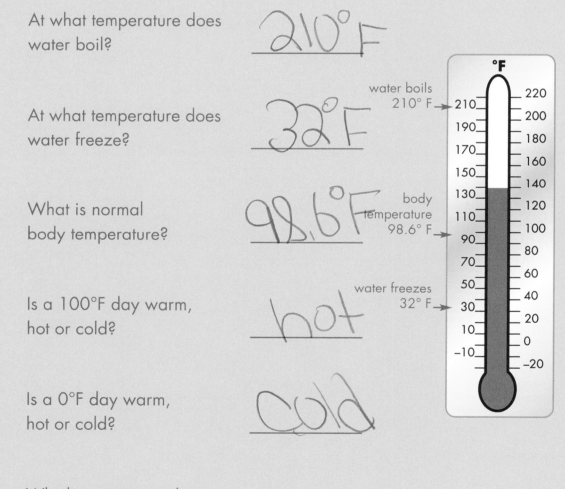

Simply Celsius

Celsius is used to measure temperature in the metric system.
°C stands for degrees Celsius.

0°C   30°C

Directions: Use the thermometer to answer these questions.

At what temperature does
water boil? _____ 100°C

At what temperature does
water boil? _____ 100°C

At what temperature does
water freeze? _____ 0°C

What is normal
body temperature? _____ 37C

Is it a hot or cold day when
the temperature is 30°C? _____ Hot

Is it a hot or cold day when
the temperature is 5°C? _____ Cold

Which temperature best
describes a hot summer day? _____ 75°C

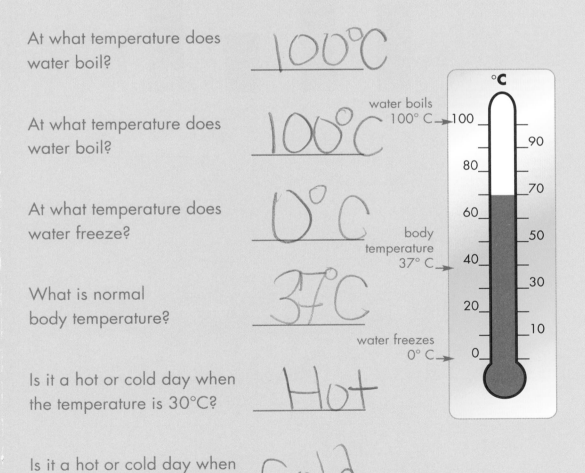

°C

water boils
100° C → 100
90
80
70
60
50
body
temperature
37° C → 40
30
20
10
water freezes
0° C → 0

Review

Do

Get Organized!

A **graph** is a drawing that shows information about changes in numbers.

Directions: Answer the questions by reading the graphs.

Bar Graph

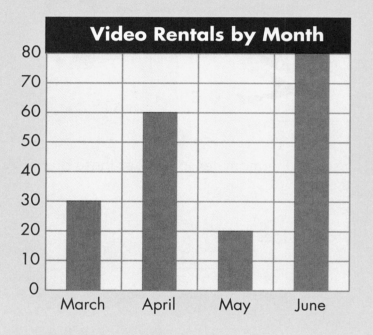

How many videos did the store rent in June? _____

In which month did the store rent the fewest videos? _____

How many videos did the store rent for all 4 months? _____

Line Graph

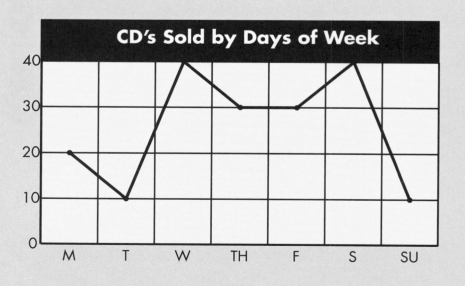

On which days did the store sell the fewest CD's? _____

How many CD's did the store sell in 1 week? _____

A Dot Marks the Spot

An **ordered pair** is a pair of numbers used to locate a point.

Example: (8, 3)

Step 1: Count across to line 8 on the graph.

Step 2: Count up to line 3 on the graph.

Step 3: Draw a dot to mark the spot.

Directions: Map the following spots on the grid using ordered pairs.

(4, 7)   (9, 10)   (2, 1)   (5, 6)   (2, 2)   (1, 5)   (7, 4)   (3, 8)

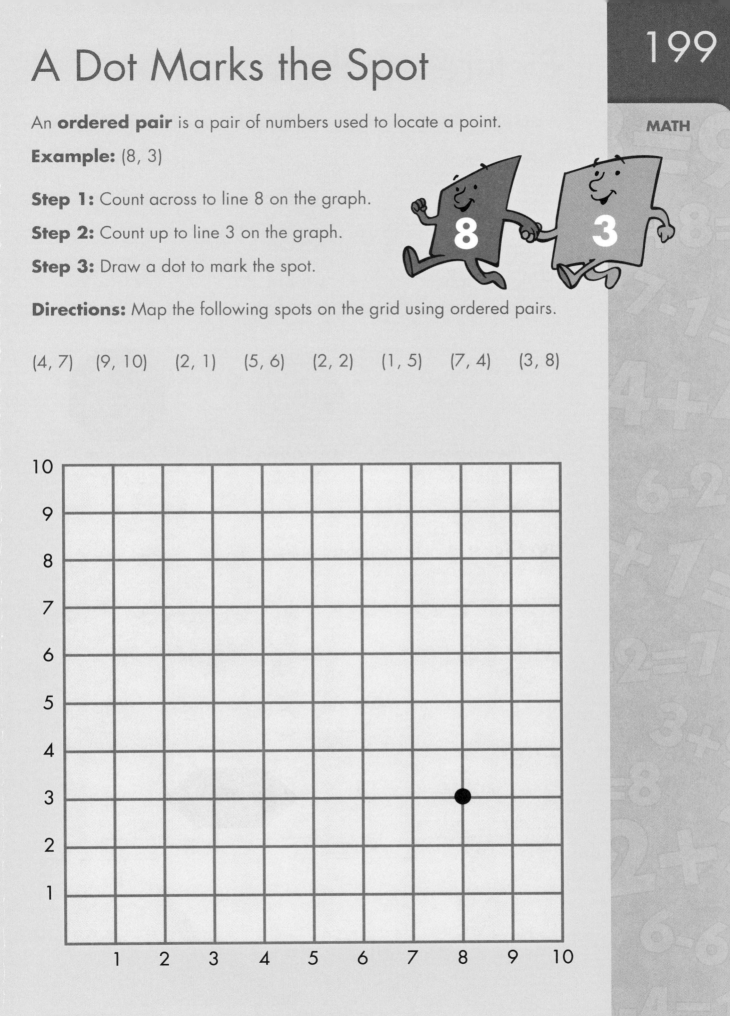

Picture a Polygon

A **polygon** is a closed figure with three or more sides.

Examples:

triangle
3 sides

square
4 equal sides

rectangle
4 sides

pentagon
5 sides

hexagon
6 sides

octagon
8 sides

Directions: Identify the polygons.

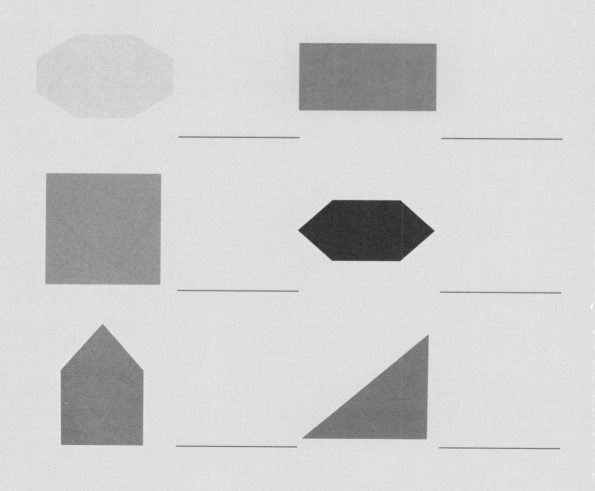

Get in Line!

A **line segment** has two end points.

A   B   Write: AB

A **line** has no end points and goes on in both directions.

C   D   Write: CD

A **ray** is part of a line and goes on in one direction. It has one end point.

E   F   Write: EF

Directions: Identify each of the following as a line, line segment, or ray.

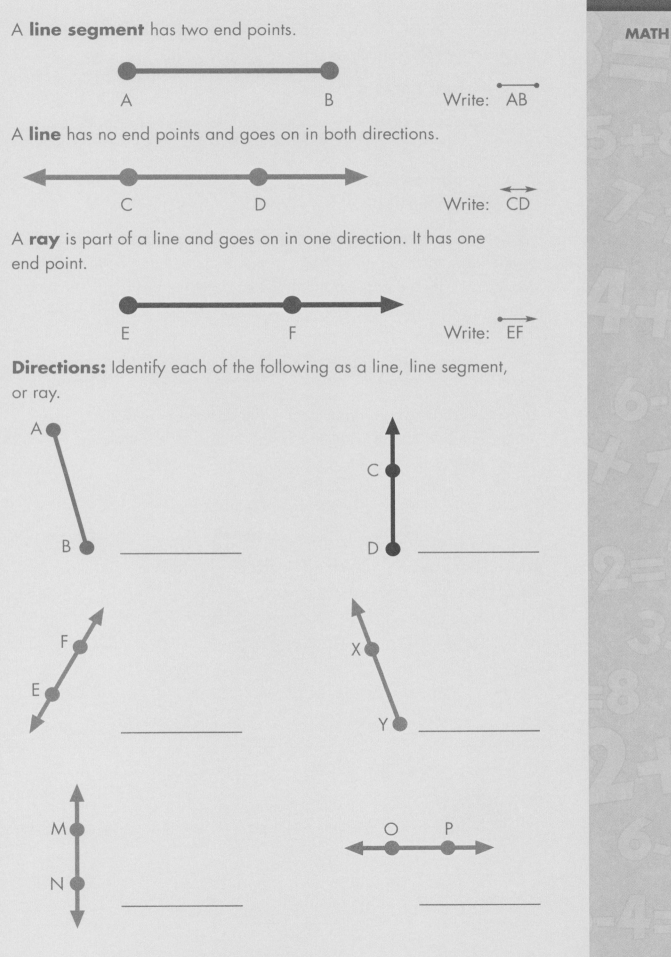

Angle Wrangler

The point at which two line segments meet is called an **angle**. There are three types of angles — right, acute and obtuse.

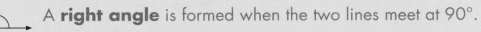 A **right angle** is formed when the two lines meet at 90°.

An **acute angle** is formed when the two lines meet at less than 90°.

An **obtuse angle** is formed when the two lines meet at greater than 90°.

Angles can be measured with a protractor or index card. With a protractor, align the bottom edge of the angle with the bottom of the protractor, with the angle point at the circle of the protractor. Note the direction of the other ray and the number of degrees of the angle.

 right   acute   obtuse

Place the corner of an index card in the corner of the angle. If the edges line up with the card, it is a right angle. If not, the angle is acute or obtuse.

 right   acute   obtuse

Directions: Use a protractor or index card to identify the following angles as right, obtuse or acute.

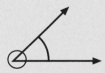

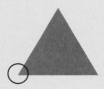

_____   _____   _____

_____   _____   _____

Send in the Circles

A **circle** is a round figure. It is named by its center. A **radius** is a line segment from the center of a circle to any point on the circle. A **diameter** is a line segment with both end points on the circle. The diameter always passes through the center of the circle.

Directions: Name the radius, diameter and circle.

Example:

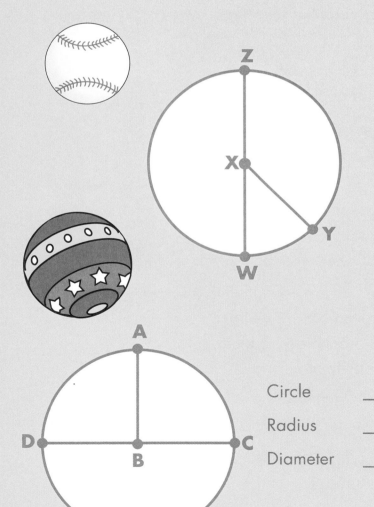

Circle ___A___

Radius ___AB___

Diameter ___DC___

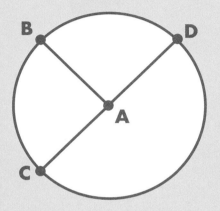

Circle _____

Radius _____

Diameter _____

Circle _____

Radius _____

Diameter _____

Heads or Tails

One thinking skill to get your brain in gear is figuring probability. **Probability** is the likelihood or chance that something will happen. Probability is expressed and written as a ratio.

The probability of tossing heads or tails on a coin is one in two (1:2).

The probability of rolling any number on a die is one in six (1:6).

The probability of getting a red on this spinner is two in four (2:4).

The probability of drawing an ace from a deck of cards is four in fifty-two (4:52).

Directions: Write the probability ratios to answer these questions.

1. There are 26 letters in the alphabet. What is the probability of drawing any letter from a set of alphabet cards? _____

2. Five of the 26 alphabet letters are vowels. What is the probability of drawing a vowel from the alphabet cards? _____

3. Matt takes 10 shots at the basketball hoop. Six of his shots are baskets. What is the probability of Matt's next shot being a basket? _____

4. A box contains 10 marbles: 2 white, 3 green, 1 red, 2 orange and 2 blue. What is the probability of pulling a green marble from the box? _____

   A red marble? _____

5. What is the probability of pulling a marble that is not blue? _____

How Does Your Garden Grow?

Grace is planting a garden. The garden will be a semi-circle in shape and have two rows. The first row will have three sections and the back row will have six sections. Grace needs to decide how many plants she can put in each section of her garden.

She wants the total number of plants in the back row to be double the total number of plants in front.

Directions: Help Grace finish her garden plan by using the numbers 1, 2, 3, 4, 5, 6, 7, 8, and 9. Each number may only be used once. Three numbers have been written in place for you.

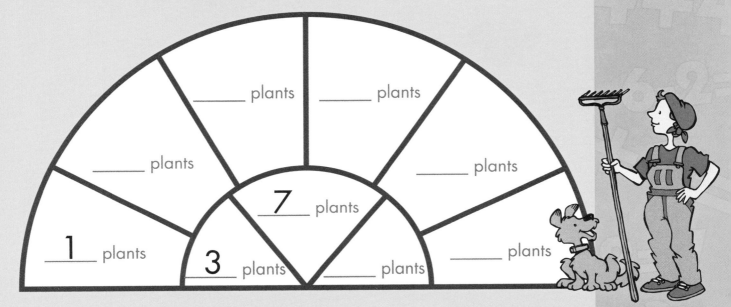

_____ plants _____ plants

_____ plants _____ plants

7 plants

1 plants 3 _____ plants _____ plants _____ plants

Directions: Arrange the digits 1 through 9 in the circles on the triangle so the numbers on each of the sides add up to 17.

What Are You Wearing?

When you have two sets of items, they can be grouped in pairs (with one item from each set) in many ways.

Example:

While shopping, Hannah bought three pairs of shorts and three blouses. How many different outfits can she make from these items?

To solve, you could draw a picture or make a list:

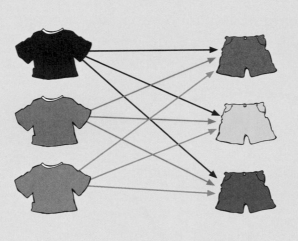

Black shirt — Blue shorts

Black shirt — Yellow shorts

Black shirt — Purple shorts

Red shirt — Blue shorts

Red shirt — Yellow shorts

Red shirt — Purple shorts

Green shirt — Blue shorts

Green shirt — Yellow shorts

Green shirt — Purple shorts

There are nine possible combinations.
3 (shirts) x 3 (shorts) = 9 (outfits)

Directions: Either draw a picture or make a list to solve the problem. Then, write the answer.

Hannah 's mom gave her $37.00 for shopping and lunch. She gave Hannah 11 bills—some are ones, some are fives and some are tens.

How many ones, fives and tens does Hannah have?

_____ ones   _____ fives   _____ tens

Abacus: A frame with sliding beads for doing math.

Acute Angle: An angle formed when two lines meet at less than 90˚.

Addition: "Putting together" or adding two or more numbers to find the sum.

Adjective: A word that describes a noun. Examples: fuzzy sweater, green car, nice boy.

Adverb: A word that tells when, where or how. Example: The train will leave early.

Analogy: A way of comparing things to show how they are similar. Example: Nose is to smell as tongue is to taste.

Angle: The point at which two line segments meet.

Antonym: A word that means the opposite of another word. Example: in and out.

Area: The number of square units needed to cover a region.

Autobiography: A book someone writes about his/her own life.

Average: The result of adding two or more quantities and dividing by the number of quantities.

Biography: A book written about the life of someone by another person.

Call Number: The number assigned to all nonfiction books in a library.

Celsius: A metric system measurement of temperature. ˚C stands for degrees Celsius.

Centimeter: A metric system measurement of length. There are 2.54 centimeters in an inch.

Cinquain: A form of poetry with five lines consisting of one noun, two adjectives, three verbs, a four-word phrase and a noun, respectively.

Circle: A round figure in which each point on the outside of the figure is equidistant from the center of the figure.

Classifying: Placing similar things into categories.

Command: A sentence that orders someone to do something. It ends with a period or exclamation mark.

Compound Predicate: A predicate with two parts joined by the word "and" or another conjunction.

Compound Subject: A subject with two parts joined by the word "and" or another conjunction.

Comprehension: Understanding what is seen, heard or read.

Conjunction: A word that joins sentences or combines ideas. "And," "but," "or," "because," "when," "after" and "so" are conjunctions.

Context: The other words in the sentence or sentences before or after a word.

Context Clues: A way to figure out the meaning of a word by relating it to other words in the sentence.

Contraction: Two words joined together as one. An apostrophe shows where some letters have been left out. **Example:** cannot—can't.

Cup: A unit of volume in the standard system equal to 8 ounces.

Decimal: A number with one or more places to the right of a decimal point, such as 6.5 or 2.25.

Decimal Point: The dot between the ones place and the tenths place in a decimal.

Denominator: The number below the fraction bar in a fraction.

Details: The who, what, when, where, why, and how of what is read.

Dewey Decimal System: A system used to file books in libraries by assigning call numbers to them and dividing them into ten main groups.

Diameter: A line segment that passes through the center of a circle and has both end points on the circle.

Difference: The answer in a subtraction problem.

Digits: The symbols used to write numbers: 0, 1, 2, 3, 4, 5, 6, 7, 8, 9.

Dividend: The larger number being divided by the smaller number, or divisor, in a division problem. **Example:** $28 \div 7 = 4$; 28 is the dividend.

Division: A way to find how many times a number is contained in another number. **Example:** $28 \div 7 = 4$ means that there are 4 groups of 7 in 28.

Encyclopedia: A set of books or CD's that gives information about different subjects in alphabetical order.

Equivalent Fractions: Two different fractions that represent the same number, such as $\frac{1}{2}$ and $\frac{2}{4}$.

Estimate: To give an approximate, rather than an exact, answer.

Exclamation: A sentence that shows strong feeling. It ends with an exclamation mark (!).

Fact: A statement that can be proven true.

Factors: The numbers multiplied together in a multiplication problem.

Fahrenheit: A standard system measurement of temperature. °F stands for degrees Fahrenheit.

Fiction: A book that contains made-up stories.

Following Directions: Doing what the directions say to do.

Foot (ft.): A unit of measure in the standard system equal to 12 inches.

Fraction: A number that names part of a whole, such as $\frac{1}{2}$ or $\frac{2}{3}$.

Future-Tense Verb: A verb form that tells what is going to happen. Examples: I will be happy. She will run fast.

Gallon: A unit of liquid measure in the standard system equal to 4 quarts.

Gram (g): A metric measurement of weight. One gram equals 0.001 kilogram, or $\frac{1}{28}$ of an ounce.

Graph: A drawing that shows information about changes in numbers.

Haiku: A form of Japanese poetry with three lines of five, seven, and five syllables, respectively.

Hexagon: A polygon with six sides.

Homophones: Two words that sound the same, but have different meanings and are usually spelled differently. **Example:** write and right.

Inch (in.): A unit of length in the standard system equal to $\frac{1}{12}$ of a foot.

Index: The section in the back of a nonfiction book or a separate volume of an encyclopedia that indicates the page number and/or volume number where information on a specific topic is located.

Kilogram (kg): A metric system measurement of weight. One kilogram equals 1,000 grams or 2.2 pounds.

Kilometer (km): A metric system measurement of length. One kilometer equals 1,000 meters or 0.62 miles.

Library Catalog: An alphabetical listing of books and other items in a library which lists items by author, title and subject and also shows their call numbers. A library catalog may be on index cards or on a computer.

Limerick: A short, silly poem with five lines, in which lines one, two and five rhyme, and lines three and four rhyme.

Line: A line with no end points that goes on in both directions.

Line Segment: A line with two end points.

Liter (L): A metric system measurement of liquid. One liter equals 1,000 milliliters or 1.06 quarts.

Main Idea: The most important idea, or main points, of a sentence, paragraph or story.

Meter (m): A metric system measurement of length. One meter equals 39.37 inches.

Mile (mi.): A unit of length in the standard system equal to 1,760 yards or 5,280 feet.

Milliliter (mL): A metric system measurement of liquid. One milliliter equals 0.001 liter or 0.03 fluid ounce.

Mixed Number: A number written as a whole number and a fraction, such as $6\frac{5}{8}$.

Multiple: The product of a specific number and any other number. Example: The multiples of 2 are 2 (2 x 1), 4 (2 x 2), 6, 8, 10, 12, and so on.

Multiplication: A short way to find the sum of adding the same number a certain amount of times, such as 7 x 4 = 28 instead of 7 + 7 + 7 + 7 = 28.

Nonfiction: A book that contains facts and information.

Noun: A word that names a person, place or thing. **Examples:** boy, town, radish.

Numerator: The number above the fraction bar in a fraction.

Obtuse Angle: An angle formed when two lines meet at greater than 90°.

Octagon: A polygon with eight sides.

Opinion: A statement that tells how someone feels or what he/she thinks about something or someone.

Ordered Pair: A pair of numbers used to locate a point.

Ounce (oz.): A unit of measure in the standard system for weight. One ounce equals $\frac{1}{16}$ of a pound.

Outline: A written plan that helps organize the writer's thoughts in preparation for writing a report.

Palindrome: A word or sentence that is spelled the same forward and backward. **Examples:** noon, dad, pop, radar.

Paragraph: A group of sentences that share the same idea.

Past-Tense Verb: A verb form that tells what has already happened. **Example:** I was happy.

Pentagon: A polygon with five sides.

Perimeter: The distance around a figure, found by adding the length of the sides.

Pint (pt.): A unit of liquid measure in the standard system equal to 2 cups.

Place Value: The value of a digit or numeral shown by where it is in a number.

Plural: A word that refers to more than one thing.

Polygon: A closed figure with three or more sides.

Pound (lb.): A unit of measure in the standard system for weight. One pound equals 16 ounces.

Predicate: The part of the sentence that tells what the subject does, did, is doing or will do. **Example:** I am happy.

Prefix: A syllable at the beginning of a word that changes its meaning.

Present-Tense Verb: A verb form that tells what is happening now.

Probability: The likelihood that something will happen, usually expressed as a ratio. **Examples:** 1:2, 6:48.

Product: The answer in a multiplication problem.

Pronoun: A word that takes the place of a noun. **Examples:** I, me, my, he, she, it, we, us, their, them.

Pronoun Referent: The noun or nouns that a pronoun refers to.

Proofreading: Searching for and correcting errors by carefully reading and rereading what has been written.

Proper Noun: Name of specific persons, places or things. **Examples:** Abe Lincoln, Empire State Building, Magna Carta.

Quart (qt.): A unit of liquid measure in the standard system equal to 4 cups or 2 pints.

Question: A sentence that asks something. It ends with a question mark (?).

Quotient: The answer in a division problem.

Radius: A line segment from the center of a circle to any point on the circle. It is equal to half the length of the diameter.

Ray: A part of a line that goes on in one direction. It has one end point.

Recognizing Details: Being able to pick out and remember who, what, when, where, why and how of what is read.

Rectangle: A figure with four 90° angles and four sides. The sides opposite one another are the same length.

Reduce: To divide by the greatest common factor in a fraction.

Regroup: To use 10 ones to form one 10, 10 tens to form one hundred, one 10 and 5 ones to form 15, and so on.

Remainder: The number left over in the quotient of a division problem.

Request: A sentence that asks someone to do something. It ends with a period or question mark.

Right Angle: An angle formed when two lines meet at 90°.

Rounding: Expressing a number to the nearest ten, hundred, thousand, and so on. **Examples:** Round 18 to 20; round 11 to 10.

Run-On Sentence: A run-on sentence occurs when two or more sentences are joined together without punctuation.

Sentence: A group of words that expresses a complete thought. It must have at least one subject and one verb.

Sequencing: Putting things or events in order.

Singular: A word that refers to only one thing.

Skip Counting: A quick way to count by skipping numbers.

Square: A figure with four 90˚ angles and four sides of equal length.

Statement: A sentence that tells something. It ends with a period (.).

Subject: The part of the sentence that tells who or what the sentence is about.

Subtraction: "Taking away" or subtracting one number from another.

Suffix: A syllable at the end of a word that changes its meaning.

Sum: The answer in an addition problem.

Summarizing: Writing a short report that gives the main points of a story or article.

Syllable: Part of a word. Each syllable has one vowel sound.

Synonym: A word that means the same, or nearly the same, as another word. **Example:** brave and courageous.

Taking Notes: Writing important information from a story, book, article, or lecture that can be used later in writing a report or taking a test.

Tanka: A Japanese poem written in response to a haiku. It has five lines of five, seven, five, seven and seven syllables, respectively.

Temperature: A unit of measurement that shows how hot or cold something is.

Ton: A unit of measure in the standard system for weight. One ton is 2,000 pounds.

Triangle: A closed figure with three angles and three sides.

Verb: A word that tells what something does or that something exists. **Example:** Pete ran down the street.

Venn Diagram: A diagram used to chart information that shows similarities and differences between two things.

Volume: The number of cubic units that fit inside a figure.

Yard (yd.): A unit of distance in the standard system. There are 3 feet in a yard.

Addition and Subtraction

Help your child practice basic facts with flash cards.

Play addition and subtraction games at the grocery store by adding and subtracting prices. Tally the total number of items to be purchased.

When adding or subtracting larger numbers, provide your child with counting sticks or another type of manipulative. When your child "carries" or "borrows" with concrete materials, he/she will better understand the operations involved.

Adjectives and Nouns

Remind your child that a noun names a person, place or thing. Have him/her write nouns on plain white index cards. Remind your child that an adjective describes a noun. Have him/her write adjectives on colored index cards. Since adjectives are describing words, this can visually help your child connect adjectives with ways to make sentences more colorful. He/she could match the cards to show nouns and adjectives that would go together.

Practice recognizing adjectives and nouns when you and your child are in the car on a trip or waiting at a traffic light. Point out an object or a building. Ask your child to name adjectives to describe it. Challenge your child to come up with 10 describing words in a specified length of time.

Adverbs

Adverbs tell place, time, or manner. Have your child label three containers with those words. One container could be decorated to represent a building (place), one to represent a clock (time), and one with a big smiley face (manner). Give your child adverb word cards and have him/her put them in the correct container. He/she could select an adverb and write a sentence using that word.

Averaging

Brainstorm daily situations with your child in which you use averaging: the cost of groceries for a month, the cost of lunches for a week, the amount of gas used in a car for a month, and so on.

Capitalization

Help your child write a letter to a relative or friend. Remind him or her that proper nouns begin with capital letters. Check the return address and the mailing address to make sure capital letters are used where needed. You may want your child to practice addressing an envelope on a sheet of paper before writing on an envelope.

Help your child develop listening skills while playing a capitalization game. Have your child listen as you say a sentence. Have him/her say which word or words need to be capitalized and why those words should begin with a capital letter.

Your child can list the days of the week or months of the year, write down names of family members, stores in your community or names of the streets in your neighborhood. This will provide good practice in writing proper nouns with capital letters.

Classifying

Play a game with your child to help him/her understand classifying. Tell your child three or four related words (oak, pine, elm, maple). Then, ask him/her to tell you the group in which they belong (trees). If your child has trouble doing this mental activity, write the words on strips of paper and have your child place them under the headings you have provided.

Invite your child to give you groups of objects to place under the headings. If your child can name several things that belong together, then he/she probably understands the concept. Your child may find that it is harder to come up with the words than it is to place them in the correct group, so use this as a challenge activity.

Comprehension

Enhance your child's understanding of a story by encouraging him/her to "picture in his/her head" what the characters look like or how a scene looks as the author describes it.

Comprehension involves understanding what is seen, heard or read. To help your child with this skill, talk about a book, movie or television program you've enjoyed together. Discuss the details of the story and ask questions to guide your child to understand something important that happened in the beginning, middle and end of the story. Many stories have a problem that needs to be solved or a situation that needs to be addressed. Discuss these details with your child to broaden his/her understanding. If your child comprehends what he/she has seen or read, he/she should be able to recount the main events in sequential order and retell the story in his/her own words. By listening to what he/she says, you can tell whether the book, movie, etc. was understood. If your child does not fully understand part of it, discuss that section further. Reread the book or watch the program again, if possible.

Ask your child questions about a story before he/she begins to read it. For example: "What do you think the people in this picture are doing?" "What do you think the title means?" "Do you think this will be a true story or a made-up story?" Then, as your child reads, he/she will already be thinking about the answers to these questions.

Your child can make an advertising poster for a book or movie. Have him/her include the important events, most exciting parts, favorite part, and reasons why someone else should read or view it.

Creating a book jacket for a book he/she has read is another way for your child to show he/she has understood what was read. The jacket should include a picture depicting a main event in the story and a brief summary on the back. If the book belongs to your child, he/she could use the cover on the book.

Decimals

Using the sports section of the newspaper, help your child locate "times" from swim meets, track meets, auto races, and so on. Point out that the times are in tenths and hundredths of seconds. Have your child practice by adding and subtracting the times of sporting events.

Details

It is important for your child to be able to recognize and remember details of what he/she has read and seen. After reading a book or watching a movie together, ask your child questions about details, like what the main character wore, when and where the story took place, names of minor characters, etc.

Play a game to help strengthen your child's attention to detail. Gather 20 to 25 common everyday objects and set them out on a table (button, dice, pen, scissors, cup, spoon, small toys, book, paper clip, straw, spool of thread, disk, etc.). Ask your child to study the objects and see how many he/she can remember. Then, cover the objects with a towel and ask him/her to name as many as possible. Do this several times with the same items, then with a different set of items.

Encourage your child to be observant about details in everyday life. After walking or driving past a building or billboard, ask your child to recall as many details as possible.

Division

Practice division facts in tandem with multiplication facts. Show your child how multiplication and division facts can be grouped into "fact families."

Examples: $7 \times 9 = 63$ $9 \times 7 = 63$ $63 \div 7 = 9$ $63 \div 9 = 7$
              $6 \times 5 = 30$ $5 \times 6 = 30$ $30 \div 6 = 5$ $30 \div 5 = 6$

Give your child three numbers, such as 7, 8, and 56, and ask him/her to name the fact family. Have your child practice with other number groups.

Drill division facts with flash cards and oral quizzes. Point out division applications in real-life situations. If mastery of facts is still a problem, have your child use counting sticks to divide large groups into smaller groups of equal size. This activity is also helpful when introducing division with remainders: $73 \div 8 = 9 \text{ R}1$. Do not go on to more difficult division problems until your child has mastered the basics.

Estimating

Use the following situations to reinforce estimating with your child:

a. Round the price of several grocery items and estimate the total cost.

b. Round the total cost at a restaurant and calculate the tip.

c. Estimate the number of miles between home and school or other destinations.

d. Use a pizza carry-out menu to estimate the costs of pizzas with various toppings.

Fables and Legends

Read fables and legends from many cultures with your child. Check your library or favorite bookstore for titles. After reading several together, make up your own. Brainstorm some ideas and write them down in the form of a question: Why is the sky blue? Why do birds fly? How did a giraffe get such a long neck? Why are hummingbirds so small? Select one and make up your story together. You can write it or tape it, then read or play it back. Encourage your child to draw an illustration for your legend or fable.

Following Directions

By fourth grade, your child should be able to listen carefully and follow directions. Before your child begins an activity, remind him/her to read carefully and make sure he/she understands the directions.

Building models and making craft projects are other ways for your child to learn to follow directions. Reading the instructions and learning to play a new board game or video game helps your child practice this skill.

Let your child help with the cooking and baking. Not only does this give your child good experience in reading and following directions, he/she also uses many math skills to measure ingredients. Have your child look for recipes in newspapers and magazines, as well as cookbooks. Most libraries have a large selection of cookbooks. It's a fun way to learn, and the results can be delicious.

Cooking is one of many daily activities that involves following directions. Whether it is heating a can of vegetables, cooking a frozen pizza, or making pudding, all involve following directions. Read the package directions with your child and have him/her help you. Explain to your child why ingredients must be mixed in a certain order and why some steps must be done before others.

Ask your child to take a turn preparing a meal for the family once a week. Write out the directions and be very specific. Remember, until he/she has had experience cooking, what seems obvious to you may not be obvious to your child. For example, if you tell your child to add a can of vegetables to make a casserole and don't mention that the vegetables should be drained first, you might end up with a very juicy casserole.

When you have a bicycle, toy, or other item to assemble, allow your child to help. Point to each step in the directions. Read each step together. Then, follow the steps in order. Like following package directions or a recipe, assembling an item enables your child to see that following directions is a skill used in everyday situations.

Fractions

Use foods such as pizza, cake, pie, and brownies to help your child identify halves, fourths, thirds, and so on. Review identification of numerators denominators. With the foods listed above, practice adding and subtracting like fractions. Example: If Sally takes $\frac{1}{6}$ of the pie and Jane takes $\frac{2}{6}$ of the pie, how much of the pie is gone? How much of the pie is left over?

Geometry

Look for shapes in everyday objects. Point out the differences in the number of angles and sides of several figures: triangles, squares, rectangles, pentagons, and so on.

Have fun using a compass and protractor to draw circles and designs. Show your child that you set the compass measure for one-half of the size of the desired circle. The compass needs to be set at the radius measure.

Grammar

On index cards or poster board pieces, write the following words: good, well, your, you're, its, it's, can, may, sit, set, they're, their, there, this, and these. On additional pieces, write sentences that have one of the above words missing. After shuffling the word cards and the sentences cards, place them facedown on two separate areas. Have the first player turn over a word card and a sentence card and see if they match. If they do, the player keeps the match and takes another turn. If there is no match, turn the cards facedown and the next player selects two cards. Play continues until all the cards have been matched.

Graphing

Show your child that graphing has many practical applications in daily life. Use the business section of the newspaper to practice reading graphs. Have your child identify whether the graph is a line graph, bar graph or pictograph. Help your child graph: weather for a month; food eaten for a week; number of books read over a specific period of time; favorite colors, music, sports, games; and so on.

Identifying Parts of Speech

Help your child learn or review parts of a sentence using a dictionary. Explain that a dictionary entry is a reference that will help identify parts of speech. Examine several dictionary entries together. When your child has difficulty recognizing what part of speech a word is, the dictionary can be a ready source.

Language Arts Challenges

Write sentences that need correcting. Your child's challenge is to correct the grammar, punctuation, spelling, capitalization, etc.

Introduce new words. Challenge your child to look up the definitions and pronunciations. Encourage him/her to use the new words in conversation and writing and to learn the spelling of the new words.

Write book titles. Have your child find the author's name, locate the book in the library and read it. Further the challenge by asking your child to tell you the main ideas of the book or to outline it.

List book character names. Challenge your child to find in what stories the characters are found. Include characters from unfamiliar books.

Main Idea

Newspapers are one of the most convenient and versatile learning tools you have around your home. Encourage your child to read parts of the newspaper every day. You might notice a headline that looks interesting and ask your child to read the article and tell you what it is about. This helps him/her find the main idea of an article.

Look for articles of interest to your child—ones about neighborhood events, people you know, items relating to school and special hobbies or sports of interest to your child.

Sometimes, it helps to cut out articles and let your child read one article a day. It can be less intimidating to start by reading one short article than to try to read an entire newspaper. Leave your newspaper folded in such a way that an interesting photo or headline is showing. That may help catch your child's attention and encourage him/her to read that article and others.

Encourage your child to read editorials and write an editorial to the paper expressing his/her views.

When an interesting story is developing in your local newspaper, encourage your child to follow it for several days to learn the latest developments. Have him/her select the main idea of the story and write it down each day. After several days, he/she will have a sequential report of the story.

Math Challenges

Write story problems with too much information. Before solving, have your child decide which information is not needed to solve the problem.

Write out number patterns like those in this book. Challenge your child to discover the pattern and write in the missing numbers.

Write story problems for your child to solve. Make sure the problems include an assortment of operations—addition, subtraction, multiplication, and division. Use the names of your child, his/her friends, relatives, pets, etc. to personalize the problems.

Measurement

Help your child see that you measurement on a daily basis. You measure ingredients for recipes, mileage to and from work and school, and so on. Allow your child to help measure whenever possible. Have him/her find the area and/or volume of his/her room. Send your child on a "measuring safari" equipped with a ruler and a list of objects to measure. Have him/her assist in cooking by measuring ingredients. Note: Do not make comparisons of standard and metric measures. This will only confuse your child. Standard/metric conversions can be learned at a later time.

Multiplication

The key to success in multiplication is the mastery of single-digit multiplication facts from 0 to 12. Help your child practice these facts with multiplication flash cards, bingo games, homemade activity sheets and timed tests. Play multiplication games with number cubes, dice or spinners. Have your child roll the number cubes and multiply the two numbers rolled or spun.

Make up multiplication story problems. Example: You make 9 cupcakes. On each cupcake you want to place 5 pieces of candy. How many pieces of candy will you need in all?

Place Value

To enhance your child's understanding of place value, have him/her practice counting and grouping craft sticks or toothpicks into bundles of tens, hundreds and thousands. Have your child manipulate these groupings on a place value chart to make various numbers. After making numbers with manipulatives, your child can write the numbers on the chart.

Poetry

Read poems you enjoyed as a child together with your own child. Ask your child to share his/her favorite poems with you. Libraries carry many good anthologies of poetry, from nursery rhymes to long, narrative poems. Sample many different kinds including both rhymed and unrhymed verse. Limericks are always fun to read and write. If your child says he/she doesn't like poetry, try authors like Ogden Nash, Shel Silverstein and Edward Lear.

Predicates and Subjects

Have your child dictate five to ten sentences to you. Write them on strips of paper. Cut the strips between the subject and the predicate. Mix up the subject sections and place them in a pile. Place the predicate sections in another pile. Have your child put the sentences back together so they make sense. Example: He / caught the ball and ran for a touchdown.

Make "silly sentences" with your child by combining a subject and a predicate that usually don't belong together. Have your child glue the silly sentence to a sheet of drawing paper and illustrate it. Example: The cuddly kitten / caught the ball and ran for a touchdown.

Your child can use these sentence strips and make new subjects for the predicates and new predicates for the subjects. Example: The running back / caught the ball and ran for a touchdown.

Proofreading

As your child writes sentences and stories, he/she needs to be able to express his/her thoughts without concern for correct spelling and punctuation. The first draft of a story should be one in which the writer doesn't worry about mechanics. He/she needs to get his/her thoughts down. When the story is completed, you can guide your child in proofreading before making a final copy.

Proofreading should consist of looking for grammatical errors, overuse of words (synonyms could be used instead), misspellings, punctuation mistakes and capitalization errors. Work with your child without being critical to enable him/her to see the types of mistakes he/she made. Make the corrections together until you see that your child is able to handle proofreading on his/her own.

You could do some practice sentences, providing written work with obvious mistakes and have your child correct them. The mistakes, at first, could be names of family members or pets. Help your child rewrite them with the corrections made. You may want to write sentences with blank spaces and have your child write the missing proper nouns. Progress to other types of errors such as commas, quotation marks, question marks and misspelled words.

Rounding

Give your child several numbers to round to the nearest ten, hundred or thousand. Have him/her determine where the numbers would fall on the respective number lines. Then, he/she can round the number by deciding to which ten, hundred or thousand it comes closest.

To help build your child's understanding of rounding numbers, make several number lines on adding machine tape. Number each as follows:

   a.   from 0 to 100, counting by tens (for rounding to the nearest ten).

   b.   from 0 to 1,000, counting by hundreds (for rounding to the nearest hundred).

   c.   from 0 to 10,000, counting by thousands (for rounding to the nearest thousand).

Sequencing

Sequencing can be done in several ways. Words can be arranged in alphabetical order. Events can be arranged in chronological order. Steps to complete a task can be arranged in logical order. Items can be arranged by size or shape from largest to smallest.

Remind your child that letters have to be in a certain order to make words, words have to be in a certain order to make sentences that make sense and paragraphs and story events have to be in a certain order.

As you are traveling, tell a story together. Begin the story. After a few sentences, have your child continue the story. Take turns until you arrive at your destination or get to the end of the story.

Present a math word problem for your child to solve. Have him/her explain and write in sequence how to solve the problem.

Find a comic strip that has three or four sections and read it with your child. Cut the sections apart and have your child put them back together.

Encourage your child to tell you about events that have occurred at school or other places where you were not present. As he/she recalls what happened, encourage him/her to recall the events in order and add details.

Have your child keep a journal. This not only helps with sequencing but is also a good way to record what is happening in his/her life for the future. Each night in the journal, have your child write in order four things that he/she did during the day. When the journal is full, put it away in a safe place and save it for your child to reread when he/she is a few years older.

Skip Counting

To help your child practice skip counting, make a large number line on several sheets of construction paper, using one sheet per number. Number the sheets from 0 to 100. As your child practices skip counting, he/she can literally "skip" from one number to the next. The physical movement of skip counting will enhance your child's understanding of this concept.

Vocabulary Building

Encourage your child to learn a new word each week. He/she should learn its meaning and use it when applicable throughout the week. You may select the word from those your child brings home from his/her science, math, reading, spelling or social studies school work.

Be aware of words your child may overuse in his/her language and writing. Decide together on synonyms that can be used in place of the overused words. Buy a thesaurus and help your child use it when he/she is doing homework. This handy reference can also be used to decide on new "words of the week."

Play a matching game with your child. Write new vocabulary words on tagboard cut into playing-card size pieces. For each word card, make a definition card (synonym, antonym, and so on). Place the cards facedown on a table. Turn over two cards at a time to see if they match. If they don't match, the next player tries to locate a match.

225

ANSWER KEY

---

8 READING

Say It Short

Vowels are the letters **a, e, i, o, u** and sometimes **y**. There are five short vowels: **ă** as in **apple**, **ĕ** as in **egg** and **breath**, **ĭ** as in **sick**, **ŏ** as in **top** and **ŭ** as in **up**.

Directions: Complete the exercises using words from the box.

blend	insist	health	pump	crop
fact	pinch	pond	hatch	plug

1. Write each word under its vowel sound.

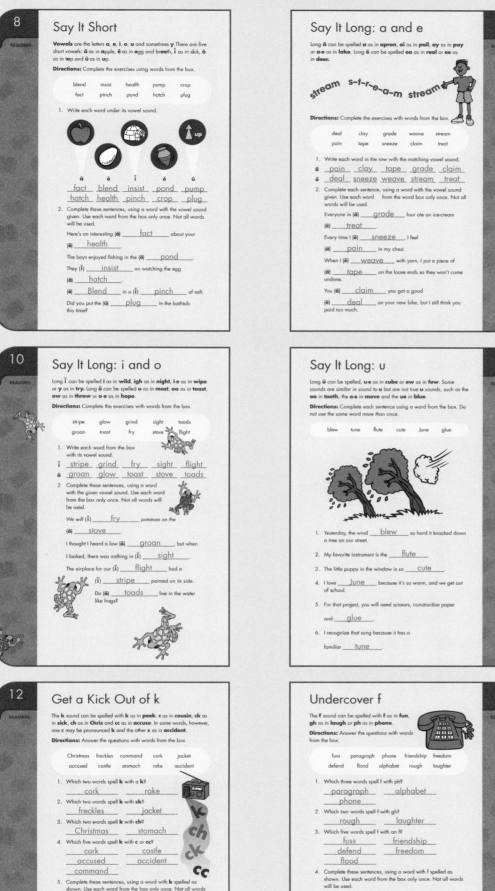

ă	ĕ	ĭ	ŏ	ŭ
fact	blend	insist	pond	pump
hatch	health	pinch	crop	plug

2. Complete these sentences, using a word with the vowel sound given. Use each word from the box only once. Not all words will be used.

Here's an interesting (ă) ___fact___ about your

(ĕ) ___health___

The boys enjoyed fishing in the (ŏ) ___pond___.

They (ĭ) ___insist___ on watching the egg

(ă) ___hatch___

(ĕ) ___Blend___ in a (ĭ) ___pinch___ of salt.

Did you put the (ŭ) ___plug___ in the bathtub this time?

---

9 READING

Say It Long: a and e

Long **ā** can be spelled **a** as in **apron**, **ai** as in **pail**, **ay** as in **pay** or **a-e** as in **lake**. Long **ē** can be spelled **ea** as in **real** or **ee** as in **deer**.

stream s-t-r-e-a-m stream

Directions: Complete the exercises with words from the box.

deal	clay	grade	weave	stream
pain	tape	sneeze	claim	treat

1. Write each word in the row with the matching vowel sound.
ā ___pain___ ___clay___ ___tape___ ___grade___ ___claim___
ē ___deal___ ___sneeze___ ___weave___ ___stream___ ___treat___

2. Complete each sentence, using a word with the vowel sound given. Use each word from the word box only once. Not all words will be used.

Everyone in (ā) ___grade___ four ate an ice-cream

(ē) ___treat___

Every time I (ē) ___sneeze___, I feel

(ā) ___pain___ in my chest.

When I (ā) ___weave___ with yarn, I put a piece of

(ā) ___tape___ on the loose ends so they won't come undone.

You (ā) ___claim___ you got a good

(ē) ___deal___ on your new bike, but I still think you paid too much.

---

10 READING

Say It Long: i and o

Long **ī** can be spelled **i** as in **wild**, **igh** as in **night**, **i-e** as in **wipe** or **y** as in **try**. Long **ō** can be spelled **o** as in **most**, **oa** as in **toast**, **ow** as in **throw** or **o-e** as in **hope**.

Directions: Complete the exercises with words from the box.

stripe	glow	grind	sight	toads
groan	toast	fry	stove	flight

1. Write each word from the box with its vowel sound.
ī ___stripe___ ___grind___ ___fry___ ___sight___ ___flight___
ō ___groan___ ___glow___ ___toast___ ___stove___ ___toads___

2 Complete these sentences, using a word with the given vowel sound. Use each word from the box only once. Not all words will be used.

We will (ī) ___fry___ potatoes on the

(ō) ___stove___

I thought I heard a low (ō) ___groan___, but when

I looked, there was nothing in (ī) ___sight___.

The airplane for our (ī) ___flight___ had a

(ī) ___stripe___ painted on its side.

Do (ō) ___toads___ live in the water like frogs?

---

11 READING

Say It Long: u

Long **ū** can be spelled, **u-e** as in **cube** or **ew** as in **few**. Some sounds are similar in sound to **u** but are not true **u** sounds, such as the **oo** in **tooth**, the **o-e** in **move** and the **ue** in **blue**.

Directions: Complete each sentence using a word from the box. Do not use the same word more than once.

blew	tune	flute	cute	June	glue

1. Yesterday, the wind ___blew___ so hard it knocked down a tree on our street.

2. My favorite instrument is the ___flute___.

3. The little puppy in the window is so ___cute___.

4. I love ___June___ because it's so warm, and we get out of school.

5. For that project, you will need scissors, construction paper and ___glue___.

6. I recognize that song because it has a familiar ___tune___.

---

12 READING

Get a Kick Out of k

The **k** sound can be spelled with **k** as in **peek**, **c** as in **cousin**, **ck** as in **sick**, **ch** as in **Chris** and **cc** as in **accuse**. In some words, however, one **c** may be pronounced **k** and the other **s** as in **accident**.

Directions: Answer the questions with words from the box.

Christmas	freckles	command	cork	jacket
accused	castle	stomach	rake	accident

1. Which two words spell **k** with a **k**?
___cork___ ___rake___

2. Which two words spell **k** with **ck**?
___freckles___ ___jacket___

3. Which two words spell **k** with **ch**?
___Christmas___ ___stomach___

4. Which five words spell **k** with **c** or **cc**?
___cork___ ___castle___
___accused___ ___accident___
___command___

5. Complete these sentences, using a word with **k** spelled as shown. Use each word from the box only once. Not all words will be used.

Dad gave Mom a garden (k) ___rake___ for
(ch) ___Christmas___.

There are (ck) ___freckles___ on my face and
(ch) ___stomach___.

The people (cc) ___accused___ her of taking a
(ck) ___jacket___.

The police took (c) ___command___ after the
(cc) ___accident___.

---

13 READING

Undercover f

The **f** sound can be spelled with **f** as in **fun**, **gh** as in **laugh** or **ph** as in **phone**.

Directions: Answer the questions with words from the box.

fuss	paragraph	phone	friendship	freedom
defend	flood	alphabet	rough	laughter

1. Which three words spell f with ph?
___paragraph___ ___alphabet___
___phone___

2. Which two words spell f with gh?
___rough___ ___laughter___

3. Which five words spell f with an f?
___fuss___ ___friendship___
___defend___ ___freedom___
___flood___

4. Complete these sentences, using a word with f spelled as shown. Use each word from the box only once. Not all words will be used.

A (f) ___friendship___ can help you through
(gh) ___rough___ times.

The soldiers will (f) ___defend___ our
(f) ___freedom___.

Can you say the (ph) ___alphabet___ backwards?

When I answered the (ph) ___phone___, all I
could hear was (gh) ___laughter___.

If it keeps raining, we'll have a (f) ___flood___.

14 · On the Scene with s

The **s** sound can be spelled with **s** as in **super** or **ss** as in **assign**, **c** as in **city**, **ce** as in **fence** or **sc** as in **scene**. In some words, though, **sc** is pronounced **sk**, as in **scare**.

| exciting | medicine | lettuce | peace | scissors |
| slice | scientist | sauce | bracelet | distance |

Directions: Answer the questions using words from the box.

1. Which five words spell **s** with just an **s** or **ss**?
   slice   scissors
   sauce   scientist
   distance

2. Which two words spell **s** with just a **c**?
   exciting   medicine

3. Which six words spell **s** with a **ce**?
   slice   lettuce
   sauce   peace
   bracelet   distance

4. Which two words spell **s** with **sc**?
   scientist   scissors

5. Complete these sentences, using a word with **s** spelled as shown. Use each word from the box only once. Not all words will be used.
   My **(ce)** bracelet fell off my wrist into the
   tomato sauce **(s and ce)**.
   My salad was just a **(s and ce)** slice
   of **(ce)** lettuce.
   It was **(c)** exciting to see the lions, even though
   they were a long **(s and ce)** distance away.

15 · Give Me a Break

A **syllable** is a word—or part of a word—with only one vowel sound. Some words have just one syllable, such as **cat**, **dog**, and **house**. Some words have two syllables, such as **in-sist** and **be-fore**. Some words have three syllables, such as **re-mem-ber**; four syllables, such as **un-der-stand-ing**; or more. Often words are easier to spell if you know how many syllables they have.

Directions: Write the number of syllables in each word below.

	Word	Syllables		Word	Syllables
1.	amphibian	4	11.	want	1
2.	liter	2	12.	communication	5
3.	guild	1	13.	pedestrian	4
4.	chili	2	14.	kilo	2
5.	vegetarian	5	15.	autumn	2
6.	comedian	4	16.	dinosaur	3
7.	warm	1	17.	grammar	2
8.	piano	3	18.	dry	1
9.	barbarian	4	19.	solar	2
10.	chef	1	20.	wild	1

Directions: Next to each number, write words with the same number of syllables. *Syl-la-bles*

1. _____
2. _____
3. _____   *Answers will vary*
4. _____
5. _____

16 · Say It with Synonyms

A **synonym** is a word that means the same, or nearly the same, as another word.

Example: quick and **fast**

Directions: Draw lines to match the words in Column A with their synonyms in Column B.

Column A	Column B
plain	unusual
career	vocation
rare	disappear
vanish	greedy
beautiful	finish
selfish	simple
complete	lovely

Directions: Choose a word from Column A or Column B to complete each sentence below.

1. Dad was very excited when he discovered the
   rare
   unusual coin for sale on the display counter.

2. My dog is a real magician; he can   vanish   into
   disappear
   thin air when he sees me getting his bath ready!

3. Many of my classmates joined the discussion about
   career
   vocation choices we had considered.

4. "You will need to   complete   your report on
   finish
   ancient Greece before you sign up for computer time,"
   said Mr. Rastetter.

5. Your   beautiful   painting will be on display in the
   lovely
   art show.

17 · Antonyms All Around

An **antonym** is a word that means the opposite of another word.

Example: difficult and **easy**

Directions: Choose words from the box to complete the crossword puzzle.

| friend | vanish | quit | safety |
| liquids | scatter | help | noisy |

ACROSS:
2. Opposite of **gather**
3. Opposite of **enemy**
4. Opposite of **prevent**
6. Opposite of **begin**
7. Opposite of **silent**

DOWN:
1. Opposite of **appear**
2. Opposite of **danger**
5. Opposite of **solids**

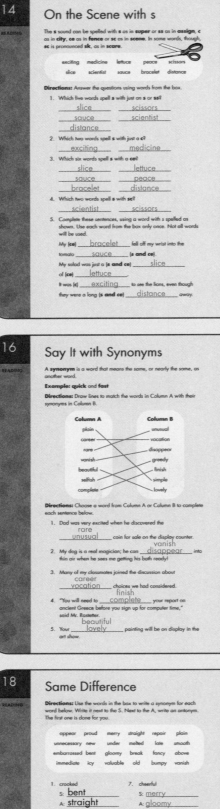

18 · Same Difference

Directions: Use the words in the box to write a synonym for each word below. Write it next to the S. Next to the A, write an antonym. The first one is done for you.

appear	proud	merry	straight	repair	plain
unnecessary	new	under	melted	late	smooth
embarrassed	bent	gloomy	break	fancy	above
immediate	icy	valuable	old	bumpy	vanish

1. crooked
   S: **bent**
   A: **straight**

2. frozen
   S: icy
   A: melted

3. instant
   S: immediate
   A: late

4. damage
   S: break
   A: repair

5. important
   S: valuable
   A: unnecessary

6. ashamed
   S: embarrassed
   A: proud

7. cheerful
   S: merry
   A: gloomy

8. elegant
   S: fancy
   A: plain

9. rough
   S: bumpy
   A: smooth

10. beneath
    S: under
    A: above

11. disappear
    S: vanish
    A: appear

12. ancient
    S: old
    A: new

19 · Madam I'm Adam

Can you think forward and backward? If so, you should have no problem with palindromes. **Palindromes** are words or sentences that are spelled the same forward or backward.

**Examples: noon, eve, mom, wow
a man, a plan, a canal, Panama**

WOW!

Directions: Read the definitions. Write the palindromes on the lines. If you get stuck, work with a partner.

1. Another name for a soft drink   pop
2. What you typically call your father   dad (or pop)
3. Short for Nancy   Nan
4. What one does with one's eyes   sees
5. Female sheep   ewe
6. An instrument used to locate airplanes   radar
7. To choke   gag
8. Boat used by Eskimos   kayak

Directions: Write as many palindromes as you can. A few have been done for you.

bib, Bob, did, dad *Answers may*
include: dud, mom, ma'am, mum,
pip, pep, pup, sis, peep

20 · Hear! Here! Homophones!

Homophones are two words that sound the same, have different meanings and are usually spelled differently.

Example: write and **right**

Directions: Write the correct homophone in each sentence below.

weight — how heavy something is
wait — to be patient

threw — tossed
through — passing between

steal — to take something that doesn't belong to you
steel — a heavy metal

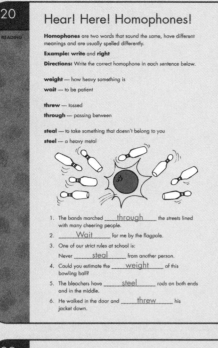

1. The bands marched ___through___ the streets lined with many cheering people.
2. ___Wait___ for me by the flagpole.
3. One of our strict rules at school is:
   Never ___steal___ from another person.
4. Could you estimate the ___weight___ of this bowling ball?
5. The bleachers have ___steel___ rods on both ends and in the middle.
6. He walked in the door and ___threw___ his jacket down.

21 · Calling All Homophones

Directions: Choose the correct word in parentheses to complete each sentence. The first one is done for you.

1. Jimmy was so ___bored___ that he fell asleep. (board, bored)
2. We'll need a ___board___ and some nails to repair the fence. (board, bored)
3. Do you want ___dessert___ after dinner? (desert, dessert)
4. Did the soldier ___desert___ his post? (desert, dessert)
5. The soldier had a ___medal___ pinned to his uniform. (medal, middle)
6. I told her not to ___meddle___ in other people's lives. (medal, middle)
7. Jack had to repair the emergency ___brake___ on his car. (brake, break)
8. Please be careful not to ___break___ my bicycle. (brake, break)
9. The race ___course___ was a very difficult one. (coarse, course)
10. We will need some ___coarse___ sandpaper to finish the job. (coarse, course)

22 · Prefix Pros

A **prefix** is a syllable at the beginning of a word that changes its meaning.

Directions: Add a prefix to the beginning of each word in the box to make a word with the meaning given in each sentence below. The first one is done for you.

PREFIX	MEANING
bi	two or twice
en	to make
in	within
mis	wrong
non	not or without
pre	before
re	again
un	not

| grown | write | information | large | cycle | sense |

1. Antonia's foot hurt because his toenail was (growing within).
   ingrown
2. If you want to see what is in the background, you will have to (make bigger) the photograph.
   enlarge
3. I didn't do a very good job on my homework, so I will have to (write it again) it.
   rewrite
4. The newspaper article about the event has some (wrong facts).
   misinformation
5. I hope I get a (vehicle with two wheels) for my birthday.
   bicycle
6. The story he told was complete (words without meaning)!
   nonsense

23 · Save the Best for Last

A **suffix** is a syllable at the end of a word that changes its meaning. In most cases, when adding a suffix that begins with a vowel, drop the final **e** of the root word. For example, **fame** becomes **famous**. Also, change a final **y** in the root word to **i** before adding any suffix except **ing**. For example, **silly** becomes **silliness**.

Directions: Add a suffix to the end of each word in the box to make a word with the meaning given (in parentheses) in each sentence below. The first one is done for you.

SUFFIX	MEANING
ful	full of
ity	quality or degree
ive	have or tend to be
less	without or lacking
able	able to be
ness	state of
ment	act of
or	person that does something
ward	in the direction of

| like | thought | pay | thank | act | happy |

1. Mike was (full of thanks) for a hot meal.
   thankful
2. I was (without thinking) for forgetting your birthday.
   thoughtless
3. Tasha is such a (able to be liked) girl!
   likable
4. Jill's wedding day was one of great (the state of being happy).
   happiness
5. The (person who performs) was very good in the play.
   actor
6. I have to make a (act of paying) for the stereo I bought.
   payment

24 · Odd One Out

Classifying is placing similar things into categories.

Directions: Classify each group by crossing out the word that does not belong.

1. factory · hotel · lodge · ~~pattern~~
2. ~~Thursday~~ · September · December · October
3. cottage · hut · ~~carpenter~~ · castle
4. cupboard · ~~orchard~~ · refrigerator · stove
5. Christmas · Thanksgiving · Easter · ~~spring~~
6. brass · copper · ~~coal~~ · tin
7. stomach · ~~breathe~~ · liver · brain
8. teacher · mother · dentist · ~~office~~
9. ~~mirror~~ · faucet · bathtub · sink
10. basement · attic · kitchen · ~~neighborhood~~

25 · TV Time!

Directions: Read the title of each TV show. Write the correct number to tell what kind of show it is.

1 — Cooking	3 — Sports	5 — Humor
2 — Nature	4 — Mystery	6 — Famous People

___4___ The Secret of the Lost Locket
___3___ Learn Tennis With the Pros
___2___ Birds in the Wild
___6___ The Life of George Washington
___1___ Great Recipes From Around the World
___5___ A Laugh a Minute

Directions: Read the description of each TV show. Write the number of each show above in the blank.

___6___ The years before he became the first president of the United States are examined.
___2___ Featured: eagles and owls
___4___ Clues lead Detective Logan to a cemetery in his search for the missing necklace.
___3___ Famous players give tips on buying a racket.
___4___ Six ways to cook chicken
___5___ Cartoon characters in short stories

26 — Come on and Compare

An **analogy** indicates how different items go together or are similar in some way.

Examples:

Petal is to **flower** as leaf is to **tree**.
Book is to **library** as food is to **grocery**.

If you study the examples, you will see how the second set of objects is related to the first set. A petal is part of a flower, and a leaf is part of a tree. A book can be found in a library, and food can be found in a grocery store.

Directions: Fill in the blanks to complete the analogies. The first one has been done for you.

1. Cup is to saucer as glass is to ___coaster___
2. Paris is to France as London is to ___England___
3. Clothes are to hangers as ___shoes___ are to boxes.
4. California is to __Pacific Ocean__ as Ohio is to Lake Erie.
5. ___Tablecloth___ is to table as blanket is to bed.
6. Pencil is to paper as ___paintbrush___ is to canvas.
7. Cow is to ___barn___ as child is to house.
8. State is to country as ___county___ is to state.
9. Governor is to state as ___president___ is to country.

Directions: Write three analogies of your own.

___Answers will vary___

27 — All About Analogies

Directions: Write a word from the box to complete the following analogies.

club	glove	saw	father
blanket	dish	rug	snow
ten	compass	hat	brake

1. Racket is to tennis as ___club___ is to golf.
2. Glass is to drink as ___dish___ is to eat.
3. Wheel is to steer as ___brake___ is to stop.
4. Roof is to house as ___rug___ is to floor.
5. Rain is to storm as ___snow___ is to blizzard.
6. Clock is to time as ___compass___ is to directions.
7. Lid is to pan as ___hat___ is to head.
8. Hammer is to pound as ___saw___ is to cut.
9. Mother is to daughter as ___father___ is to son.
10. Shoe is to foot as ___glove___ is to hand.
11. Five is to ten as ___ten___ is to twenty.
12. Shade is to lamp as ___blanket___ is to bed.

28 — Follow Me!

Directions: Follow the directions below to reach a "mystery" location on the map.

1. Begin at home.
2. Drive east on River Road.
3. Turn south on Broadway.
4. Drive to Central Street and turn west.
5. When you get to City Street, turn south.
6. Turn east on Main Street and drive one block to Park Avenue; turn north.
7. At Central Street turn east, then turn southeast on Through Way.
8. Drive to the end of Through Way. Your "mystery" location is to the east.

You are at the ___school___

Can you write an easier way to get back home?

___Answers will vary___

29 — Let's Get Cooking!

Sequencing is putting items or events in logical order.

Directions: Read the recipe. Then, number the steps in order for making brownies.

Preheat the oven to 350 degrees. Grease an 8-inch square baking dish.

In a mixing bowl, place two squares (2 ounces) of unsweetened chocolate and $\frac{1}{3}$ cup butter. Place the bowl in a pan of hot water and heat it to melt the chocolate and the butter.

When the chocolate is melted, remove the pan from the heat. Add 1 cup sugar and two eggs to the melted chocolate and beat it. Next, stir in $\frac{3}{4}$ cup sifted flour, $\frac{1}{2}$ teaspoon baking powder and $\frac{1}{2}$ teaspoon salt. Finally, mix in $\frac{1}{2}$ cup chopped nuts.

Spread the mixture in the greased baking dish. Bake for 30 to 35 minutes. The brownies are done when a toothpick stuck in the center comes out clean. Let the brownies cool. Cut them into squares.

__8__ Stick a toothpick in the center of the brownies to make sure they are done.

__5__ Mix in chopped nuts.

__2__ Melt chocolate and butter in a mixing bowl over a pan of hot water.

__9__ Cool brownies and cut into squares.

__3__ Beat in sugar and eggs.

__6__ Spread mixture in a baking dish.

__4__ Stir in flour, baking powder and salt.

__7__ Bake for 30 to 35 minutes.

__1__ Turn oven to 350 degrees and grease pan.

30 — Right on Track

Directions: Below is part of a schedule for trains leaving New York City for cities all around the country. Use the schedule to answer the questions.

Destination	Train Number	Departure Time	Arrival Time
Birmingham	958	9:00 a.m.	12:31 a.m.
Boston	611	7:15 a.m.	4:30 p.m.
Cambridge	398	8:15 a.m.	1:14 p.m.
Cincinnati	242	5:00 a.m.	7:25 p.m.
Detroit	415	1:45 p.m.	4:40 a.m.
Evansville	623	3:00 p.m.	8:28 a.m.

1. What is the number of the train that leaves latest in the day?
   ___623___
2. What city is the destination for train number 623?
   ___Evansville___
3. What time does the train for Boston leave New York?
   ___7:15 a.m.___
4. What time does train number 415 arrive in Detroit?
   ___4:40 a.m.___
5. What is the destination of the train that leaves earliest in the day?
   ___Cincinnati___

31 — Label Lingo

Directions: You should never take any medicine without your parents' permission, but it is good to know how to read the label of a medicine bottle. Read the label to answer the questions.

**Children's Cold Relief
Sneezing and Runny Nose Formula**

For relief of runny nose and sneezing due to common cold, hay fever or other allergies.

Dosage:

Children under 2 years, only as directed by a physician.

Children 2 to 6 years old, 1 teaspoon.

Children 6 to 11 years old, 2 teaspoons.

All doses may be repeated every 4 to 6 hours, but not more than four doses every 24 hours.

Warning: May cause dizziness or sleepiness
Do not give to children with heart disease.
Keep this and all medicines out of reach of children.

1. How much medicine should a 5 year old take?
   ___1 teaspoon___
2. How often can this medicine be taken?
   ___every 4 to 6 hours___
3. How do you know how much medicine to give a 1 year old?
   ___ask a physician___
4. Who should not take this medicine?
   ___children with heart disease___

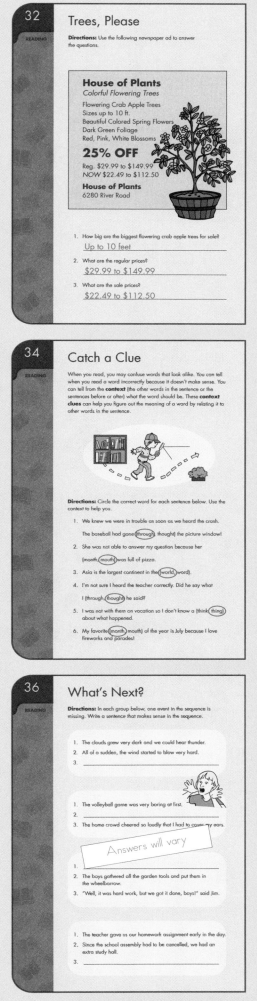

32 — Trees, Please

READING

Directions: Use the following newspaper ad to answer the questions.

House of Plants
Colorful Flowering Trees

Flowering Crab Apple Trees
Sizes up to 10 ft.
Beautiful Colored Spring Flowers
Dark Green Foliage
Red, Pink, White Blossoms

25% OFF

Reg. $29.99 to $149.99
NOW $22.49 to $112.50

House of Plants
6280 River Road

1. How big are the biggest flowering crab apple trees for sale?
   Up to 10 feet

2. What are the regular prices?
   $29.99 to $149.99

3. What are the sale prices?
   $22.49 to $112.50

33 — That's a Fact!

READING

Facts are statements or events that have happened and can be proven to be true.

Example: George Washington was the first president of the United States.

This statement is a fact. It can be proven to be true by researching the history of our country.

Opinions are statements that express how someone thinks or feels.

Example: George Washington was the greatest president the United States has ever had.

This statement is an opinion. Many people agree that George Washington was a great president, but not everyone agrees he was the greatest president. In some people's opinion, Abraham Lincoln was our greatest president.

Directions: Read each sentence. Write **F** for fact or **O** for opinion.

F   1. There is three feet of snow on the ground.
O   2. A lot of snow makes the winter enjoyable.
O   3. Chris has a better swing set than Mary.
F   4. Both Chris and Mary have swing sets.
F   5. California is a state.
O   6. California is the best state in the west.

Directions: Write three facts and three opinions.

Facts:
1)
2)
3)

Opinions:
1)
2)
3)

Answers will vary

34 — Catch a Clue

READING

When you read, you may confuse words that look alike. You can tell when you read a word incorrectly because it doesn't make sense. You can tell from the **context** (the other words in the sentence or the sentences before or after) what the word should be. These **context clues** can help you figure out the meaning of a word by relating it to other words in the sentence.

Directions: Circle the correct word for each sentence below. Use the context to help you.

1. We knew we were in trouble as soon as we heard the crash. The baseball had gone (through) thought) the picture window!

2. She was not able to answer my question because her (month, (mouth)) was full of pizza.

3. Asia is the largest continent in the ((world,) word).

4. I'm not sure I heard the teacher correctly. Did he say what I (through, (thought)) he said?

5. I was not with them on vacation so I don't know a (think, (thing)) about what happened.

6. My favorite ((month,) mouth) of the year is July because I love fireworks and parades!

35 — What Nonsense!

READING

Directions: In each sentence below, circle the correct meaning for the nonsense word.

1. Be careful when you put that plate back on the shell— it is **quibbable**.
   flexible   colorful   (breakable)

2. What is your favorite kind of **tonn**, pears or bananas?
   (fruit)   salad   purple

3. The **dinlay** outside this morning was very chilly; I needed my sweater.
   tree   vegetable   (temperature)

4. The whole class enjoyed the **weat**. They wanted to see it again next Friday.
   colorful   plant   (video)

5. Ashley's mother brought in a **zundy** she made by hand.
   temperature   (quilt)   plant

6. "Why don't you sit over here, Ronnie? That **sloey** is not very comfortable," said Mr. Gross.
   (chair)   car   cat

36 — What's Next?

READING

Directions: In each group below, one event in the sequence is missing. Write a sentence that makes sense in the sequence.

1. The clouds grew very dark and we could hear thunder.
2. All of a sudden, the wind started to blow very hard.
3. _____

1. The volleyball game was very boring at first.
2. _____
3. The home crowd cheered so loudly that I had to cover my ears.

Answers will vary

1. _____
2. The boys gathered all the garden tools and put them in the wheelbarrow.
3. "Well, it was hard work, but we got it done, boys!" said Jim.

1. The teacher gave us our homework assignment early in the day.
2. Since the school assembly had to be cancelled, we had an extra study hall.
3. _____

37 — Living a Double Life

READING

Directions: Read about how a tadpole becomes a frog. Then, number the stages in order below.

Frogs and toads belong to a group of animals called *amphibians* (am-FIB-ee-ans). This means "living a double life." Frogs and toads live a "double life" because they live part of their lives in water and part on land. They are able to do this because their bodies change as they grow. This series of changes is called *metamorphosis* (met-a-MORE-fa-sis).

A mother frog lays her eggs in water and then leaves them on their own to grow. The eggs contain cells—the tiny "building blocks" of all living things—that multiply and grow. Soon the cells grow into a swimming tadpole. Tadpoles breathe through gills—small holes in their sides—like fish do. They spend all of their time in the water.

The tadpole changes as it grows. Back legs slowly form. Front legs begin inside the tadpole under the gill holes. They pop out when they are fully developed. At the same time, lungs, which a frog uses to breathe instead of gills, are almost ready to be used.

As the tadpole reaches the last days of its life in the water, its tail seems to disappear. When all of the tadpole's body parts are ready for life on land, it has become a frog.

6   The front legs pop out. The lungs are ready to use for breathing.
2   The cells in the egg multiply and grow.
8   The tadpole has become a frog.
4   Back legs slowly form.
3   Soon the cells grow into a swimming tadpole.
5   Front legs develop inside the tadpole.
7   The tadpole's tail seems to disappear.
1   A mother frog lays her eggs in water.

38 — Get to the Point

The **main idea** is the most important idea, or main point, in a sentence, paragraph, or story.

Directions: Circle the main idea for each sentence.

1. Emily knew she would be late if she watched the end of the TV show.
   a. Emily likes watching TV.
   b. Emily is always running late.
   c. (circled) If Emily didn't leave, she would be late.

2. The dog was too strong and pulled Jason across the park on his leash.
   a. (circled) The dog is stronger than Jason.
   b. Jason is not very strong.
   c. Jason took the dog for a walk.

3. Jennifer took the book home so she could read it over and over.
   a. Jennifer loves to read.
   b. (circled) Jennifer loves the book.
   c. Jennifer is a good reader.

4. Jerome threw the baseball so hard it broke the window.
   a. (circled) Jerome throws baseballs very hard.
   b. Jerome was mad at the window.
   c. Jerome can't throw very straight.

5. Lori came home and decided to clean the kitchen for her parents.
   a. Lori is a very nice person.
   b. (circled) Lori did a favor for her parents.
   c. Lori likes to cook.

6. It was raining so hard that it was hard to see the road through the windshield.
   a. It always rains hard in April.
   b. (circled) The rain blurred our vision.
   c. It's hard to drive in the rain.

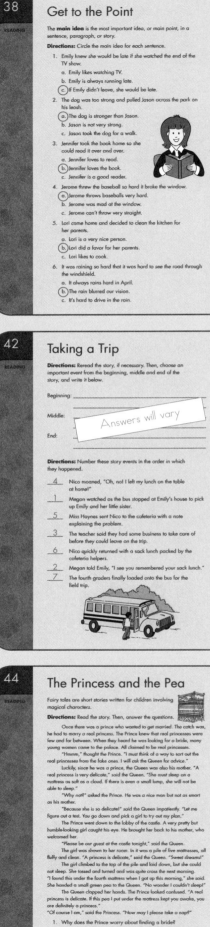

39 — Winter Wonderland

The **main idea** of a story or report is a sentence that summarizes the most important point. If a story or report is only one paragraph in length, then the main idea is usually stated in the first sentence (topic sentence). If it is longer than one paragraph, then the main idea is a general sentence including all the important points of the story or report.

Directions: Read the story about snow fun. Then, draw an X in the blank for the main idea.

> After a big snowfall, my friends and I enjoy playing in the snow. We bundle up in snow clothes at our homes, then meet with sleds at the hill by my house.
> One by one, we take turns sledding down the hill to see who will go the farthest and the fastest. Sometimes we have a contest to see whose sled will reach the fence at the foot of the hill first.
> When we tire of sledding, we may build a snowman or snowforts. Sometimes we have a friendly snowball fight.
> The end of our snow fun comes too quickly, and we head home to warm houses, dry clothes and hot chocolate.

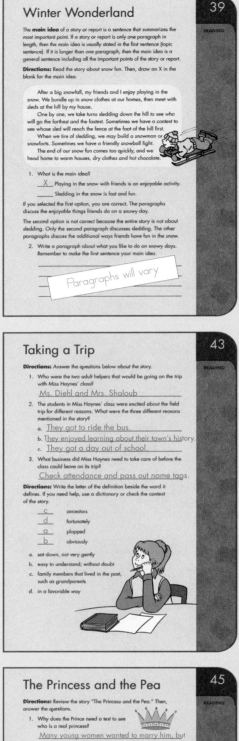

1. What is the main idea?
   __X__ Playing in the snow with friends is an enjoyable activity.
   _____ Sledding in the snow is fast and fun.

If you selected the first option, you are correct. The paragraphs discuss the enjoyable things friends do on a snowy day.

The second option is not correct because the entire story is not about sledding. Only the second paragraph discusses sledding. The other paragraphs discuss the additional ways friends have fun in the snow.

2. Write a paragraph about what you like to do on snowy days. Remember to make the first sentence your main idea.

Paragraphs will vary

42 — Taking a Trip

Directions: Reread the story, if necessary. Then, choose an important event from the beginning, middle and end of the story, and write it below.

Beginning: _____

Middle: _____ *Answers will vary*

End: _____

Directions: Number these story events in the order in which they happened.

_4_ Nico moaned, "Oh, no! I left my lunch on the table at home!"

_1_ Megan watched as the bus stopped at Emily's house to pick up Emily and her little sister.

_5_ Miss Haynes sent Nico to the cafeteria with a note explaining the problem.

_3_ The teacher said they had some business to take care of before they could leave on the trip.

_6_ Nico quickly returned with a sack lunch packed by the cafeteria helpers.

_2_ Megan told Emily, "I see you remembered your sack lunch."

_7_ The fourth graders finally loaded onto the bus for the field trip.

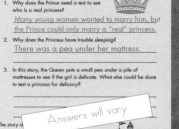

43 — Taking a Trip

Directions: Answer the questions below about the story.

1. Who were the two adult helpers that would be going on the trip with Miss Haynes' class?
   Ms. Diehl and Mrs. Shaloub

2. The students in Miss Haynes' class were excited about the field trip for different reasons. What were the three different reasons mentioned in the story?
   a. They got to ride the bus.
   b. They enjoyed learning about their town's history.
   c. They got a day out of school.

3. What business did Miss Haynes need to take care of before the class could leave on its trip?
   Check attendance and pass out name tags.

Directions: Write the letter of the definition beside the word it defines. If you need help, use a dictionary or check the context of the story.

_c_ ancestors
_d_ fortunately
_a_ plopped
_b_ obviously

a. sat down, not very gently
b. easy to understand; without doubt
c. family members that lived in the past, such as grandparents
d. in a favorable way

44 — The Princess and the Pea

Fairy tales are short stories written for children involving magical characters.

Directions: Read the story. Then, answer the questions.

Once there was a prince who wanted to get married. The catch was, he had to marry a real princess. The Prince knew that real princesses were few and far between. When they heard he was looking for a bride, many young women came to the palace. All claimed to be real princesses.

"Hmmm," thought the Prince. "I must think of a way to sort out the real princesses from the fake ones. I will ask the Queen for advice."

Luckily, since he was a prince, the Queen was also his mother. "A real princess is very delicate," said the Queen. "She must sleep on a mattress as soft as a cloud. If there is even a small lump, she will not be able to sleep."

"Why not?" asked the Prince. He was a nice man but not as smart as his mother.

"Because she is so delicate!" said the Queen impatiently. "Let me figure out a test. You go down and pick a girl to try out my plan."

The Prince went down to the lobby of the castle. A very pretty but humble-looking girl caught his eye. He brought her back to his mother, who welcomed her.

"Please be our guest at the castle tonight," said the Queen.

The girl was shown to her room. In it was a pile of five mattresses, all fluffy and clean. "A princess is delicate," said the Queen. "Sweet dreams!"

The girl climbed to the top of the pile and laid down, but she could not sleep. She tossed and turned and was quite cross the next morning. "I found this under the fourth mattress when I got up this morning," she said. She handed a small green pea to the Queen. "No wonder I couldn't sleep!"

The Queen clapped her hands. The Prince looked confused. "A real princess is delicate. If this pea I put under the mattress kept you awake, you are definitely a princess."

"Of course I am," said the Princess. "Now may I please take a nap?"

1. Why does the Prince worry about finding a bride?
   Real princesses are hard to find.

2. According to the Queen, how can the Prince tell who is a real princess?
   A real princess is very delicate.

3. Who hides something under the girl's mattress? the Queen

45 — The Princess and the Pea

Directions: Review the story "The Princess and the Pea." Then, answer the questions.

1. Why does the Prince need a test to see who is a real princess?
   Many young women wanted to marry him, but the Prince could only marry a "real" princess.

2. Why does the Princess have trouble sleeping?
   There was a pea under her mattress.

3. In this story, the Queen puts a small pea under a pile of mattresses to see if the girl is delicate. What else could be done to test a princess for delicacy?

   Answers will vary

The story ... Prince and ... ...med and live happily ever after, only that the Princess wants to take a nap.

Directions: Write a new ending to the story.

4. What do you think happens after the Princess wakes up?

   Answers will vary

46 — The Frog Prince

Directions: Read the story "The Frog Prince." Then, answer the questions.

Once upon a time, there lived a beautiful princess who liked to play alone in the woods. One day, as she was playing with her golden ball, it rolled into a lake. The water was so deep she could not see the ball. The Princess was very sad. She cried out, "I would give anything to have my golden ball back!"

Suddenly, a large ugly frog popped out of the water. "Anything?" he croaked. The Princess looked at him with distaste. "Yes," she said, "I would give anything."

"I will get your golden ball," said the frog. "In return, you must take me back to the castle. You must let me live with you and eat from your golden plate."

"Whatever you want," said the Princess. She thought the frog was very ugly, but she wanted her golden ball.

The frog dove down and brought the ball to the Princess. She put the frog in her pocket and took him home. "He is ugly," the Princess said. "But a promise is a promise. And a princess always keeps her word."

The Princess changed her clothes and forgot all about the frog. That evening, she heard a tapping at her door. She ran to the door to open it and a handsome prince stepped in.

"Who are you?" asked the Princess, already half in love.

"I am the prince you rescued at the lake," said the handsome Prince. "I was turned into a frog one hundred years ago today by a wicked lady. Because they always keep their promises, only a beautiful princess could break the spell. You are a little forgetful, but you did keep your word!"

Can you guess what happened next? Of course, they were married and lived happily ever after.

1. What does the frog ask the Princess to promise? <u>to take him back to the castle, let him live with her and eat from her golden plate</u>
2. Where does the Princess put the frog when she leaves the lake? <u>in her pocket</u>
3. Why could only a princess break the spell? <u>Because they always keep their promises.</u>

47 — The Frog Prince

Directions: Review the story "The Frog Prince." Then, answer the questions.

1. What does the Princess lose in the lake? <u>a golden ball</u>
2. How does she get it back? <u>A frog dove to the bottom of the lake and got it for her in return for a promise from the Princess.</u>
3. How does the frog turn back into a prince? <u>The spell is broken when the Princess keeps her word.</u>
4. What phrases are used to begin and end this story? <u>"once upon a time" and "happily ever after"</u>
5. Are these words used frequently to begin and end fairy tales? <u>Yes</u>

There is more than one version of most fairy tales. In another version of this story, the Princess has to kiss the frog in order for him to change back into a prince.

Directions: Write your answers.

6. What do you think would happen in a story where the Princess kisses the frog, but he remains a frog?

Answers will vary

7. Rewrite the ending to "The Frog Prince" so that the frog remains a frog and does not turn into a handsome prince. Continue your story on another sheet of paper.

48 — Review

Directions: Think of fairy tales you know from books or videos, like "Cinderella," "Snow White," "Sleeping Beauty," "Rapunzel" and "Beauty and the Beast." Then, answer the questions.

1. What are some common elements in all fairy tales? <u>Answers may include: a hero or heroine, a villian, a problem, a happy ending</u>
2. How do fairy tales usually begin? <u>"Once upon a time"</u>
3. How do fairy tales usually end? <u>with a happy ending</u>

Directions: Locate and read several different versions of the same fairy tale. For example, "Cinderella," "Princess Furball," "Cinderlad" and "Yeh Shen." Then, answer the questions.

4. How are the stories alike? _____
5. How are they different? _____

Answers will vary

6. Which story is best developed by the author? _____
7. Which story did you like best? Why? _____

49 — Review

Most of us have read many fairy tales and have seen them in movies. Fairy tales have a certain style and format they usually follow.

Directions: Use another sheet of paper to write another fairy tale. Use the following questions to help you brainstorm ideas.

1. What is the name of the kingdom? _____
2. What is the size of the kingdom, its climate, trees, plants, animals, etc.? _____
3. What kind of magic happens there? _____
4. Who are the characters?
   Good guys   Bad

Answers will vary

5. What does the character look like? _____
6. What kind of spell is cast on a particular character and why? _____
7. What happens to the good characters and the bad characters in the end? _____

50 — Kanati's Son

A legend is a story or group of stories handed down through generations. Legends are usually about an actual person.

Directions: Read about Kanati's son. Then, number the events in order.

This legend is told by a tribe called the *Cherokee* (chair-oh-key).
Long ago, soon after the world was made, a hunter and his wife lived on a big mountain with their son. The father's name was Kanati (kah-na-tee), which means "lucky hunter." The mother's name was Selu (see-loo), which means "corn." No one remembers the son's name.

The little boy used to play alone by the river each day. One day, elders of the tribe told the boy's parents they had heard two children playing. Since their boy was the only child around, the parents were puzzled. They told their son what the elders had said.

"I do have a playmate," the boy said. "He comes out of the water. He says he is the brother that mother threw in the river."

Then, Selu knew what had happened.

"He is formed from the blood of the animals I washed in the river," she told Kanati. "After you kill them, I wash them in the river before I cook them."

Here is what Kanati told his boy: "Tomorrow when the other boy comes, wrestle with him. Hold him to the ground and call for us."

The boy did as his parents told him. When he called, they came running and grabbed the wild boy. They took him home and tried to tame him. The boy grew up with magic powers. The Cherokee called this "adawehi" (ad-do-we-hi). He was always getting into mischief! But he saved himself with his magic.

<u>5</u> Selu and Kanati try to tame the boy from the river.
<u>3</u> The little boy tells Selu and Kanati about the other boy.
<u>2</u> The little boy's parents are puzzled.
<u>6</u> The new boy grows up with magic powers.
<u>1</u> The elders tell Selu and Kanati they heard two children playing.
<u>4</u> The little boy wrestles his new playmate to the ground.

51 — Why Bear Has a Short Tail

Some stories try to explain the reasons why certain things occur in nature.

Directions: Read the legend "Why Bear Has a Short Tail." Then, answer the questions.

Long ago, Bear had a long tail like Fox. One winter day, Bear met Fox coming out of the woods. Fox was carrying a long string of fish. He had stolen the fish, but that is not what he told Bear.

"Where did you get those fish?" asked Bear, rubbing his paws together. Bear loved fish. It was his favorite food.

"I was out fishing and caught them," replied Fox.

Bear did not know how to fish. He had only tasted fish that others gave him. He was eager to learn to catch his own.

"Please Fox, will you tell me how to fish?" asked Bear.

So, the mean old Fox said to Bear, "Cut a hole in the ice and stick your tail in the hole. It will get cold, but soon the fish will begin to bite. When you can stand it no longer, pull your tail out. It will be covered with fish!"

"Will it hurt?" asked Bear, patting his tail.

"It will hurt some," admitted Fox. "But the longer you leave your tail in the water, the more fish you will catch."

Bear did as Fox told him. He loved fish, so he left his tail in the icy water a very, very long time. The ice froze around Bear's tail. When he pulled free, his tail remained stuck in the ice. That is why bears today have short tails.

1. How does Fox get his string of fish? <u>He stole it.</u>
2. What does he tell Bear to do? <u>to put his tail in a hole in the ice to catch fish</u>
3. Why does Bear do as Fox told him? <u>He loves to eat fish but doesn't know how to catch them.</u>
4. How many fish does Bear catch? <u>none</u>
5. What happens when Bear tries to pull his tail out? <u>His tail remains stuck in the ice.</u>

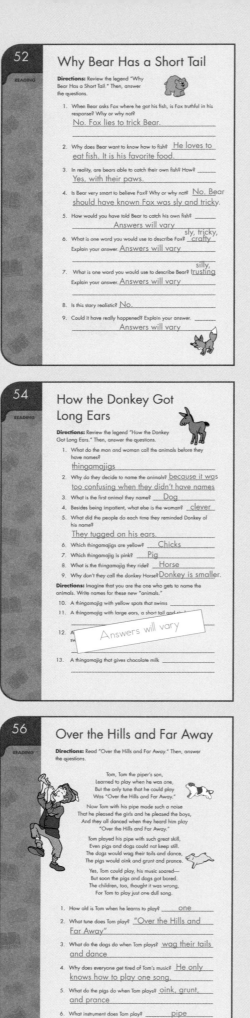

52 — Why Bear Has a Short Tail

Directions: Review the legend "Why Bear Has a Short Tail." Then, answer the questions.

1. When Bear asks Fox where he got his fish, is Fox truthful in his response? Why or why not? **No. Fox lies to trick Bear.**

2. Why does Bear want to know how to fish? **He loves to eat fish. It is his favorite food.**

3. In reality, are bears able to catch their own fish? How? **Yes, with their paws.**

4. Is Bear very smart to believe Fox? Why or why not? **No. Bear should have known Fox was sly and tricky.**

5. How would you have told Bear to catch his own fish? **Answers will vary**

6. What is one word you would use to describe Fox? **sly, tricky, crafty** Explain your answer. **Answers will vary**

7. What is one word you would use to describe Bear? **silly, trusting** Explain your answer. **Answers will vary**

8. Is this story realistic? **No.**

9. Could it have really happened? Explain your answer. **Answers will vary**

53 — How the Donkey Got Long Ears

Directions: Write your predictions to answer these questions.

1. How do you think animals ~~got their~~ **Answers will vary**

2. W~~...~~ ~~...~~ did not have names?

Directions: Read the legend "How the Donkey Got Long Ears." Then, answer the questions.

In the beginning, when the world was young, animals had no names. It was very confusing! A woman would say, "Tell the thingamajig to bring in the paper." The man would say, "What thingamajig?" She was talking about the dog, of course, but the man didn't know that.

Together, they decided to name the animals on their farm. First, they named their pet thingamajig Dog. They named the pink thingamajig that oinked Pig. They named the red thingamajig that crowed Rooster. They named the white thingamajig that laid eggs Hen. They named the little yellow thingamajigs that cheeped Chicks. They named the big brown thingamajig they rode Horse.

Then, they came to another thingamajig. It looked like Horse, but was smaller. It would be confusing to call the smaller thingamajig Horse, they decided. "Let's name it Donkey," said the woman. So they did.

Soon all the animals knew their names. All but Donkey, that is. Donkey kept forgetting.

"What kind of a thingamajig am I again?" he would ask the man.

"You are Donkey!" the man would answer. Each time Donkey forgot, the man tugged on Donkey's ears to help him remember.

Soon, however, Donkey would forget his name again.

"Uh, what's my name?" he would ask the woman.

She would answer, "Donkey! Donkey! Donkey!" and pull his ears each time. She was a clever woman but not very patient.

At first, the man and woman did not notice that Donkey's ears grew longer each time they were pulled. Donkey was patient but not very clever. It took him a long time to learn his name. By the time he remembered his name was Donkey, his ears were much longer than Horse's ears. That is why donkeys have long ears.

3. What words could you use to describe Donkey? **forgetful, patient**

54 — How the Donkey Got Long Ears

Directions: Review the legend "How the Donkey Got Long Ears." Then, answer the questions.

1. What do the man and woman call the animals before they have names? **thingamajigs**

2. Why do they decide to name the animals? **because it was too confusing when they didn't have names**

3. What is the first animal they name? **Dog**

4. Besides being impatient, what else is the woman? **clever**

5. What did the people do each time they reminded Donkey of his name? **They tugged on his ears.**

6. Which thingamajigs are yellow? **Chicks**

7. Which thingamajig is pink? **Pig**

8. What is the thingamajig they ride? **Horse**

9. Why don't they call the donkey Horse? **Donkey is smaller.**

Directions: Imagine that you are the one who gets to name the animals. Write names for these new "animals."

10. A thingamajig with yellow spots that swims _____

11. A thingamajig with large ears, a short tail and ~~...~~

12. A ~~...~~ **Answers will vary** ~~...~~ sw~~...~~

13. A thingamajig that gives chocolate milk _____

55 — Mr. Nobody

Directions: After reading the poem "Mr. Nobody," number in order the things people blame him for.

I know a funny little man
As quiet as a mouse,
Who does the mischief that is done
In everybody's house!
No one ever sees his face.
And yet we all agree
That every plate we break was cracked
By Mr. Nobody.

It's he who always tears out books,
Who leaves the door ajar,
He pulls the buttons from our shirts,
And scatters pins afar;
That squeaking door will always squeak,
The reason is, you see,
We leave the oiling to be done
By Mr. Nobody.

The finger marks upon the wall
By none of us are made;
We never leave the blinds unclosed
To let the carpet fade.
The bowl of soup we do not spill,
It's not our fault, you see
These mishaps—every one is caused
By Mr. Nobody.

7	Putting finger marks on walls	**5**	Scattering pins
3	Leaving the door ajar	**1**	Breaking plates
9	Spilling soup	**4**	Tearing out books
2	Squeaking doors	**6**	Pulling buttons off shirts
8	Leaving the blinds open		

56 — Over the Hills and Far Away

Directions: Read "Over the Hills and Far Away." Then, answer the questions.

Tom, Tom the piper's son,
Learned to play when he was one,
But the only tune that he could play
Was "Over the Hills and Far Away."

Now Tom with his pipe made such a noise
That he pleased the girls and he pleased the boys,
And they all danced when they heard him play
"Over the Hills and Far Away."

Tom played his pipe with such great skill,
Even pigs and dogs could not keep still.
The dogs would wag their tails and dance,
The pigs would oink and grunt and prance.

Yes, Tom could play, his music soared—
But soon the pigs and dogs got bored.
The children, too, thought it was wrong,
For Tom to play just one dull song.

1. How old is Tom when he learns to play? **one**

2. What tune does Tom play? **"Over the Hills and Far Away"**

3. What do the dogs do when Tom plays? **wag their tails and dance**

4. Why does everyone get tired of Tom's music? **He only knows how to play one song.**

5. What do the pigs do when Tom plays? **oink, grunt, and prance**

6. What instrument does Tom play? **pipe**

57 — The Spider and the Fly

Directions: Read the poem "The Spider and the Fly." Then, number the events in order.

"Won't you come into my parlor?" said the spider to the fly.
"It's the nicest little parlor that you will ever spy.
The way into my parlor is up a winding stair,
I have so many pretty things to show you inside there."

The little fly said, "No! No! No! To do so is not sane.
For those who travel up your stair do not come down again."

The spider turned himself around and went back in his den—
He knew for sure the silly fly would visit him again.
The spider wove a tiny web, for he was very sly
He was making preparations to trap the silly fly.

Then, out his door the spider came and merrily did sing,
"Oh, fly, oh lovely, lovely fly with pearl and silver wings."

Alas! How quickly did the fly come buzzing back to hear
The spider's words of flattery, which drew the fly quite near.

The fly was trapped within the web, the spider's winding stair,
Then, the spider jumped upon him, and ate the fly right there!

4	The spider sings a song about how beautiful the fly is.
7	The spider jumps on the fly.
1	The spider invites the fly into his parlor.
3	The spider spins a tiny new web to catch the fly.
6	The fly becomes caught in the spider's web.
2	The fly says he knows it's dangerous to go into the spider's parlor.
8	The spider eats the fly.
5	The fly comes near the web to hear the song.

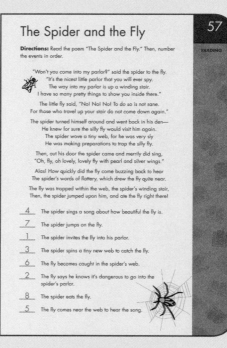

58 The Pueblo People

Directions: Read about the Pueblo people. Then, answer the questions.

Long ago, Native Americans occupied all the land that is now Arizona, New Mexico, Utah and parts of California and Colorado. Twenty-five different tribes lived in this southwestern area. Several of the tribes lived in villages called pueblos. The Hopi (hope-ee) Indians lived in pueblos. So did the Zuñi (zoo-nee) and the Laguna (lah-goon-noh). These and other tribes who lived in villages were called the "Pueblo people."

When it was time for the Pueblo people to plant crops, everyone helped. The men kept the weeds pulled. Native Americans prayed for rain to make their crops grow. As part of their worship, they also had special dances called rain dances. When it was time for harvest, the women helped.

The land was bountiful to the Pueblo people. They grew many different crops. They planted beans, squash and 19 different kinds of corn. They gathered wild nuts and berries. They hunted for deer and rabbits. They also traded with other tribes for things they could not grow or hunt.

The Pueblo people lived in unusual houses. Their homes were made of adobe brick. Adobe is a type of mud. They shaped the mud into bricks, dried them, then built with them. Many adobe homes exist today in the Southwest.

The adobe homes of long ago had no doors. The Pueblo people entered through a type of trapdoor at the top. The homes were three or four stories high. The ground floor had no windows and was used for storage. These adobe homes were clustered around a central plaza. Each village had several clusters of homes. Villages also had two or three clubhouses where people could gather for celebrations. Each village also had special places for worship.

1. What were the five states where the Pueblo people lived?
<u>Arizona, Utah, New Mexico, California, Colorado</u>

2. What were three crops the Pueblo people grew?
<u>beans, squash, corn</u>

3. The early pueblo houses had no
☐ yards.   ☐ windows.   ☒ doors.

59 The Pueblo People

Directions: Read more about the Pueblo people. Then, answer the questions.

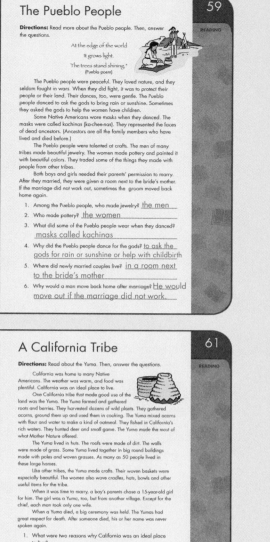

At the edge of the world
It grows light.
The trees stand shining.
(Pueblo poem)

The Pueblo people were peaceful. They loved nature, and they seldom fought in wars. When they did fight, it was to protect their people or their land. Their dances, too, were gentle. The Pueblo people danced to ask the gods to bring rain or sunshine. Sometimes they asked the gods to help the women have children.

Some Native Americans wore masks when they danced. The masks were called kachinas (ka-chee-nas). They represented the faces of dead ancestors. (Ancestors are all the family members who have lived and died before.)

The Pueblo people were talented at crafts. The men of many tribes made beautiful jewelry. The women made pottery and painted it with beautiful colors. They traded some of the things they made with people from other tribes.

Both boys and girls needed their parents' permission to marry. After they married, they were given a room next to the bride's mother. If the marriage did not work out, sometimes the groom moved back home again.

1. Among the Pueblo people, who made jewelry? <u>the men</u>

2. Who made pottery? <u>the women</u>

3. What did some of the Pueblo people wear when they danced?
<u>masks called kachinas</u>

4. Why did the Pueblo people dance for the gods? <u>to ask the gods for rain or sunshine or help with childbirth</u>

5. Where did newly married couples live? <u>in a room next to the bride's mother</u>

6. Why would a man move back home after marriage? <u>He would move out if the marriage did not work.</u>

60 The Pueblo People

Directions: Review what you learned about the Pueblo people. Then, answer the questions.

1. How many different tribes lived in the Southwestern part of the United States? <u>25</u>

2. The article specifically names three of the Pueblo tribes. Where could you find the names of the other Pueblo tribes?
<u>reference sources like encyclopedias or the Internet</u>

3. How did the Pueblo people build their adobe homes? <u>They shaped mud into bricks, dried them, then built with them.</u>

4. How did the location and climate affect their lifestyle? <u>Location and climate affected what they wore, what crops they grew, the animals they hunted and materials used for building homes.</u>

5. How were the jobs of the men and women of a Pueblo tribe alike? <u>Both helped care for crops.</u>

6. How were their jobs different? <u>Men made jewelry, women made pottery.</u>

7. How do the responsibilities of the Pueblo men and women discussed differ from those of men and women today?
<u>Answers will vary</u>

61 A California Tribe

Directions: Read about the Yuma. Then, answer the questions.

California was home to many Native Americans. The weather was warm, and food was plentiful. California was an ideal place to live.

One California tribe that made good use of the land was the Yuma. The Yuma farmed and gathered roots and berries. They harvested dozens of wild plants. They gathered acorns, ground them up and used them in cooking. The Yuma mixed acorns with flour and water to make a kind of oatmeal. They fished in California's rich waters. They hunted deer and small game. The Yuma made the most of what Mother Nature offered.

The Yuma lived in huts. The roofs were made of dirt. The walls were made of grass. Some Yuma lived together in big round buildings made with poles and woven grasses. As many as 50 people lived in these large homes.

Like other tribes, the Yuma made crafts. Their woven baskets were especially beautiful. The women also wove cradles, hats, bowls and other useful items for the tribe.

When it was time to marry, a boy's parents chose a 15-year-old girl for him. The girl was a Yuma, too, but from another village. Except for the chief, each man took only one wife.

When a Yuma died, a big ceremony was held. The Yumas had great respect for death. After someone died, his or her name was never spoken again.

1. What were two reasons why California was an ideal place to live?
<u>The weather was warm and food was plentiful.</u>

2. What did the Yuma use acorns for? <u>They ground them up and used them for cooking.</u>

3. What was a beautiful craft made by the Yuma? <u>woven baskets</u>

4. How old was a Yuma bride? <u>15</u>

5. What types of homes did the Yuma live in? <u>dirts and grass huts</u>

6. How did the Yuma feel about death? <u>They had great respect for death.</u>

62 A California Tribe

Directions: Review what you read about the Yuma. Write the answers.

1. How did the Yuma make good use of the land? <u>They farmed and gathered roots, acorns and berries. They fished and hunted.</u>

2. How were the Yuma like the Pueblo people? <u>Both hunted deer and small game, farmed, gathered berries and made crafts.</u>

3. How were they different? <u>The Yuma fished, made baskets and lived in huts. The Pueblos made pottery and jewelry and lived in adobe homes.</u>

4. Why did the Yuma have homes different than those of the Pueblo tribes?
<u>Answers should indicate differences in natural materials available due to different climates.</u>

5. When it was time for a young Yuma man to marry, his parents selected a fifteen-year-old bride for him from another tribe. Do you think this is a good idea? Why or why not?

6. Why do you suppose the Yuma _____ after he/she died? <u>Answers will vary</u>

7. Do you think this would be an easy thing to do? Explain your answer.

63 Setting Sail

Directions: Read about the Sailor Native Americans of Puget Sound. Then, work the puzzle.

Three tribes lived on Puget (pew-jit) Sound in Washington state. They made their living from the sea. People later called them the "Sailor" Indians.

These Native Americans fished for salmon. They trapped the salmon in large baskets. Sometimes they used large nets. The sea was filled with fish. Their nets rarely came up empty.

The Sailor Native Americans also gathered roots and berries. They hunted deer, black bear and ducks.

Their homes were amazing! They built big wooden buildings without nails. They did not use saws to cut the wood. The walls and roofs were tied together. Each building had different homes inside. As many as 50 families lived in each big building.

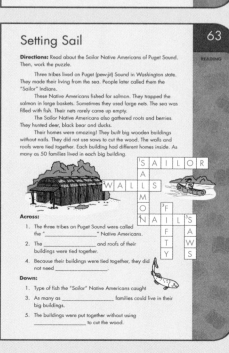

Crossword puzzle:
- S A I L O R
- W A L L S
- S A L M O N
- F
- N A I L S
- F I F T Y
- S A W S

Across:

1. The three tribes on Puget Sound were called the "_____" Native Americans.

2. The _____ and roofs of their buildings were tied together.

4. Because their buildings were tied together, they did not need _____.

Down:

1. Type of fish the "Sailor" Native Americans caught

3. As many as _____ families could live in their big buildings.

5. The buildings were put together without using _____ to cut the wood.

64 Setting Sail

Directions: Review what you read about the Sailor Native Americans. Write your answers.

1. How were the housing arrangements of the Puget Sound Native Americans similar to those of the Yuma?
   Many families lived together in large buildings.

2. How was the diet of the Sailor Native Americans like those of the Yuma and Pueblo?
   All three hunted and gathered berries.

3. How was it different? Yumas and Pueblos grew their own crops.

4. The Sailor Native Americans made a living from the sea, and their nets were rarely empty. What type of transportation do you think these Native Americans used to get their nets to the sea?
   canoes, boats or rafts

5. Where could you find more information on this group of Native Americans to check your answer? reference sources like encyclopedias and the Internet

6. Verify your answer. Were you correct? Answers will vary

7. Who do you think performed the many tasks in the Sailor village? Write men, women, boys and/or girls for your answers.

   Built homes? _____

   Made fishing baskets? _____

   Fished? _____

   Ga[t] _____

   Hunt _____

   Made fishing nets? _____

Answers will vary

65 Review

Review what you read about Native Americans. Then, answer the questions.

1. Of the tribes discussed, which one would you most like to have been a member of? Explain your answer.
   Answers will vary

2. Why did each of the tribes have a different lifestyle?
   because of their location, different climates and resources were available

3. How did their location influence how each of the tribes functioned?
   Food, plants, animals, fish, climate and building materials all influenced the people and how they lived.

Directions: Select two of the Native American tribes you read about. Compare and contrast their homes, clothing and lifestyle in the Venn diagram. Write words and phrases that were unique to one group or the other in the correct parts of the circle. Write words and phrases that are common to both groups in the section where the circles intersect.

Answers will vary

66 Wild and Free

Directions: Read about wild horses. Then, answer the questions.

Have you ever heard of a car called a Mustang? It is named after a type of wild horse.

In the 1600s, the Spanish explorers who came to North America brought horses with them. Some of these horses escaped onto the prairies and plains. With no one to feed them or ride them, they became wild. Their numbers quickly grew, and they roamed in herds. They ran free and ate grass on the prairie.

Later, when the West was settled, people needed horses. They captured wild ones. This was not easy to do. Wild horses could run very fast. They did not want to be captured!

Some men made their living by capturing wild horses, taming them and selling them. These men were called mustangers. Can you guess why?

After cars were invented, people did not need as many horses. Not as many mustangers were needed to catch them. More and more wild horses roamed the western prairies. In 1925, about a million mustangs were running loose.

The government was worried that the herds would eat too much grass. Ranchers who owned big herds of cattle complained that their animals didn't have enough to eat because the mustangs ate all the grass. Permission was given to ranchers and others to kill many of the horses. Thousands were killed and sold to companies that made them into pet food.

Now, wild horses live in only 12 states. The largest herds are in California, New Mexico, Oregon, Wyoming, and Nevada. Most people who live in these states never see wild horses. The herds live away from people in the distant plains and mountains. They are safer there.

1. What is one type of wild horse called? a mustang

2. What were men called who captured wild horses? mustangers

3. About how many wild horses were running free in the U.S. in 1925? one million

4. The wild mustangs were killed and turned into
   ☐ cars. ☒ pet food. ☐ lunch meat.

5. The largest herds of wild horses are now in
   ☒ Oregon. ☐ Ohio. ☒ New Mexico. ☒ Wyoming.
   ☒ California. ☒ Nevada. ☐ Kansas. ☐ Arkansas.

67 Wild and Free

Directions: Read more about wild horses. Then, answer the questions.

Have you noticed that in any large group, one person seems to be the leader? This is true for wild horses, too. The leader of a band of wild horses is a stallion. Stallions are adult male horses.

The stallion's job is important. He watches out for danger. If a bear or other animal comes close, he lets out a warning cry. This helps keep the other horses safe. Sometimes they all run away together. Other times, the stallion protects the other horses. He shows his teeth. He rears up on his back legs. Often, he scares the other animal away. Then, the horses can safely continue eating grass.

Much of the grass on the prairies is gone now. Wild horses must move around a lot to find new grass. They spend about half their time eating and looking for food. If they cannot find prairie grass, wild horses will eat tree bark. They will eat flowers. If they can't find these either, wild horses will eat anything that grows!

Wild horses also need plenty of water. It is often hot in the places where they roam. At least twice a day, they find streams and take long, long drinks. Like people, wild horses lose water when they sweat. They run and sweat a lot in hot weather. To survive, they need as much water as they can get.

Wild horses also use water another way. When they find deep water, they wade into it. It feels good! It cools their skin.

1. What is the main idea? (Check one.)
   _____ Wild horses need plenty of water.
   __X__ Wild horses move in bands protected by a stallion.
   _____ Wild horses eat grass.

2. What are two reasons why wild horses need water? to drink and to cool their skin

3. Why do wild horses move around so much? to find new grass

4. What do wild horses most like to eat? prairie grass

5. What do wild horses spend half their time doing?
   eating and looking for food

68 Wild and Free

Directions: Review what you read about wild horses. Then, answer the questions.

1. How did horses come to North America and become wild?
   Spanish explorers brought them. Some escaped and became wild.

2. Why is it so difficult to capture, tame and train wild horses?
   Wild horses can run very fast and do not want to be captured.

3. Do you think it was right of the government to allow the killing of wild horses? _____
   Explain your answer.
   Answers will vary

4. Do [you think wild] horses should be protected?
   Explain your answer. _____

5. What is the role of the lead stallion in a wild horse herd?
   to watch out for danger and protect the herd

6. What are some things wild horses have in common with giraffes?
   _____

7. What do you think will happen [to] lands [as] [more people build] homes? Answers will vary

69 Space Pioneer

Neil Armstrong is one of the great pioneers of space. On July 20, 1969, Armstrong was commander of Apollo 11, the first manned American spacecraft to land on the Moon. He was the first person to walk on the Moon.

Armstrong was born in Ohio in 1930. He took his first airplane ride when he was 6 years old. As he grew older, he did jobs to earn money to learn to fly. On his 16th birthday, he received his student pilot's license.

Armstrong served as a Navy fighter pilot during the Korean War. He received three medals. Later, he was a test pilot. He was known as one of the best pilots in the world. He was also an engineer. He contributed much to the development of new methods of flying. In 1962, he was accepted into an astronaut training program.

Armstrong had much experience when he was named to command the historic flight to the Moon. It took four days to fly to the Moon. As he climbed down the ladder to be the first person to step onto the Moon, he said these now famous words: "That's one small step for (a) man, one giant leap for mankind."

Directions: Answer these questions about Neil Armstrong.

1. What did Neil Armstrong do before any other person in the world?
   He walked on the moon.

2. How old was Neil Armstrong when he got his student pilot's license?
   16 years old

3. What did Armstrong do during the Korean War?
   served as a Navy fighter pilot

4. On what date did a person first walk on the Moon?
   July 20, 1969

70 — A Ride in Space

Directions: Read about Sally Ride. Then, answer the questions.

Sally Ride was the first American woman in space. She was only 31 years old when she went into space in 1982. Besides being the first American woman, she was also the youngest person ever to go into space!

Many people wanted to be astronauts. When Sally Ride was chosen, there were 8,000 people who wanted to be in the class. Only 35 were selected. Six of those people were women.

Sally Ride rode in the spaceship *Challenger*. She was called a *Mission Specialist*. Like any astronaut, Sally Ride had to study for several years before she went into space. She spent 6 days on her journey. She has even written a book for children about her adventure! It is called *To Space and Back*.

1. What was significant about Sally Ride's journey into space?
   <u>She was the first American woman and the youngest person in space.</u>
2. How old was Sally ride when she went into space? <u>31</u>
3. What was the name of her spaceship? <u>Challenger</u>
4. What was her title on the trip into space? <u>mission specialist</u>
5. How long did Sally Ride's journey last? <u>6 days</u>
6. What was the name of the book she wrote?
   <u>To Space and Back</u>
7. Why do you think many people want to be astronauts?
   <u>Answers will vary</u>

71 — Floating Free

Directions: Read about life in space. Then, answer the questions.

Life in space is very different from life on Earth. There is no gravity in space. Gravity is what holds us to the ground. In space, everything floats around.

Astronauts wear suction cups on their shoes to hold them to the floor of their spaceships. At night, they do not crawl into bed like you do. Instead, they climb into sleeping bags that hang on the wall and then they zip themselves in.

If an astronaut is thirsty, he or she cannot simply pour a glass of water. The water would form little balls that would float around the spaceship! Instead, water has to be squirted into the astronauts' mouths from bottles or containers.

When astronauts are in space, they do a lot of floating around outside their spaceship. Astronauts always have special jobs to do in space. One astronaut is the pilot of the spaceship. The other astronauts do experiments, make repairs and gather information about their trip.

1. What is the main idea?
   <u>X</u> Life in space is much different than it is on Earth.
   _____ Without gravity, people on Earth would float around.
   _____ Gravity makes life on Earth much different than life in space.
2. What does gravity do? <u>Gravity holds us to the ground.</u>
3. How do astronauts sleep? <u>They climb into sleeping bags that hang on the wall and zip themselves in.</u>
4. What do astronauts do in space? <u>One astronaut is the pilot. Others do experiments, make repairs and gather information.</u>
5. How do astronauts drink water? <u>squirt it into their mouths</u>
6. Would you like to be an astronaut? Why or why not? <u>Answers will vary</u>

72 — Review

Directions: Read about early ideas for space travel. Then, answer the questions.

People have dreamed about going into space for thousands of years. There are legends that tell about inventors who wanted to get birds to fly to the Moon. In 1864, a French author named Jules Verne wrote a book called *From the Earth to the Moon*. In the book, he wrote about men being shot into space from a huge cannon.

Jules Verne made up that story. Other writers also made up stories about going to the Moon. During the 1920s, several scientists wrote about sending rockets into space. They decided that liquid fuel was needed. Since then, space exploration has come a long way!

A Russian named Yuri A. Gagarin was the first person in space. An American, Alan B. Shepard, Jr., went into space next. Both men did experiments that later helped other astronauts in their trips to outer space!

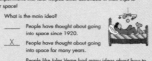

1. What is the main idea?
   _____ People have thought about going into space since 1920.
   <u>X</u> People have thought about going into space for many years.
   _____ People like Jules Verne had many ideas about how to get to the Moon.
2. Who wrote a book called *From the Earth to the Moon*?
   <u>Jules Verne</u>
3. What did he write about?
   <u>men being shot into space from a huge cannon</u>
4. When was that book written? <u>1864</u>
5. In what country did Jules Verne live? <u>France</u>
6. What did scientists in the 1920s think we needed to go to space?
   <u>liquid fuel</u>
7. How did Yuri Gagarin and Alan Shepard help future astronauts?
   <u>They did experiments.</u>

74 — Ask It, State It

A **statement** tells some kind of information. It is followed by a period (.).
Examples: It is a rainy day. We are going to the beach next summer.

A **question** asks for a specific piece of information. It is followed by a question mark (?).
Examples: What is the weather like today? When are you going to the beach?

Directions: Write whether each sentence is a statement or question. The first one has been done for you.

1. Jamie went for a walk at the zoo. <u>statement</u>
2. The leaves turn bright colors in the fall. <u>statement</u>
3. When does the Easter Bunny arrive? <u>question</u>
4. Madeleine went to the new art school. <u>statement</u>
5. Is school over at 3:30? <u>question</u>
6. Grandma and Grandpa are moving. <u>statement</u>
7. Anthony went home. <u>statement</u>
8. Did Malia go to Amy's house? <u>question</u>
9. Who went to work late? <u>question</u>
10. Ms. Gomez is a good teacher. <u>statement</u>

Directions: Write two statements and two questions below.
Statements:

Questions:

<u>Answers will vary</u>

75 — Taking Command

A **command** tells someone to do something. It is followed by a period (.).
Examples: Get your math book. Do your homework.

An **exclamation** shows strong feeling or excitement. It is followed by an exclamation mark (!).
Examples: Watch out for that car! Oh, no! There's a snake!

Directions: Write whether each sentence is a command or exclamation. The first one has been done for you.

1. Please clean your room. <u>command</u>
2. Wow! Those fireworks are beautiful! <u>exclamation</u>
3. Come to dinner now. <u>command</u>
4. Color the sky and water blue. <u>command</u>
5. Trim the paper carefully. <u>command</u>
6. Hurry, here comes the bus! <u>exclamation</u>
7. Isn't that a lovely picture! <u>exclamation</u>
8. Time to stop playing and clean up. <u>command</u>
9. Brush your teeth before bedtime. <u>command</u>
10. Wash your hands before you eat! <u>exclamation</u>

Directions: Write two commands and two exclamations below.
Commands:

Exclamations:

<u>Answers will vary</u>

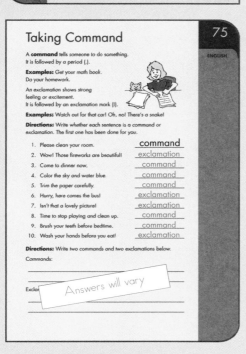

76 — Subject Matters

The **subject** of a sentence tells you who or what the sentence is about. A subject is either a common noun, a proper noun or a pronoun.

Examples: Li went to the store.
Li is the subject of the sentence.

The tired boys and girls walked home slowly.
The tired boys and girls is the subject of the sentence.

Directions: Underline the subject of each sentence. The first one has been done for you.

1. <u>The birthday cake</u> was pink and white.
2. <u>Anthony</u> celebrated his fourth birthday.
3. <u>The tower of building blocks</u> fell over.
4. On Saturday, <u>our family</u> will go to a movie.
5. <u>The busy editor</u> was writing sentences.
6. <u>Seven children</u> painted pictures.
7. <u>Two happy dolphins</u> played cheerfully on the surf.
8. <u>A sand crab</u> buried itself in the dunes.

Directions: Write a subject for each sentence.

1. <u>Chocolate-chip ice cream</u> was melting in the heat.
2. _____ ran down the hill.
3. _____
4. _____
5. _____ made her a beautiful dress.
6. _____ hopped, skipped and jumped all the way home.

<u>Answers will vary</u>

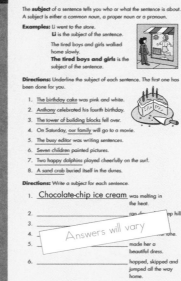

Find the Action

The **predicate** of a sentence tells what the subject is doing. The predicate contains the action, linking and/or helping verb.

Examples: Li went to the store.
Went to the store is the predicate.

The tired boys and girls walked home slowly. **Walked home slowly** is the predicate.

Hint: When identifying the predicate, look for the verb. The verb is usually the first word of the predicate.

Directions: Underline the predicate in each sentence with two lines. The first one has been done for you.

1. The choir sang joyfully.
2. Their song had both high and low notes.
3. Sal played the piano while they sang.
4. This Sunday the orchestra will have a concert in the park.
5. John is working hard on his homework.
6. He will write a report on electricity.
7. The report will tell about Ben Franklin's kite experiment.
8. Elena, Lily, and Amy played on the swings.

Directions: Write a predicate for each sentence.

1. Sam and Libby
2. At school, the children
3. The
4. Seven silly serpents

Answers will vary

Sentence Superstars

The **subject** tells who or what the sentence is about. The **predicate** tells what the subject does, did, is doing, or will do. A complete sentence must have a subject and a predicate.

Examples:

Subject	Predicate
Sharon	writes to her grandmother every week.
The horse	ran around the track quickly.
My mom's car	is bright green.
Bella	will be here after lunch.

Directions: Circle the subject of each sentence. Underline the predicate.

1. My sister is a very happy person.
2. I wish we had more holidays in the year.
3. Laura is one of the nicest girls in our class.
4. Samir is fun to have as a friend.
5. The rain nearly ruined our picnic!
6. My birthday present was exactly what I wanted.
7. Your bicycle is parked beside my skateboard.
8. The printer will need to be filled with paper before you use it.
9. Six dogs chased my cat home yesterday!

Sentence Starters

Directions: Write subjects to complete the following sentences.

1. _____ went to school last Wednesday.
2. _____ did not understand the joke.
3. _____ barked so loudly that no one could sleep a wink.
4. _____
5. _____ wonder what happened at the end of the book.
6. _____ jumped for joy when she won the contest.

Answers will vary

Directions: Write predicates to complete the following sentences.

7. Everyone
8. Dogs
9. I
10. J
11. Jokes
12. Twelve people

Answers will vary

Double Duty

A **compound subject** is a subject with two parts joined by the word **and** or another conjunction. Compound subjects share the same predicate.

Example:

Her shoes were covered with mud. Her ankles were covered with mud, too.

Compound subject:
Her shoes and ankles were covered with mud.

The predicate in both sentences is **were covered with mud.**

Directions: Combine each pair of sentences into one sentence with a compound subject.

1. Bill sneezed. Kassie sneezed.
   Bill and Kassie sneezed.
2. Carmen made cookies. Joey made cookies.
   Carmen and Joey made cookies.
3. Fruit flies are insects. Ladybugs are insects.
   Fruit flies and ladybugs are insects.
4. The girls are planning a dance. The boys are planning a dance.
   The girls and boys are planning a dance.
5. Our dog ran after the ducks. Our cat ran after the ducks.
   Our dog and cat ran after the ducks.
6. Joshua got lost in the parking lot. DeShaun got lost in the parking lot.
   Joshua and DeShaun got lost in the parking lot.

It's Fine to Combine

A **compound predicate** is a predicate with two parts joined by the word **and** or another conjunction. Compound predicates share the same subject.

Example:

The baby grabbed the ball. The baby threw the ball.

Compound predicate:
The baby grabbed the ball and threw it.

The subject in both sentences is **the baby.**

Directions: Combine each pair of sentences into one sentence to make a compound predicate.

1. Leah jumped on her bike. Leah rode around the block.
   Leah jumped on her bike and rode around the block.
2. Father rolled out the pie crust. Father put the pie crust in the pan.
   Father rolled out the pie crust and put it in the pan.
3. Colin slipped on the snow. Colin nearly fell down.
   Colin slipped on the snow and nearly fell down.
4. My friend lives in a green house. My friend rides a red bicycle.
   My friend lives in a green house and rides a red bicycle.
5. I opened the magazine. I began to read it quietly.
   Father rolled out the pie crust and put it in the pan.
6. My father bought a new plaid shirt. My father wore his new red tie.
   My father bought a new plaid shirt and wore his new red tie.

Review

Directions: Circle the subjects.

1. Everyone felt the day had been a great success.
2. No one really understood why he was crying.
3. Mr. Winston, Ms. Fuller, and Ms. Rosenberg took us on a field trip.

Directions: Underline the predicates.

4. Who can tell what will happen tomorrow?
5. Mark was a carpenter by trade and a talented painter, too.
6. The animals yelped and whined in their cages.

Directions: Combine the sentences to make one sentence with a compound subject.

9. Elizabeth ate everything in sight. George ate everything in sight.
   Elizabeth and George ate everything in sight.
10. Wishing something will happen won't make it so. Dreaming something will happen won't make it so.
    Wishing and dreaming something will happen won't make it so.

Directions: Combine the sentences to make one sentence with a compound predicate.

11. I jumped for joy. I hugged all my friends.
    I jumped for joy and hugged all of my friends.
12. She ran around the track before the race. She warmed up before the race.
    She ran around the track and warmed up before the race.

Nouns All Around

83 ENGLISH

Common nouns name general people, places and things.

Examples: boy, girl, cat, dog, park, city, building

Proper nouns name specific persons, places and things.

Examples: Owen, Mary, Fluffy, Rover, Central Park, Chicago, Empire State Building

Proper nouns begin with capital letters.

Directions: Read the following nouns. On the blanks, indicate whether the nouns are common or proper. The first two have been done for you.

1. New York City — proper
2. house — common
3. car — common
4. Ohio — proper
5. river — common
6. Rocky Mountains — proper
7. Dr. DiCarlo — proper
8. man — common
9. Rock River — proper
10. building — common
11. lawyer — common
12. Grand Canyon — proper

On another sheet of paper, write proper nouns for the above common nouns. *Answers will vary*

Directions: Read the following sentences. Underline the common nouns. Circle the proper nouns.

1. (Addy's) birthday is (Friday,) (October) 7.
2. She likes having her birthday in a fall month.
3. Her friends will meet her at the (Video Arcade) for a party.
4. (Ms. McCarthy) and (Mr. Landry) will help with the birthday party games.
5. (Addy's) friends will play video games all afternoon.

A Capital Idea

84 ENGLISH

Proper nouns always begin with a capital letter.

Examples:

Monday
Texas
Karen
Mr. Antonelli
Hamburger Avenue
Rover

MICHIGAN HAMBURGER AVE.

Directions: Cross out the lower-case letters at the beginning of the proper nouns. Write capital letters above them. The first one has been done for you.

1. My teddy bear's name is ~~c~~ocoa. **C**
2. ~~m~~rs. ~~b~~ernhard does an excellent job at ~~c~~restview ~~e~~lementary ~~s~~chool. **M B   C E S**
3. ~~a~~nh, ~~e~~lizabeth, and ~~m~~egan live on ~~m~~ain ~~s~~treet. **A E   M   M S**
4. I am sure our teacher said the book report is due on ~~m~~onday. **M**
5. I believe you can find ~~l~~ake ~~s~~treet if you turn left at the next light. **L S**
6. Will your family be able join our family for dinner at ~~b~~urger ~~b~~arn? **B B**
7. The weather forecasters think the storm will hit the coast of ~~l~~ouisiana ~~f~~riday afternoon. **L F**
8. My family went to ~~w~~ashington, ~~dc~~ this summer. **W   DC**

Plural Power

85 ENGLISH

Nouns come in two forms: singular and plural. When a noun is **singular**, it means there is only one person, place, or thing.

Examples: car, swing, box, truck, slide, bus

When a noun is **plural**, it means there is more than one person, place, or thing.

Examples: two cars, four trucks, three swings, five slides, six boxes, three buses

Usually an **s** is added to most nouns to make them plural. However, if the noun ends in **s, x, ch** or **sh**, then **es** is added to make it plural.

Directions: Write the singular or plural form of each word.

	Singular	Plural		Singular	Plural
1.	car	cars	7.	trick	tricks
2.	bush	bushes	8.	mess	messes
3.	wish	wishes	9.	box	boxes
4.	fox	foxes	10.	dish	dishes
5.	rule	rules	11.	boat	boats
6.	stitch	stitches	12.	path	paths

Directions: Rewrite the following sentences and change the bold nouns from singular to plural or from plural to singular. The first one has been done for you.

1. She took a **book** to school.
   She took books to school.
2. Tommy made **wishes** at his birthday party.
   Tommy made a wish at his birthday party.
3. The **fox** ran away from the **hunters**.
   The foxes ran away from the hunters.
4. The **houses** were painted white.
   The house was painted white.

Plural Power

86 ENGLISH

When a word ends with a consonant before **y**, to make it plural, drop the **y** and add **ies**.

Examples:

party	parties
cherry	cherries
daisy	daisies

However, if the word ends with a vowel before **y**, just add **s**.

Examples:

boy	boys
toy	toys
monkey	monkeys

Directions: Write the singular or plural form of each word.

	Singular	Plural		Singular	Plural
1.	fly	flies	7.	decoy	decoys
2.	boy	boys	8.	candy	candies
3.	joy	joys	9.	toy	toys
4.	spy	spies	10.	cry	cries
5.	key	keys	11.	monkey	monkeys
6.	dry	dries	12.	daisy	daisies

Directions: Write six sentences of your own using any of the plurals above.

Sentences will vary

Breaking the Rules

87 ENGLISH

Some words in the English language do not follow any of the plural rules discussed earlier. These words may not change at all from singular to plural, or they may completely change spellings.

No Change		Complete Change	
Examples:		**Examples:**	
Singular	**Plural**	**Singular**	**Plural**
deer	deer	goose	geese
pants	pants	ox	oxen
scissors	scissors	man	men
moose	moose	child	children
sheep	sheep	leaf	leaves

Directions: Write the singular or plural form of each word. Use a dictionary to help if necessary.

	Singular	Plural		Singular	Plural
1.	moose	moose	6.	leaf	leaves
2.	woman	women	7.	sheep	sheep
3.	deer	deer	8.	scissors	scissors
4.	child	children	9.	tooth	teeth
5.	hoof	hooves	10.	wharf	wharves or wharfs

Directions: Write four sentences of your own using two singular and two plural words from above.

Sentences will vary

Pronoun Lowdown

88 ENGLISH

A **pronoun** is a word that takes the place of a noun in a sentence.

Examples:

I, my, mine, me
we, our, ours, us
you, your, yours
he, his, him
she, her, hers
it, its
they, their, theirs, them

I, ME, YOU. WE! HIM, HER, THEM.

Directions: Underline the pronouns in each sentence.

1. Bring <u>them</u> to <u>us</u> as soon as <u>you</u> are finished.
2. <u>She</u> has been <u>my</u> best friend for many years.
3. <u>They</u> should be here soon.
4. <u>We</u> enjoyed <u>our</u> trip to the Mustard Museum.
5. Would <u>you</u> be able to help <u>us</u> with the project on Saturday?
6. <u>Our</u> homeroom teacher will not be here tomorrow.
7. <u>My</u> uncle said that <u>he</u> will be leaving soon for Australia.
8. Harry! Could <u>you</u> please open the door for <u>him</u>?

Verb Alert

Verbs are the action words in a sentence. There are three kinds of verbs: action verbs, linking verbs, and helping verbs.

An **action verb** tells the action of a sentence.

Examples: run, hop, skip, sleep, jump, talk, snore

Michael **ran** to the store. **Ran** is the action verb.

A **linking verb** joins the subject and predicate of a sentence.

Examples: am, is, are, was, were

Michael **was** at the store. **Was** is the linking verb.

A **helping verb** is used with an action verb to "help" the action of the sentence.

Examples: am, is, are, was, were

Matthew **was** helping Michael. **Was** helps the action verb **helping**.

Directions: Read the following sentences. Underline the verbs. Above each, write **A** for action verb, **L** for linking verb and **H** for helping verb. The first one has been done for you.

1. Amy jumps rope. — A
2. Kahlil was jumping rope, too. — H A
3. They were working on their homework. — H A
4. The math problem requires a lot of thinking. — A
5. Addition problems are fun to do. — L
6. The baby sleeps in the afternoon. — A
7. Grandma is napping also. — H A
8. Sam is going to bed. — H A
9. Jackson paints a lovely picture of the sea. — A
10. The colors in the picture are soft and pale. — L

Tense Tips

Not only do verbs tell the action of a sentence but they also tell when the action takes place. This is called the **verb tense**. There are three verb tenses: past, present and future tense.

Present-tense verbs tell what is happening now.

Example: Jane **spells** words with long vowel sounds.

Past-tense verbs tell about action that has already happened. Past-tense verbs are usually formed by adding **ed** to the verb.

Example: stay — stayed
Vidas **stayed** home yesterday.

Past-tense verbs can also be made by adding helping verbs **was** or **were** before the verb and adding **ing** to the verb.

Example: talk — was talking
Sally **was talking** to her mom.

Future-tense verbs tell what will happen in the future. Future-tense verbs are made by putting the word **will** before the verb.

Example: paint — will paint
Amelia and Ana-Maria **will paint** the house.

Directions: Read the following verbs. Write whether the verb tense is past, present or future.

	Verb	Tense		Verb	Tense
1.	watches	present	8.	writes	present
2.	wanted	past	9.	vaulted	past
3.	will eat	future	10.	were sleeping	past
4.	was squawking	past	11.	will sing	future
5.	yawns	present	12.	is speaking	present
6.	crawled	past	13.	will cook	future
7.	will hunt	future	14.	likes	present

Writing with "ing"

Remember, use **is** and **are** when describing something happening right now. Use **was** and **were** when describing something that already happened.

Directions: Use the verb in bold to complete each sentence. Add **ing** to the verb and use **is, are, was,** or **were**.

Examples:

When it started to rain,
we **were raking** the leaves. — rake

When the soldiers marched up that hill,
Captain Stevens **was commanding** them. — command

1. Now, the police **are accusing** them of stealing the money. — accuse
2. Look! The eggs **are hatching**. — hatch
3. A minute ago, the sky **was glowing**. — glow
4. My dad says he **is treating** us to ice cream! — treat
5. She **was sneezing** the whole time we were at the mall. — sneeze
6. While we were playing outside at recess, he **was grading** our tests. — grade

Put It in the Past

To make many verbs past tense, add **ed**.

Examples:

cook + ed = cooked   wish + ed = wished   play + ed = played

When a verb ends in a **silent e**, drop the **e** and add **ed**.

Examples:

hope + ed = hoped   hate + ed = hated

When a verb ends in **y** after a consonant, change the **y** to **i** and add **ed**.

Examples:

hurry + ed = hurried   marry + ed = married

When a verb ends in a single consonant after a single short vowel, double the final consonant before adding **ed**.

Examples:

stop + ed = stopped   hop + ed = hopped

Directions: Write the past tense of the verb correctly. The first one has been done for you.

1.	call	called	9.	reply	replied
2.	copy	copied	10.	top	topped
3.	frown	frowned	11.	clean	cleaned
4.	smile	smiled	12.	scream	screamed
5.	live	lived	13.	clap	clapped
6.	talk	talked	14.	mop	mopped
7.	name	named	15.	soap	soaped
8.	list	listed	16.	choke	choked

That's History!

Irregular verbs change completely in the past tense. Unlike regular verbs, past-tense forms of irregular verbs are not formed by adding **ed**.

Example: The past tense of **go** is **went**.

Other verbs change some letters to form the past tense.

Example: The past tense of **break** is **broke**.

A **helping verb** helps to tell about the past. **Has, have** and **had** are helping verbs used with action verbs to show the action occurred in the past. The past-tense form of the irregular verb sometimes changes when a helping verb is added.

Present Tense Irregular Verb	Past Tense Irregular Verb	Past Tense Irregular Verb With Helper
go	went	have/has/had gone
see	saw	have/has/had seen
do	did	have/has/had done
bring	brought	have/has/had brought
sing	sang	have/has/had sung
drive	drove	have/has/had driven
swim	swam	have/has/had swum
sleep	slept	have/has/had slept

Directions: Choose four words from the chart. Write one sentence using the past-tense form of the verb without a helping verb. Write another sentence using the past-tense form with a helping verb.

1. _____
2. _____
3. _____   Sentences will vary
4. _____

It's Meant to Be!

Be is an irregular verb. The present-tense forms of **be** are **be, am, is** and **are**. The past-tense forms of **be** are **was** and **were**.

Directions: Write the correct form of **be** in the blanks. The first one has been done for you.

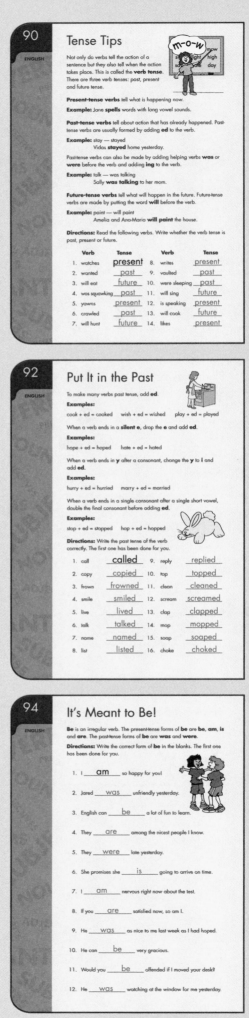

1. I **am** so happy for you!
2. Jared **was** unfriendly yesterday.
3. English can **be** a lot of fun to learn.
4. They **are** among the nicest people I know.
5. They **were** late yesterday.
6. She promises she **is** going to arrive on time.
7. I **am** nervous right now about the test.
8. If you **are** satisfied now, so am I.
9. He **was** as nice to me last week as I had hoped.
10. He can **be** very gracious.
11. Would you **be** offended if I moved your desk?
12. He **was** watching at the window for me yesterday.

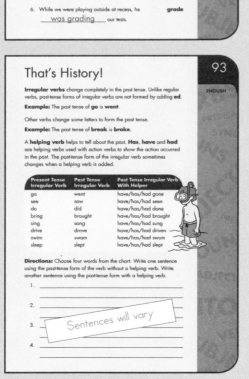

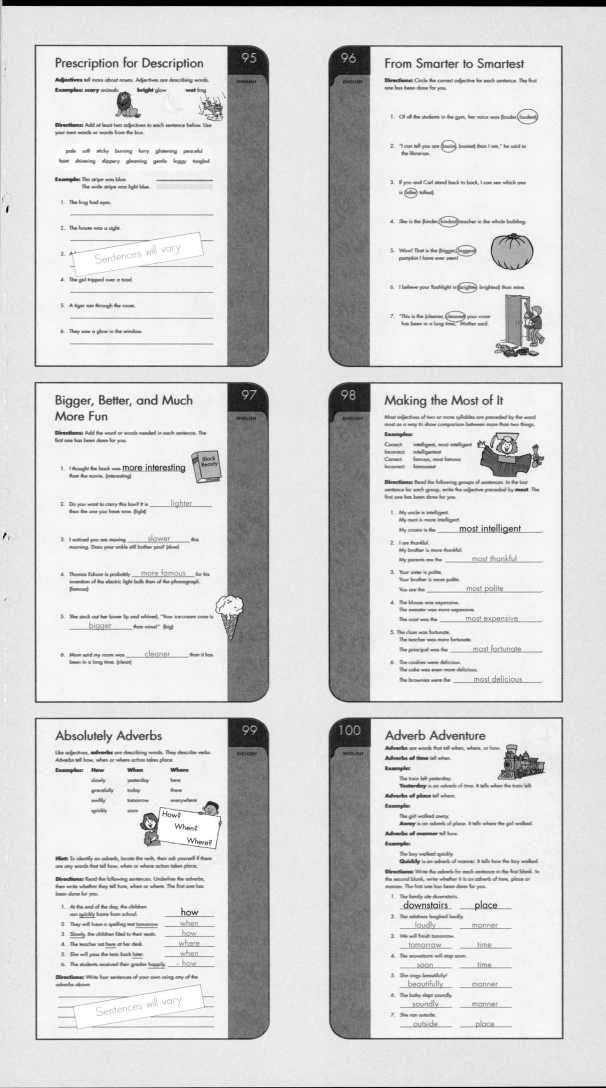

Prescription for Description

95

ENGLISH

Adjectives tell more about nouns. Adjectives are describing words.

Examples: **scary** animals   **bright** glow   **wet** frog

Directions: Add at least two adjectives to each sentence below. Use your own words or words from the box.

pale soft sticky burning furry glistening peaceful
faint shivering slippery gleaming gentle foggy tangled

Example: The stripe was blue. _____
The wide stripe was light blue. _____

1. The frog had eyes.
   _____

2. The house was a sight.
   _____

3. A _____

   Sentences will vary

4. The girl tripped over a toad.
   _____

5. A tiger ran through the room.
   _____

6. They saw a glow in the window.
   _____

From Smarter to Smartest

96

ENGLISH

Directions: Circle the correct adjective for each sentence. The first one has been done for you.

1. Of all the students in the gym, her voice was (louder, *loudest*)

2. "I can tell you are (*busier*, busiest) than I am," he said to the librarian.

3. If you and Carl stand back to back, I can see which one is (*taller*, tallest).

4. She is the (kinder, *kindest*) teacher in the whole building.

5. Wow! That is the (bigger, *biggest*) pumpkin I have ever seen!

6. I believe your flashlight is (*brighter*, brightest) than mine.

7. "This is the (cleaner, *cleanest*) your room has been in a long time," Mother said.

Bigger, Better, and Much More Fun

97

ENGLISH

Directions: Add the word or words needed in each sentence. The first one has been done for you.

1. I thought the book was **more interesting** than the movie. (interesting)

2. Do you want to carry this box? It is ___**lighter**___ than the one you have now. (light)

3. I noticed you are moving ___**slower**___ this morning. Does your ankle still bother you? (slow)

4. Thomas Edison is probably ___**more famous**___ for his invention of the electric light bulb than of the phonograph. (famous)

5. She stuck out her lower lip and whined, "Your ice-cream cone is ___**bigger**___ than mine!" (big)

6. Mom said my room was ___**cleaner**___ than it has been in a long time. (clean)

Making the Most of It

98

ENGLISH

Most adjectives of two or more syllables are preceded by the word **most** as a way to show comparison between more than two things.

Examples:

Correct: intelligent, most intelligent
Incorrect: intelligentest
Correct: famous, most famous
Incorrect: famousest

Directions: Read the following groups of sentences. In the last sentence for each group, write the adjective preceded by **most**. The first one has been done for you.

1. My uncle is intelligent.
   My aunt is more intelligent.
   My cousin is the ___**most intelligent**___

2. I am thankful.
   My brother is more thankful.
   My parents are the ___**most thankful**___

3. Your sister is polite.
   Your brother is more polite.
   You are the ___**most polite**___.

4. The blouse was expensive.
   The sweater was more expensive.
   The coat was the ___**most expensive**___.

5. The class was fortunate.
   The teacher was more fortunate.
   The principal was the ___**most fortunate**___

6. The cookies were delicious.
   The cake was even more delicious.
   The brownies were the ___**most delicious**___

Absolutely Adverbs

99

ENGLISH

Like adjectives, **adverbs** are describing words. They describe verbs. Adverbs tell how, when or where action takes place.

Examples:

How	When	Where
slowly	yesterday	here
gracefully	today	there
swiftly	tomorrow	everywhere
quickly	soon	

How?
When?
Where?

Hint: To identify an adverb, locate the verb, then ask yourself if there are any words that tell how, when or where action takes place.

Directions: Read the following sentences. Underline the adverbs, then write whether they tell how, when or where. The first one has been done for you.

1. At the end of the day, the children ran quickly home from school. ___**how**___
2. They will have a spelling test tomorrow. ___**when**___
3. Slowly, the children filed to their seats. ___**how**___
4. The teacher sat here at her desk. ___**where**___
5. She will pass the tests back later. ___**when**___
6. The students received their grades happily. ___**how**___

Directions: Write four sentences of your own using any of the adverbs above.

Sentences will vary

Adverb Adventure

100

ENGLISH

Adverbs are words that tell when, where, or how.

Adverbs of time tell when.

Example:
The train left yesterday.
Yesterday is an adverb of time. It tells when the train left.

Adverbs of place tell where.

Example:
The girl walked away.
Away is an adverb of place. It tells where the girl walked.

Adverbs of manner tell how.

Example:
The boy walked quickly.
Quickly is an adverb of manner. It tells how the boy walked.

Directions: Write the adverb for each sentence in the first blank. In the second blank, write whether it is an adverb of time, place or manner. The first one has been done for you.

1. The family ate downstairs.
   ___**downstairs**___   ___**place**___
2. The relatives laughed loudly.
   ___**loudly**___   ___**manner**___
3. We will finish tomorrow.
   ___**tomorrow**___   ___**time**___
4. The snowstorm will stop soon.
   ___**soon**___   ___**time**___
5. She sings beautifully!
   ___**beautifully**___   ___**manner**___
6. The baby slept soundly.
   ___**soundly**___   ___**manner**___
7. She ran outside.
   ___**outside**___   ___**place**___

---

101 — Tell Me More
ENGLISH

Directions: Write **ADJ** on the line if the bold word is an adjective. Write **ADV** if the bold word is an adverb. The first one has been done for you.

ADV 1. That road leads **nowhere**.

ADJ 2. The squirrel was **nearby**.

ADJ 3. Her **delicious** cookies were all eaten.

ADV 4. Everyone rushed **indoors**.

ADV 5. He **quickly** zipped his jacket.

ADJ 6. She hummed a **popular** tune.

ADJ 7. Her **sunny** smile warmed my heart.

ADV 8. I hung your coat **there**.

ADV 9. Bring that **here** this minute!

ADV 10. We all walked **back** to school.

ADJ 11. The **skinniest** boy ate the most food!

ADJ 12. She acts like a **famous** person.

ADJ 13. The **silliest** jokes always make me laugh.

---

102 — Review
ENGLISH

Directions: Write the correct words to complete the sentences. Use the words on the presents at the bottom of the page.

1. The suffix ___er___ and the word ___more___ are used when comparing two things.
2. One example of an adverb of time is ___tomorrow___.
3. When an adjective ends with ___y___, you change the **y** to **i** before adding er or est.
4. An ___adverb___ is a word that tells when, where or how.
5. An example of an adverb of place is ___there___.
6. The suffix ___est___ and the word ___most___ are used when comparing more that two things.
7. An ___adjective___ is a word that describes a noun.
8. An example of an adverb of manner is ___softly___.

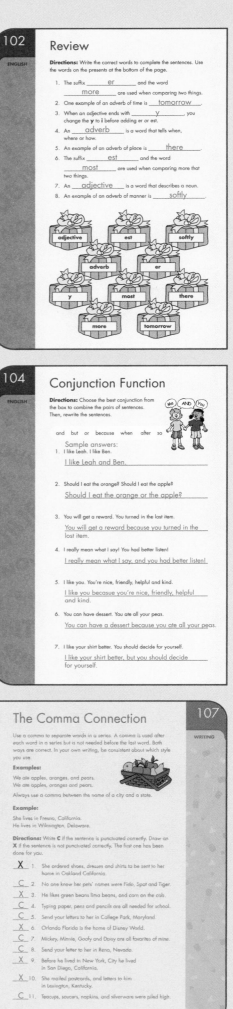

adjective · est · softly · adverb · er · y · most · there · more · tomorrow

---

103 — Join the Fun
ENGLISH

Conjunctions are joining words that can be used to combine sentences. Words such as **and**, **but**, **or**, **when** and **after** are conjunctions.

Examples:

Kaitlyn went to the mall. She went to the movies.
Kaitlyn went to the mall, and she went to the movies.

We can have our vacation at home. We can vacation at the beach.
We can have our vacation at home, or we can vacation at the beach.

Jada fell on the playground. She did not hurt herself.
Jada fell on the playground, but she did not hurt herself.

Note: The conjunctions **after** or **when** are usually placed at the beginning of the sentence.

Example: Amrita went to the store. She went to the gas station.
After Amrita went to the store, she went to the gas station.

Directions: Combine the following sentences using a conjunction.
Sample answers:
1. Peter fell down the steps. He broke his foot. (and)
   Peter fell down the steps, and broke his foot.
2. I visited New York. I would like to see Chicago. (but)
   I visited New York, but I would like to see Chicago.
3. Rosie can edit books. She can write stories. (or)
   Rosie can edit books, or she can write stories.
4. He played in the barn. John started to sneeze. (when)
   When John played in the barn, he started to sneeze.
5. The team won the playoffs. They went to the championships. (after)
   After the team won the playoffs, they went to the championships.

Directions: Write three sentences of your own using the conjunctions **and**, **but**, **or**, **when** and **after**.

Sentences will vary

---

104 — Conjunction Function
ENGLISH

Directions: Choose the best conjunction from the box to combine the pairs of sentences. Then, rewrite the sentences.

and · but · or · because · when · after · so

Sample answers:
1. I like Leah. I like Ben.
   I like Leah and Ben.
2. Should I eat the orange? Should I eat the apple?
   Should I eat the orange or the apple?
3. You will get a reward. You turned in the lost item.
   You will get a reward because you turned in the lost item.
4. I really mean what I say! You had better listen!
   I really mean what I say, and you had better listen!
5. I like you. You're nice, friendly, helpful and kind.
   I like you becasue you're nice, friendly, helpful and kind.
6. You can have dessert. You ate all your peas.
   You can have a dessert because you ate all your peas.
7. I like your shirt better. You should decide for yourself.
   I like your shirt better, but you should decide for yourself.

---

106 — Common Commas
WRITING

Use a comma to separate the number of the day of a month and the year. Do not use a comma to separate the month and year if no day is given.

Examples:

June 14, 2010

June 2009

Use a comma after **yes** or **no** when it is the first word in a sentence.

Examples:

Yes, I will do it right now.

No, I don't want any.

Directions: Write **C** if the sentence is punctuated correctly. Draw an **X** if the sentence is not punctuated correctly. The first one has been done for you.

C 1. No, I don't plan to attend.

C 2. I told them, oh yes, I would go.

C 3. Her birthday is March 13, 1995.

X 4. He was born in May, 2008.

C 5. Yes, of course I like you!

X 6. No I will not be there.

X 7. They left for vacation on February, 14.

C 8. No, today is Monday.

C 9. The program was first shown on August 12, 1991.

X 10. In September, 2015 how old will you be!

X 11. He turned 12 years old on November, 13.

X 12. I said no, I will not come no matter what!

---

107 — The Comma Connection
WRITING

Use a comma to separate words in a series. A comma is used after each word in a series but is not needed before the last word. Both ways are correct. In your own writing, be consistent about which style you use.

Examples:

We ate apples, oranges, and pears.
We ate apples, oranges and pears.

Always use a comma between the name of a city and a state.

Example:

She lives in Fresno, California.
He lives in Wilmington, Delaware.

Directions: Write **C** if the sentence is punctuated correctly. Draw an **X** if the sentence is not punctuated correctly. The first one has been done for you.

X 1. She ordered shoes, dresses and shirts to be sent to her home in Oakland California.

C 2. No one knew her pets' names were Fido, Spot and Tiger.

X 3. He likes green beans lima beans, and corn on the cob.

C 4. Typing paper, pens and pencils are all needed for school.

C 5. Send your letters to her in College Park, Maryland.

X 6. Orlando Florida is home of Disney World.

C 7. Mickey, Minnie, Goofy and Daisy are all favorites of mine.

C 8. Send your letter to her in Reno, Nevada.

X 9. Before he lived in New York, City he lived in San Diego, California.

X 10. She mailed postcards, and letters to him in Lexington, Kentucky.

C 11. Teacups, saucers, napkins, and silverware were piled high.

---

108 WRITING

Good Reads

All words in the title of a book are underlined. Underlined words also mean italics.

Examples:

The Hunt for Red October was a best-seller!
(The Hunt for Red October)

Have you read Lost in Space?
(Lost in Space)

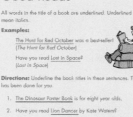

Directions: Underline the book titles in these sentences. The first one has been done for you.

1. The Dinosaur Poster Book is for eight year olds.

2. Have you read Lion Dancer by Kate Waters?

3. Baby Dinosaurs and Giant Dinosaurs were both written by Peter Dodson.

4. Have you heard of the book That's What Friends Are For by Carol Adorjan?

5. J.B. Stamper wrote a book called The Totally Terrific Valentine Party Book.

6. The teacher read Almost Ten and a Half aloud to our class.

7. Marrying Off Mom is about a girl who tries to get her widowed mother to start dating.

8. The Snow and The Fire are the second and third books by author Caroline Cooney.

9. The title sounds silly, but Goofbang Value Daze really is the name of a book!

10. A book about space exploration is The Day We Walked on the Moon by George Sullivan.

11. Alice and the Birthday Giant tells about a giant who came to a girl's birthday party.

---

109 WRITING

Hooked on Books

Capitalize the first and last word of book titles. Capitalize all other words of book titles except short prepositions, such as **of**, **at** and **in**; conjunctions, such as **and**, **or** and **but**; and articles, such as **a**, **an** and **the**.

Examples:

Have you read War and Peace?

Pippi Longstocking in Moscow is her favorite book.

Directions: Underline the book titles. Circle the words that should be capitalized. The first one has been done for you.

1. murder in the blue room by Elliot Roosevelt

2. growing up in a divided society by Sandra Burnham

3. the corn king and the spring queen by Naomi Mitchison

4. new kids on the block by Grace Catalano

5. best friends don't tell lies by Linda Barr

6. turn your kid into a computer genius by Carole Gerber

7. 50 simple things you can do to save the earth by Earth Works Press

8. garfield goes to waist by Jim Davis

9. the hunt for red october by Tom Clancy

10. fall into darkness by Christopher Pike

11. oh the places you'll go by Dr. Seuss

12. amy the dancing bear by Carly Simon

---

110 WRITING

You Said It!

Use quotation marks (" ") before and after the exact words of a speaker.

Examples:

I asked Aunt Martha, "How do you feel?"
"I feel awful," Aunt Martha replied.

Do not put quotation marks around words that report what the speaker said.

Examples:

Aunt Martha said she felt awful.
I asked Aunt Martha how she felt.

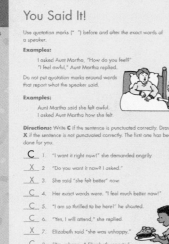

Directions: Write **C** if the sentence is punctuated correctly. Draw an **X** if the sentence is not punctuated correctly. The first one has been done for you.

C 1. "I want it right now!" she demanded angrily.

X 2. "Do you want it now? I asked."

X 3. She said "she felt better" now.

C 4. Her exact words were, "I feel much better now!"

C 5. "I am so thrilled to be here!" he shouted.

C 6. "Yes, I will attend," she replied.

X 7. Elizabeth said "she was unhappy."

C 8. "I'm unhappy," Elizabeth reported.

C 9. "Did you know her mother?" I asked.

X 10. I asked "whether you knew her mother."

C 11. I wondered, "What will dessert be?"

C 12. "Which will it be, salt or pepper?" the waiter asked.

---

111 WRITING

Sing Me a Song

Use quotation marks around the titles of songs and poems.

Examples:

Have you heard "Still Cruising" by the Beach Boys?
"Ode To a Nightingale" is a famous poem.

Directions: Write **C** if the sentence is punctuated correctly. Draw an **X** if the sentence is not punctuated correctly. The first one has been done for you.

C 1. Do you know "My Bonnie Lies Over the Ocean"?

X 2. We sang The Stars and Stripes Forever" at school.

C 3. Her favorite song is "The Eensy Weensy Spider."

X 4. Turn the music up when "A Hard Day's "Night comes on!

C 5. "Yesterday" was one of Paul McCartney's most famous songs.

C 6. "Mary Had a Little Lamb" is a very silly poem!

C 7. A song everyone knows is "Happy Birthday."

C 8. "Swing Low, Sweet Chariot" was first sung by slaves.

X 9. Do you know the words to Home on "the Range"?

C 10. "Hiawatha" is a poem many older people had to memorize.

X 11. "Happy Days Are Here Again! is an upbeat tune.

C 12. Frankie Valli and the Four Seasons sang "Sherry."

---

112 WRITING

Review

Directions: The following sentences have errors in punctuation, capitalization or both. The number in parentheses ( ) at the end of each sentence tells you how many errors it contains. Correct the errors by rewriting each sentence.

1. I saw mr. Johnson reading War And Peace to his class. (3)

   I saw Mr. Johnson reading _War And Peace_ to his class.

2. Do you like to sing "Take me Out to The Ballgame"? (2)

   Do you like to sing "Take Me Out to the Ballgame?"

3. He recited Hiawatha to Miss. Simpson's class. (2)

   He recited _Hiawatha_ to Miss Simpson's class.

4. Bananas, and oranges are among Dr patel's favorite fruits. (3)

   Bananas and oranges are among Dr. Patel's favorite fruits.

5. "Daisy, daisy is a song about a bicycle built for two. (2)

   "Daisy, Daisy" is a song about a bicycle built for two.

6. Good Morning, Granny Rose is about a woman and her dog. (1)

   "Good Morning, Granny Rose" is about a woman and her dog.

7. Garfield goes to waist is a very funny book! (3)

   Garfield Goes to Waist is a very funny book!

8. Peanut butter, jelly, and bread are miss. Lee's favorite treats. (1)

   Peanut butter, jelly, and bread are Miss Lee's favorite treats.

---

113 WRITING

Proof It!

Proofreading means searching for and correcting errors by carefully reading and rereading what has been written. Use the proofreading marks below when correcting your writing or someone else's.

To insert a word or a punctuation mark that has been left out, use this mark: ∧. It is called a caret.

Example: We ∧to the dance together. *went*

To show that a letter should be capitalized, put three lines under it.

Example: Mrs. Jones drove us to school.

To show a capital letter should be small or lowercase, draw a diagonal line through it.

Example: Mrs. Jones Ɗrove us to school.

To show that a word is spelled incorrectly, draw a horizontal line through it and write the correct spelling above it.

Example: The walros is an amazing animal. *walrus*

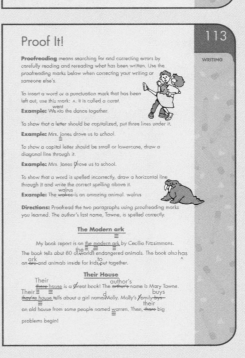

Directions: Proofread the two paragraphs using proofreading marks you learned. The author's last name, Towne, is spelled correctly.

The Modern ark

My book report is on the modern ark by Cecilia Fitzsimmons. The book tells about 80 of the world's endangered animals. The book also has an ark and animals inside for kids to put together.

Their House

Their house is a great book! The author's name is Mary Towne. Their house tells about a girl named Molly. Molly's family buys an old house from some people named warren. Then, their big problems begin!

114 Key Facts

WRITING

Directions: Proofread the sentences. Write **C** if the sentence has no errors. Draw an **X** if the sentence contains missing words or other errors. The first one has been done for you.

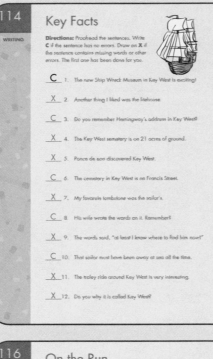

C 1. The new Ship Wreck Museum in Key West is exciting!

X 2. Another thing I liked was the lirehouse.

C 3. Do you remember Hemingway's address in Key West?

X 4. The Key West sematary is on 21 acres of ground.

X 5. Ponce de son discovered Key West.

C 6. The cemetery in Key West is on Francis Street.

X 7. My favorate tombstone was the sailor's.

C 8. His wife wrote the words on it. Remember?

X 9. The words said, "at least I know where to find him now!"

C 10. That sailor must have been away at sea all the time.

X 11. The troley ride around Key West is very interesting.

X 12. Do you why it is called Key West?

115 A Tropical Paradise

WRITING

Directions: Proofread the paragraphs, using the proofreading marks you learned. There are seven capitalization errors, three missing words and eleven errors in spelling or word usage.

Key West

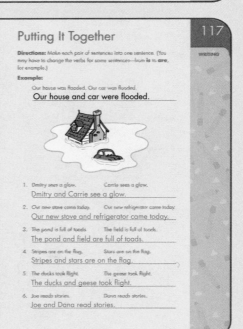

Key West has been, tropical paradise ever since Ponce de Leon first saw the set of islands called the keys in 1513. Two streets in Key West are named duval and whitehead. You will find the city cemetery on Francis Street. The tombstones are funny!

The message on one is, "I told you I was sick!" On sailor's tombstone is this message from his widow: "At least I no where to find him now."

The cemetery is on 21 acres in the middle of town. The most famous home in key west is that of the author Ernest Hemingway. Hemingway's home was at 907 whitehead Street. He lived there for 30 years.

116 On the Run

WRITING

A **run-on sentence** occurs when two or more sentences are joined together without punctuation.

Examples:

Run-on sentence:
I lost my way once did you?

Two sentences with correct punctuation:
I lost my way once. Did you?

Run-on sentence:
I found the recipe it was not hard to follow.

Two sentences with correct punctuation:
I found the recipe. It was not hard to follow.

Directions: Rewrite the run-on sentences correctly with periods, exclamation points, and question marks. The first one has been done for you.

1. Did you take my umbrella I can't find it anywhere!
   Did you take my umbrella? I can't find it anywhere!

2. How can you stand that noise I can't!
   How can you stand that noise? I can't!

3. The cookies are gone I see only crumbs.
   The cookies are gone. I see only crumbs.

4. The dogs were barking they were hungry.
   The dogs were barking. They were hungry.

5. She is quite ill please call a doctor immediately!
   She is quite ill. Please call the doctor immediately!

6. The clouds came up we knew the storm would hit soon.
   The clouds came up. We knew the storm would hit soon.

7. You weren't home he stopped by this morning.
   You weren't home. He stopped by this morning.

117 Putting It Together

WRITING

Directions: Make each pair of sentences into one sentence. (You may have to change the verbs for some sentences—from **is** to **are**, for example.)

Example:

Our house was flooded. Our car was flooded.
Our house and car were flooded.

1. Dmitry sees a glow.   Carrie sees a glow.
   Dmitry and Carrie see a glow.

2. Our new stove came today.   Our new refrigerator came today.
   Our new stove and refrigerator came today.

3. The pond is full of toads.   The field is full of toads.
   The pond and field are full of toads.

4. Stripes are on the flag.   Stars are on the flag.
   Stripes and stars are on the flag.

5. The ducks took flight.   The geese took flight.
   The ducks and geese took flight.

6. Joe reads stories.   Dana reads stories.
   Joe and Dana read stories.

118 Frosty Fun

WRITING

A **paragraph** is a group of sentences that share the same idea.

Directions: Rewrite the paragraph by combining the simple sentences into larger sentences.

Jason awoke early. He threw off his covers. He ran to his window. He looked outside. He saw snow. It was white and fluffy. Jason thought of something. He thought of his sled. His sled was in the garage. He quickly ate breakfast. He dressed warmly. He got his sled. He went outside. He went to play in the snow.

Jason awoke early and threw off his covers. He ran to his window and looked outside. He saw white and fluffy snow. Jason thought of his sled in the garage. He quickly ate breakfast and dressed warmly. He got his sled and went outside to play in the snow.

Answers will vary

119 Friends to the End

WRITING

A **paragraph** is a group of sentences that tells about one main idea. A **topic sentence** tells the main idea of a paragraph.

Many topic sentences come first in the paragraph. The topic sentence in the paragraph below is underlined. Do you see how it tells the reader what the whole paragraph is about?

Friendships can make you happy or make you sad. You feel happy to do things and go places with your friends. You get to know each other so well that you can almost read each others' minds. But friendships can be sad when your friend moves away—or decides to be best friends with someone else.

Directions: Underline the topic sentence in the paragraph below.

We have two rules about using the phone at our house. Our whole family agreed on them. The first rule is not to talk longer than 10 minutes. The second rule is to take good messages if you answer the phone for someone else.

Directions: After you read the paragraph below, write a topic sentence for it.

There are many ways you can earn money.

For one thing, you could ask your neighbors if they need any help. They might be willing to pay you for walking their dog or mowing their grass or weeding their garden. Maybe your older brothers or sisters would pay you to do some of their chores. You also could ask your parents if there's an extra job you could do around the house to make money.

Directions: Write a topic sentence for a paragraph on each of these subjects.

Homework:

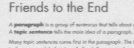

Sentences will vary

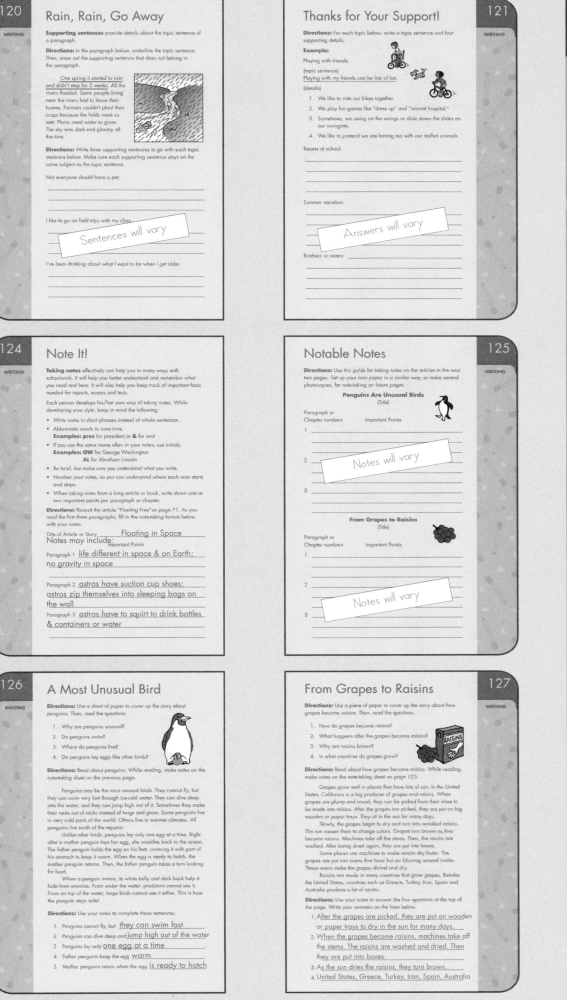

128

WRITING

Garden Growing

Outlines are plans that help you organize your thoughts. If you are writing an essay, an outline helps you decide what to write. An outline should look similar to this:

I. First main idea
  A. A smaller idea
    1. An example
    2. An example
II. Second main idea
  A. A smaller idea
  B. Another smaller idea
III. Third main idea
  A. A smaller idea
  B. Another smaller idea
    1. An example

I. Planting a garden
  A. Choosing seeds
    1. Tomatoes
    2. Lettuce
II. Taking care of the garden
  A. Pulling the weeds
  B. Watering the garden
III. Harvesting
  A. Are they ripe?
  B. How to pick them
    1. Pick only the tomato off the vine

Directions: Use the outline for planting a garden to answer the questions.

1. What are the three main ideas?
  1) _Planting a garden_
  2) _Taking care of the garden_
  3) _Harvesting_

2. What are the two smaller ideas listed under "Taking care of the garden"?
  1) _Pulling the weeds_
  2) _Watering the garden_

3. What are the smaller ideas listed under "Harvesting"?
  1) _Are they ripe?_
  2) _How to pick them_

4. What is listed under the smaller idea "How to pick them"?
  Pick only the tomato off the vine.

129

WRITING

At Home in the Trees

Directions: Study the sample outline for building a tree house. Then, use words and phrases from the box to fill in the missing parts of the outline on how to build a tree house.

I. Find land
  A. On a hill
  B. By a lake
  C. In the city
II. Gather materials
  A. Buy wood
  B. Buy nails
  C. Buy tools
    1. Hammer
    2. Screwdriver
    3. Drill
    4. Saw
III. Build the house
  A. Who will use the tools?
  B. Who will carry the wood?

Collect wood scraps
Who will hold the boards?
Who will use the hammer?
Gather tools
Can we climb it easily?
Saw
How will we get things off the ground?

I. Find a tree
  A. Is it sturdy?
  B. _Can we climb it easily?_
II. Gather supplies
  A. _Collect wood scraps_
  B. _Gather tools_
    1. Hammer and nails
    2. _Saw_
III. Build the tree house
  A. _Who will hold the boards?_
  B. _Who will use the hammer?_
  C. _How will we get things off the ground?_

130

WRITING

House Rules

Directions: Use words and phrases from the box to fill in the missing parts of the outline of what to do once your tree house is built.

Sisters and brothers   When can they visit?
Parents   Spray paint
Tables   Choose a kind of paint
Chairs   Who can visit?

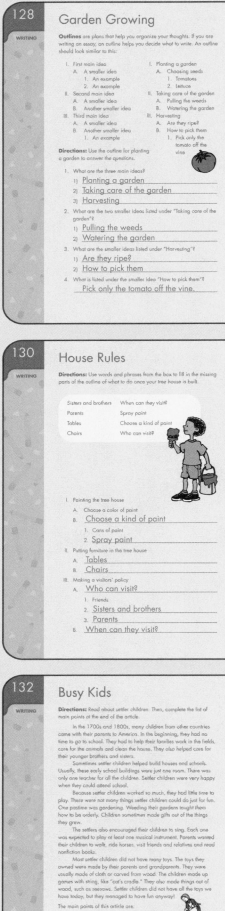

I. Painting the tree house
  A. Choose a color of paint
  B. _Choose a kind of paint_
    1. Cans of paint
    2. _Spray paint_
II. Putting furniture in the tree house
  A. _Tables_
  B. _Chairs_
III. Making a visitors' policy
  A. _Who can visit?_
    1. Friends
    2. _Sisters and brothers_
    3. _Parents_
  B. _When can they visit?_

131

WRITING

All About Me

When you summarize an article, book or speech, you are simply writing a shorter article that contains only the main points. This shorter article of main points is called a summary.

To prepare for writing a summary of your life, you would begin with an outline. Since a summary is a brief account of main points, you will not be able to include every detail of your life. Your summary should include only basic facts.

I. Yourself
  A. Name
  B. Age and grade in school
    1. Subjects you like in school
    2. Subjects you do not like in school
  C. Looks
    1. Eye color
    2. Hair color
    3. Other features
II. Your family
  A. Parents
  B. Brothers/sisters
  C. Pets
III. Hobbies and interests
  A. Sports
  B. Clubs

Directions: Follow the format above to write an outline about your life. Feel free to add more main ideas, smaller ideas, or examples.

Outline should follow format

132

WRITING

Busy Kids

Directions: Read about settler children. Then, complete the list of main points at the end of the article.

In the 1700s and 1800s, many children from other countries came with their parents to America. In the beginning, they had no time to go to school. They had to help their families work in the fields, care for the animals and clean the house. They also helped care for their younger brothers and sisters.

Sometimes settler children helped build houses and schools. Usually, these early school buildings were just one room. There was only one teacher for all the children. Settler children were very happy when they could attend school.

Because settler children worked so much, they had little time to play. There were not many things settler children could do just for fun. One pastime was gardening. Weeding their gardens taught them how to be orderly. Children sometimes made gifts out of the things they grew.

The settlers also encouraged their children to sing. Each one was expected to play at least one musical instrument. Parents wanted their children to walk, ride horses, visit friends and relatives and read nonfiction books.

Most settler children did not have many toys. The toys they owned were made by their parents and grandparents. They were usually made of cloth or carved from wood. The children made up games with string, like "cat's cradle." They also made things out of wood, such as seesaws. Settler children did not have all the toys we have today, but they managed to have fun anyway!

The main points of this article are:

1. Settler children worked hard.
2. Settler children had many jobs.
3. _Settler children liked school._
4. _Settler children had little time to play._
5. _Settler children had few toys._

Directions: Use the main points to write a summary of this article on a separate sheet of paper.

133

WRITING

Who Comes First

Authors are alphabetized by their last names first. In a library catalog, Blume, Judy would come before Voirst, Judith. Books are alphabetized by title. If a title begins with **The**, **A**, or **An**, ignore it, and use the second word of the title.

Directions: Look at the list of authors, subjects and titles. Write **A** for author, **S** for subject or **T** for title in the blanks. Then, write each on the card where it belongs in alphabetical order. Some have been done for you.

_A_   Gallant, Roy A.
_S_   Native Americans
_T_   Animals of Long Ago
_S_   gardens
_T_   The White House
_A_   Sandak, Cass R.
_T_   The Pony Express
_A_   Herbst, Judith
_S_   Pilgrims
_T_   The Hobbit
_A_   Dicerto, Joseph J.
_S_   planets

Author
Dicerto, Joseph J.
Gallant, Roy A.
Herbst, Judith
Sandak, Cass R.

Title
Animals of Long Ago
The Hobbit
The Pony Express
The White House

Subject
gardens
Native Americans
Pilgrims
planets

134 Know Your Numbers

The **call number** of a book tells where it can be found among nonfiction books.

Information is presented differently on the title, subject and author card for the same book. A computer listing for this book would look quite similar.

Author card
567.91 VanCleave, Janice
V278 Dinosaurs for Every Kid
John Wiley & Sons, Inc., 1994

Subject card
567.91 DINOSAURS
V278 VanCleave, Janice
Dinosaurs for Every Kid
John Wiley & Sons, Inc., 1994

Title card
567.91 Dinosaurs for Every Kid
V278 VanCleave, Janice
John Wiley & Sons, Inc., 1994

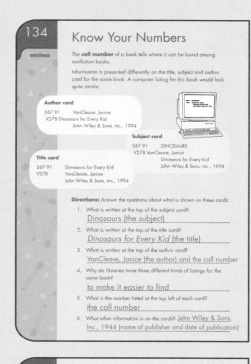

Directions: Answer the questions about what is shown on these cards.

1. What is written at the top of the subject card?
   Dinosaurs (the subject)

2. What is written at the top of the title card?
   Dinosaurs for Every Kid (the title)

3. What is written at the top of the author card?
   VanCleave, Janice (the author) and the call number

4. Why do libraries have three different kinds of listings for the same book?
   to make it easier to find

5. What is the number listed at the top left of each card?
   the call number

6. What other information is on the cards? John Wiley & Sons, Inc., 1944 (name of publisher and date of publication)

135 Doing the Dewey

All libraries that use the Dewey Decimal System follow the same order. All books between 500 and 599 are related to science. All books between 900 and 999 are history.

Each library divides its system even further. For example, one library may have kites at 796.15, while another library may have kites at 791.13.

Directions: Look at the number on each book. Then, use the Dewey Decimal System directory at the bottom of the page to find out what the book is about. Write the subject on the line.

560	915.2	391	612	599
Fossils	Japan	Costumes	Human Body	Big Foot

793.8	796.41	923.1	636.9	581
Magic	Gymnastics	Presidents	Pets	Plants

Dewey Decimal System directory:

390–399	Costumes	630–639	Pets
560–569	Fossils	790–795	Magic
580–589	Plants	796–799	Gymnastics
590–599	Big Foot	910–919	Japan
610–619	Human Body	920–929	Presidents

136 Sort It Out

Some books in a library are not filed by the Dewey Decimal System. Those books include biographies, autobiographies and fiction. Biographies and autobiographies may be filed together in the 920s or be assigned a call number by subject.

Fiction books are stories that someone has made up. They are filed in alphabetical order by the author's last name in the fiction section of the library.

Directions: For each title, write **B** if it is a biography, **A** if it is an autobiography or **F** if it is fiction. Then, circle the titles that would not be filed by the Dewey Decimal System.

F (Tales of a Fourth Grade Nothing)

B The Real Tom Thumb

F (Ramona the Pest)

A Bill Peet: An Autobiography

B Abraham Lincoln

F (Charlotte's Web)

A The King and I

A My Life With Chimpanzees

F (Sara Plain and Tall)

B Michael Jordan, Basketball's Soaring Star

B The First Book of Presidents

B The Helen Keller Story

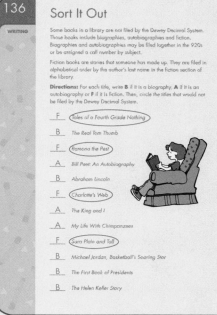

137 Out of This World

The history of the American space program is a very fascinating topic. The articles presented earlier in this book (pages 69–72) provided many interesting facts about some of the astronauts, what their jobs were and what space travel was like.

Besides books and encyclopedias, magazine articles and the Internet are other good reference sources you can use to learn more about a topic.

Directions: Neil Armstrong was the first man to walk on the Moon in July 1969. Use reference sources to answer these questions.

1. What two other astronauts were with him?
   Edwin Aldrin and Michael Collins

2. What was the name of the Apollo mission that went to the Moon? Apollo 11

3. What was the exact date of the first Moon landing?
   July 20, 1969

4. Why was the U.S. racing Russia to the Moon?
   Answers will vary

Directions: John Glenn first orbited Earth in 1962. Use reference sources to answer these questions.

5. How old was he then? 41

6. When did John Glenn return to space? 1998

7. How old was he on his second trip? 77

8. Why did he return to space?
   to assist in the study of the effects of no gravity and aging

Directions: Compare and contrast Glenn's two trips.

9. Answers will vary

138 Out of This World

Directions: Use reference sources to answer these questions.

1. What caused the "Space Race" in the 1950s?
   Answers may include: the launching of *Sputnik I* by Russia in 1957

2. In testing rockets, why were chimps used instead of other animals?
   They are physically much like humans

3. What is the astronaut training program like?

4. Why do you think the training is so difficult?

Answers will vary

Directions: Use reference sources to answer these questions.

5. Do you think being an astronaut is a career for you? Explain.

6. What do you think life would be like on a space station or in a space colony?

139 Haiku and You

Haiku is a form of unrhymed Japanese poetry. A haiku poem has only three lines. Each line has a specific number of syllables.

Haiku poems usually describe a season or something in nature. Sometimes haiku are written about feelings.

The Haiku pattern:	Example haiku:
Line 1 — 5 syllables	Winter snow slides from
Line 2 — 7 syllables	The eave. Drops—plop—on my head.
Line 3 — 5 syllables	As I walk under. —D.S. Underwood

When writing haiku you do not count words per line. Count only the number of syllables.

Directions: To prepare for writing your poem, think of words about a snowy day. Write them on the lines. After each word, write the number of syllables in the word.

frosty (2)   white (1)   snowflakes (2)

Answers will vary

When writing any type of poetry, it is a good idea to start on scrap paper so you can write, erase, cross out and rewrite.

Directions: Write a haiku poem about a snowy day on scrap paper. When you are satisfied with your poem, rewrite it below. At the end of each line, write the number of syllables in the line.

Poems will vary

5
7
5

246

ANSWER KEY

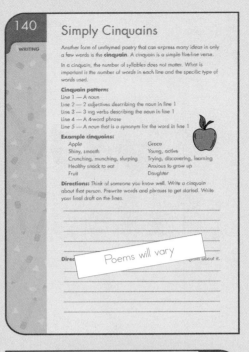

140 WRITING

Simply Cinquains

Another form of unrhymed poetry that can express many ideas in only a few words is the **cinquain**. A cinquain is a simple five-line verse.

In a cinquain, the number of syllables does not matter. What is important is the number of words in each line and the specific type of words used.

Cinquain pattern:
Line 1 — A noun
Line 2 — 2 adjectives describing the noun in line 1
Line 3 — 3 ing verbs describing the noun in line 1
Line 4 — A 4-word phrase
Line 5 — A noun that is a synonym for the word in line 1

Example cinquains:

Apple	Grace
Shiny, smooth	Young, active
Crunching, munching, slurping	Trying, discovering, learning
Healthy snack to eat	Anxious to grow up
Fruit	Daughter

Directions: Think of someone you know well. Write a cinquain about that person. Prewrite words and phrases to get started. Write your final draft on the lines.

Poems will vary

---

142 MATH

Finding Your Place

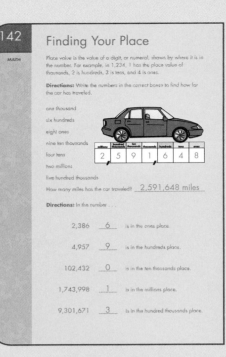

Place value is the value of a digit, or numeral, shown by where it is in the number. For example, in 1,234, 1 has the place value of thousands, 2 is hundreds, 3 is tens, and 4 is ones.

Directions: Write the numbers in the correct boxes to find how far the car has traveled.

one thousand
six hundreds
eight ones
nine ten thousands
four tens
two millions
five hundred thousands

millions	hundred thousands	ten thousands	thousands	hundreds	tens	ones
2	5	9	1	6	4	8

How many miles has the car traveled? __2,591,648 miles__

Directions: In this number . . .

2,386	6	is in the ones place.
4,957	9	is in the hundreds place.
102,432	0	is in the ten thousands place.
1,743,998	1	is in the millions place.
9,301,671	3	is in the hundred thousands place.

---

143 MATH

Going in Circles

Directions: Where the circles meet, write the sum of the numbers from the circles on the right and left and above and below. The first row shows you what to do.

7	16	**9**	21	**12**	20	**8**
11		15		17		9
4	10	**6**	11	**5**	6	**1**
4		9		7		11
0	3	**3**	5	**2**	12	**10**
11		18		22		22
11	26	**15**	35	**20**	32	**12**
24		31		34		29
13	29	**16**	30	**14**	31	**17**

---

144 MATH

Adding On

When adding two-, three- and four-digit numbers, add the ones first, then tens, hundreds, thousands, and so on.

Example:

Tens	Ones		Tens	Ones
5	4		5	4
+2	5		+2	5
	9		7	9

Directions: Add the following numbers.

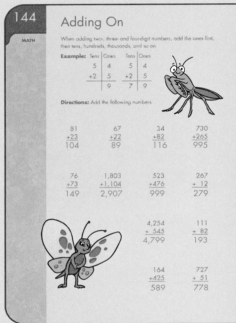

81	67	34	730
+23	+22	+82	+265
104	89	116	995

76	1,803	523	267
+73	+1,104	+476	+ 12
149	2,907	999	279

4,254	111
+ 545	+ 82
4,799	193

164	727
+425	+ 51
589	778

---

145 MATH

In the Doghouse

Regrouping uses 10 ones to form one 10, 10 tens to form one hundred, one 10 and 5 ones to form 15, and so on.

Directions: Add using regrouping. Color in all the boxes with a 5 in the answer to help the dog find its way home.

	63 +22 85	5,268 4,910 +1,683 11,861	248 +463 711	291 +543 834	2,934 + 112 3,046
1,736 +5,367 7,103	2,946 +7,384 10,330	3,245 1,239 + 981 5,465	738 +692 1,430	896 +728 1,624	594 +738 1,332
2,603 +5,004 7,607	4,507 + 289 4,796	1,483 +6,753 8,236	1,258 +6,301 7,559	27 469 +6,002 6,498	4,637 +7,531 12,168
782 + 65 847	485 +276 761	3,421 +8,064 11,485			
48 93 +26 167	90 263 +864 1,217	362 453 +800 1,615			

---

146 MATH

Subtraction Action

Subtraction is "taking away" or subtracting one number from another.

Directions: Complete the following problems as quickly and as accurately as you can.

18	13	12	17	16
− 9	− 6	− 5	− 8	− 8
9	7	7	9	8

12	10	5	14	15
− 5	− 4	−3	− 6	− 9
7	6	2	8	6

9	8	6	5	10
−5	−3	−2	−4	− 7
4	5	4	1	3

11	12	16	11	10
−4	− 8	− 9	− 8	−10
7	4	7	3	0

How quickly did you complete this page? _____

Take It Away! — 147

MATH

When you subtract larger numbers, subtract the ones first, then the tens, hundreds, thousands, and so on.

Example:

Tens	Ones		Tens	Ones
9	4		9	4
−2	1		−2	1
			3	7

Tens	Ones
9	4
−2	1
7	3

Directions: Solve these subtraction problems.

29	99	359
−26	−58	− 55
3	41	304

735	849	7,678
−734	−726	−4,321
1	123	3,357

865	55	9,876
−731	−25	−1,234
134	30	8,642

Regrouping Roundup — 148

MATH

Directions: Subtract using regrouping.

Examples:

23		243	
−18		− 96	
5		147	

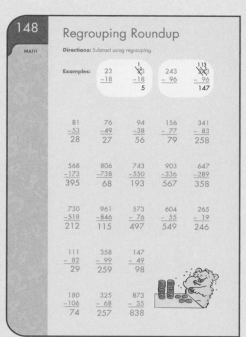

81	76	94	156	341
−53	−49	−38	− 77	− 83
28	27	56	79	258

568	806	743	903	647
−173	−738	−550	−336	−289
395	68	193	567	358

730	961	573	604	265
−518	−846	− 76	− 55	− 19
212	115	497	549	246

111	358	147
− 82	− 99	− 49
29	259	98

180	325	873
−106	− 68	− 35
74	257	838

Pond Play — 149

MATH

Directions: Add or subtract, using regrouping when needed.

38	1,269		629	
43	2,453	5,792	491	4,697
+21	+8,219	−4,814	+308	−2,988
102	11,941	978	1,428	1,709

	68	197		
5,280	27	436	7,321	456
−3,147	+42	+213	−2,789	+974
2,133	137	846	4,532	1,430

	492			
3,932	863	9,873	4,978	6,235
+4,681	+ 57	+5,483	+2,131	+2,986
8,613	1,412	15,356	7,109	9,221

Elena stocked her pond with 263 bass and 187 trout. 97 fish swam away in a flood. How many fish are left? __353 fish__

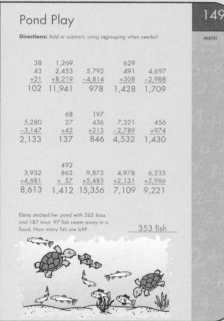

Turtles All A-Round — 150

MATH

Rounding a number means expressing it to the nearest ten, hundred, thousand, and so on. Knowing how to round numbers makes estimating sums, differences and products easier. When rounding to the nearest ten, the key number is in the ones place. If the ones digit is 5 or larger, round up to the next highest ten. If the ones digit is 4 or less, round down to the nearest ten.

Examples:

- Round 81 to the nearest ten.
- 1 is the key digit.
- If it is less than 5, round down.
- **Answer:** 80

- Round 246 to the nearest ten.
- 6 is the key digit.
- If it is more than 5, round up.
- **Answer:** 250

Directions: Round these numbers to the nearest ten.

41 → 40	32 → 30
75 → 80	481 → 480	165 → 170
89 → 90	29 → 30	17 → 20	38 → 40	68 → 70
87 → 90	52 → 50	573 → 570	98 → 100
43 → 40	12 → 10

Round Up, Round Down — 151

MATH

When rounding to the nearest hundred, the key number is in the tens place. If the tens digit is 5 or larger, round up to the nearest hundred. If the tens digit is 4 or less, round down to the nearest hundred.

Examples:

Round 871 to the nearest hundred.
7 is the key digit.
If it is more than 5, round up.
Answer: 900

Round 421 to the nearest hundred.
2 is the key digit.
If it is less than 4, round down.
Answer: 400

Directions: Round these numbers to the nearest hundred.

255 __300__	368 __400__	443 __400__
562 __600__	698 __700__	99 __100__
812 __800__	592 __600__	124 __100__

When rounding to the nearest thousand, the key number is in the hundreds place. If the hundreds digit is 5 or larger, round up to the nearest thousand. If the hundreds digit is 4 or less, round down to the nearest thousand.

Examples:

Round 7,932 to the nearest thousand.
9 is the key digit.
If it is more than 5, round up.
Answer: 8,000

Round 1,368 to the nearest thousand.
3 is the key digit.
If it is less than 4, round down.
Answer: 1,000

Directions: Round these numbers to the nearest thousand.

8,631 __9,000__	1,248 __1,000__	798 __1,000__
999 __1,000__	6,229 __6,000__	8,461 __8,000__
9,654 __10,000__	4,963 __5,000__	99,923 __100,000__

Can't Wait to Estimate! — 152

MATH

Estimating is used for certain mathematical calculations. For example, to figure the cost of several items, round their prices to the nearest dollar, then add up the approximate cost. A store clerk, on the other hand, needs to know the exact prices in order to charge the correct amount. To estimate to the nearest hundred, round up numbers over 50. **Example:** 251 is rounded up to 300. Round down numbers less than 50. **Example:** 128 is rounded down to 100.

Directions: In the following situations, write whether an exact or estimated answer should be used.

Example:
You make a deposit in your bank account. Do you want an estimated total or an exact total? __Exact__

1. Your family just ate dinner at a restaurant. Your parents are trying to calculate the tip for your server. Should they estimate by rounding or use exact numbers?
   __Estimate__

2. You are at the store buying candy, and you want to know if you have enough money to pay for it. Should you estimate or use exact numbers?
   __Estimate__

3. Some friends are planning a trip from New York City to Washington, D.C. They need to know about how far they will travel in miles. Should they estimate or use exact numbers?
   __Estimate__

4. You plan a trip to the zoo. Beforehand, you call the zoo for the price of admission. Should the person at the zoo tell you an estimated or exact price?
   __Exact__

5. The teacher is grading your papers. Should your scores be exact or estimated?
   __Exact__

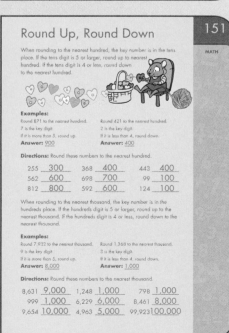

Game On! 153
MATH

Directions: Round the numbers to the nearest hundred. Then, solve the problems.

Example:

Jack and Alex were playing a computer game. Jack scored 428 points. Alex scored 132. About how many more points did Jack score than Alex?

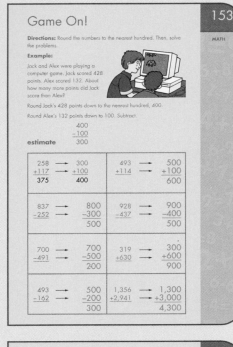

Round Jack's 428 points down to the nearest hundred, 400.

Round Alex's 132 points down to 100. Subtract.

```
            400
           -100
estimate    300
```

258 +117 = **375** → 300 +100 = **400**	493 +114 → 500 +100 = **600**
837 -252 → 800 -300 = **500**	928 -437 → 900 -400 = **500**
700 -491 → 700 -500 = **200**	319 +630 → 300 +600 = **900**
493 -162 → 500 -200 = **300**	1,356 +2,941 → 1,300 +3,000 = **4,300**

154 Missing Multiples
MATH

A multiple is the product of a specific number and any other number. For example, the multiples of 2 are 2 (2 x 1), 4 (2 x 2), 6, 8, 10, 12, and so on.

Directions: Write the missing multiples.

Example: Count by 5's.

5, 10, 15, 20, 25, 30, 35. These are multiples of 5.

Caterpillar: 5, 10, 15, 20, 25, 30, 35, 40, 45, 50, 55, 60

Sailboats: 10, 20, 30, 40, 50, 60

Bubbles: 4, 8, 12, 16, 20, 24, 28

Fact Factory 155
MATH

Factors are the numbers multiplied together in a multiplication problem. The product is the answer.

Directions: Write the missing factors or products.

x5		x9		x7		x3		x1		x8	
1	5	8	72	2	14	7	21	1	1	9	72
5	25	3	27	5	35	4	12	12	12	8	64
4	20	4	36	6	42	2	6	10	10	4	32
6	30	9	81	8	56	1	3	3	3	5	40
3	15	6	54	7	49	9	27	5	5	6	48
2	10	7	63	4	28	2	6	7	7	7	56
7	35	2	18	3	21	5	15	6	6	3	24
9	45	1	9	0	0	8	24	4	4	2	16

x2		x4		x6		x10		x11		x12	
12	24	2	8	7	42	2	20	4	44	1	12
1	2	4	16	6	36	3	30	7	77	2	24
11	22	6	24	5	30	9	90	9	99	3	36
2	4	8	32	4	24	5	50	10	110	4	48
10	20	1	4	3	18	6	60	5	55	5	60
3	6	3	12	2	12	3	30	6	66	6	72
9	18	5	20	1	6	8	80	7	77	7	84
4	8	7	28	0	0	9	90	8	88	8	96

156 Multiplication Mania
MATH

Multiplication is a short way to find the sum of adding the same number a certain amount of times, such as 7 x 4 = 28 instead of 7 + 7 + 7 + 7 = 28.

Directions: Multiply as quickly and as accurately as you can.

4 x7 = 28	7 x6 = 42	0 x8 = 0	7 x2 = 14	9 x5 = 45	1 x5 = 5
8 x3 = 24	7 x1 = 7	4 x2 = 8	9 x6 = 54	8 x5 = 40	6 x7 = 42
3 x5 = 15	7 x8 = 56	3 x9 = 27	5 x6 = 30	9 x9 = 81	7 x5 = 35
			3 x6 = 18	2 x8 = 16	8 x6 = 48
				0 x7 = 0	3 x3 = 9

How quickly did you complete this page? _____

Don't Count Your Eggs— Multiply! 157
MATH

Follow the steps for multiplying a one-digit number by a two-digit number using regrouping.

Example:

Step 1: Multiply the ones. Regroup.
```
 2
54
x 7
 8
```

Step 2: Multiply the tens. Add two tens.
```
  2
 54
x 7
378
```

Directions: Multiply.

27 x3 = 81	63 x4 = 252	52 x5 = 260	91 x9 = 819	45 x7 = 315
64 x5 = 320	76 x3 = 228	93 x6 = 558	87 x4 = 348	66 x7 = 462
		47 x8 = 376	64 x9 = 576	51 x8 = 408

The chickens on the Boudreaux farm produce 48 dozen eggs each day. How many dozen eggs do they produce in 7 days? **336**

158 Dairy Delights
MATH

Follow the steps for multiplying a two-digit number by a two-digit number using regrouping.

Example:

Step 1: Multiply the ones. Regroup.
```
  2
 63
x68
504
```

Step 2: Multiply the tens. Regroup. Add.
```
   1
  63
 x68
 504
+3,780
4,284
```

Directions: Multiply.

12 x55 = 660	27 x15 = 405	65 x27 = 1,755	19 x39 = 741	99 x13 = 1,287
43 x26 = 1,118	38 x17 = 646	53 x86 = 4,558	47 x72 = 3,384	57 x62 = 1,584
27 x54 = 1,458	93 x45 = 4,185	64 x16 = 1,024	53 x23 = 1,219	

The Polanski farm has 24 cows that each produce 52 quarts of milk a day. How many quarts are produced each day altogether? **1,248 quarts**

At the Pumpkin Patch
159

MATH

Directions: Multiply. Regroup when needed.

Example:

```
    563
   x248
  4,504
 22,520
+112,600
 139,624
```

Hint: When Multiplying by the tens, start writing the number in the tens place. When multiplying by the hundreds, start in the hundreds place.

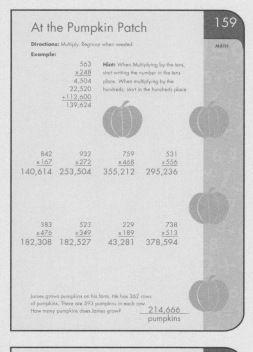

842	932	759	531
x167	x272	x468	x556
140,614	253,504	355,212	295,236

383	523	229	738
x476	x349	x189	x513
182,308	182,527	43,281	378,594

James grows pumpkins on his farm. He has 362 rows of pumpkins. There are 593 pumpkins in each row. How many pumpkins does James grow?   __214,666__ pumpkins

Caterpillar Crawl
160

MATH

Division is a way to find out how many times one number is contained in another number. For example, 28 ÷ 7 = 4 means that there are 4 groups of 7 in 28.

Division problems can be written two ways: 36 ÷ 6 = 6 or 6)36

These are the parts of a division problem:

dividend → 36 ÷ 6 = 6 ← quotient
divisor

6 ← quotient
divisor → 6)36 ← dividend

Directions: Divide.

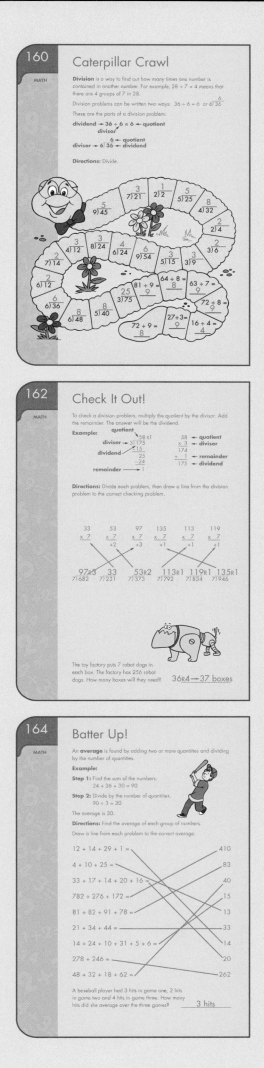

Leftovers
161

MATH

Sometimes groups of objects or numbers cannot be divided into equal groups. The **remainder** is the number left over in the quotient of a division problem. The remainder must be smaller than the divisor.

Example:

Divide 18 butterflies into groups of 5. You have 3 equal groups, with 3 butterflies left over.

18 ÷ 5 = 3 R3

or

```
   3 R3
5)18
  -15
   3
```

Directions: Divide. Some problems may have remainders.

9 R3	9 R2	3 R1	7	6 R4
9)84	7)65	8)25	5)35	5)34

6 R1	9 R2	1 R3	4	4 R5
4)25	6)56	4)7	4)16	8)37

3 R6	2 R1	2	9 R1	2 R1
7)27	2)5	2)4	8)73	4)9

5 R1	3 R2	1 R1	3 R1	5
9)46	5)17	2)3	4)13	5)25

Check It Out!
162

MATH

To check a division problem, multiply the quotient by the divisor. Add the remainder. The answer will be the dividend.

Example:

```
          quotient
        58 R1            58 ← quotient
divisor → 3)175          x 3 ← divisor
dividend   -15          174
            25          + 1 ← remainder
           -24          175 ← dividend
remainder → 1
```

Directions: Divide each problem, then draw a line from the division problem to the correct checking problem.

33	53	97	135	113	119
x 7	x 7	x 7	x 7	x 7	x 7
+2	+3	+1	+1	+1	+1

97 R3	33	53 R2	113 R1	119 R1	135 R1
7)682	7)231	7)373	7)792	7)834	7)946

The toy factory puts 7 robot dogs in each box. The factory has 256 robot dogs. How many boxes will they need?   36 R4 → __37 boxes__

The Drive to Divide
163

MATH

Directions: Divide. Then, check each answer on another sheet of paper by multiplying it by the divisor and adding the remainder.

Example:

```
    2              21 R4          Check:
12)256         12)256            21
   -24            -24           x12
    1              16            42
                  -12          +210
                   4            252
                               + 4
                               256
```

32 R16	11 R22	12 R10	16 R2	12 R19
27)880	81)913	65)790	42)674	67)823

13 R41	13 R41	19 R8	18	20 R12
72)977	54)743	45)863	24)432	18)372

6 R7	10 R48	12 R12	16 R11	13 R16
28)175	49)538	77)936	37)603	63)835

The Allen farm has 882 chickens. The chickens are kept in 21 coops. How many chickens are there in each coop?   __42 chickens__

Batter Up!
164

MATH

An **average** is found by adding two or more quantities and dividing by the number of quantities.

Example:

Step 1: Find the sum of the numbers.
24 + 36 + 30 = 90

Step 2: Divide by the number of quantities.
90 ÷ 3 = 30

The average is 30.

Directions: Find the average of each group of numbers. Draw a line from each problem to the correct average.

12 + 14 + 29 + 1 =	410
4 + 10 + 25 =	83
33 + 17 + 14 + 20 + 16 =	40
782 + 276 + 172 =	15
81 + 82 + 91 + 78 =	13
21 + 34 + 44 =	33
14 + 24 + 10 + 31 + 5 + 6 =	14
278 + 246 =	20
48 + 32 + 18 + 62 =	262

A baseball player had 3 hits in game one, 2 hits in game two and 4 hits in game three. How many hits did she average over the three games?   __3 hits__

250

ANSWER KEY

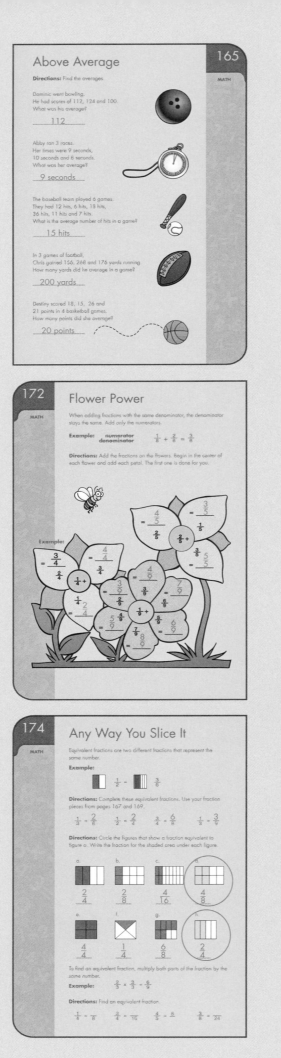

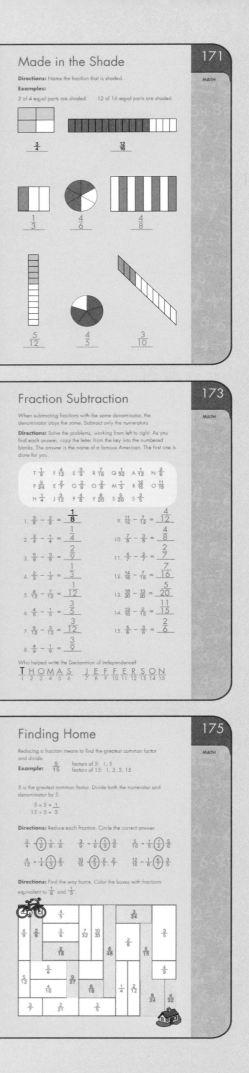

Above Average — 165

Directions: Find the averages.

Dominic went bowling. He had scores of 112, 124 and 100. What was his average?

112

Abby ran 3 races. Her times were 9 seconds, 10 seconds and 6 seconds. What was her average?

9 seconds

The baseball team played 6 games. They had 12 hits, 6 hits, 18 hits, 36 hits, 11 hits and 7 hits. What is the average number of hits in a game?

15 hits

In 3 games of football, Chris gained 156, 268 and 176 yards running. How many yards did he average in a game?

200 yards

Destiny scored 18, 15, 26 and 21 points in 4 basketball games. How many points did she average?

20 points

Made in the Shade — 171

Directions: Name the fraction that is shaded.

Examples:

3 of 4 equal parts are shaded.   12 of 16 equal parts are shaded.

$\frac{3}{4}$ $\frac{12}{16}$

$\frac{1}{3}$ $\frac{4}{6}$ $\frac{4}{8}$

$\frac{5}{12}$ $\frac{4}{5}$ $\frac{3}{10}$

172 — Flower Power

When adding fractions with the same denominator, the denominator stays the same. Add only the numerators.

Example: $\frac{\text{numerator}}{\text{denominator}}$ $\frac{1}{8} + \frac{2}{8} = \frac{3}{8}$

Directions: Add the fractions on the flowers. Begin in the center of each flower and add each petal. The first one is done for you.

Fraction Subtraction — 173

When subtracting fractions with the same denominator, the denominator stays the same. Subtract only the numerators.

Directions: Solve the problems, working from left to right. As you find each answer, copy the letter from the key into the numbered blanks. The answer is the name of a famous American. The first one is done for you.

1. $\frac{3}{8} - \frac{2}{8} = \frac{1}{8}$ 9. $\frac{11}{12} - \frac{7}{12} = \frac{4}{12}$
2. $\frac{2}{4} - \frac{1}{4} = \frac{1}{4}$ 10. $\frac{7}{8} - \frac{3}{8} = \frac{4}{8}$
3. $\frac{5}{9} - \frac{3}{9} = \frac{2}{9}$ 11. $\frac{4}{7} - \frac{2}{7} = \frac{2}{7}$
4. $\frac{2}{3} - \frac{1}{3} = \frac{1}{3}$ 12. $\frac{14}{16} - \frac{7}{16} = \frac{7}{16}$
5. $\frac{8}{12} - \frac{7}{12} = \frac{1}{12}$ 13. $\frac{16}{20} - \frac{11}{20} = \frac{5}{20}$
6. $\frac{4}{5} - \frac{1}{5} = \frac{3}{5}$ 14. $\frac{13}{15} - \frac{2}{15} = \frac{11}{15}$
7. $\frac{6}{12} - \frac{3}{12} = \frac{3}{12}$ 15. $\frac{5}{6} - \frac{3}{6} = \frac{2}{6}$
8. $\frac{4}{9} - \frac{1}{9} = \frac{3}{9}$

Who helped write the Declaration of Independence?

T H O M A S   J E F F E R S O N

174 — Any Way You Slice It

Equivalent fractions are two different fractions that represent the same number.

Example: $\frac{1}{2}$ $\frac{3}{6}$

Directions: Complete these equivalent fractions. Use your fraction pieces from pages 167 and 169.

$\frac{1}{3} = \frac{2}{6}$ $\frac{1}{2} = \frac{2}{4}$ $\frac{3}{4} = \frac{6}{8}$ $\frac{1}{3} = \frac{3}{9}$

Directions: Circle the figures that show a fraction equivalent to figure a. Write the fraction for the shaded area under each figure.

a. $\frac{2}{4}$ b. $\frac{2}{8}$ c. $\frac{4}{16}$ d. $\frac{4}{8}$

e. $\frac{4}{4}$ f. $\frac{1}{4}$ g. $\frac{6}{8}$ h. $\frac{2}{4}$

To find an equivalent fraction, multiply both parts of the fraction by the same number.

Example: $\frac{2}{3} \times \frac{3}{3} = \frac{6}{9}$

Directions: Find an equivalent fraction.

$\frac{1}{4} = \frac{}{8}$ $\frac{3}{4} = \frac{}{16}$ $\frac{4}{5} = \frac{}{6}$ $\frac{3}{8} = \frac{}{24}$

Finding Home — 175

Reducing a fraction means to find the greatest common factor and divide.

Example: $\frac{5}{15}$ factors of 5: 1, 5   factors of 15: 1, 3, 5, 15

5 is the greatest common factor. Divide both the numerator and denominator by 5.

$5 \div 5 = 1$
$15 \div 5 = 3$

Directions: Reduce each fraction. Circle the correct answer.

$\frac{2}{4} = \frac{1}{2}$ $\frac{1}{6}$ $\frac{3}{9} = \frac{1}{3}$ $\frac{1}{2}$ $\frac{5}{10} = \frac{1}{5}$ $\frac{1}{2}$

$\frac{4}{12} = \frac{1}{3}$ $\frac{2}{3}$ $\frac{10}{15} = \frac{3}{5}$ $\frac{2}{7}$ $\frac{4}{7} = \frac{1}{8}$ $\frac{9}{5}$

Directions: Find the way home. Color the boxes with fractions equivalent to $\frac{1}{6}$ and $\frac{1}{3}$.

176 — Mix It up!

A mixed number is a number written as a whole number and a fraction, such as $6\frac{1}{8}$.

To change a fraction into a mixed number, divide the denominator (bottom number) into the numerator (top number). Write the remainder over the denominator.

Example: $\frac{14}{6} = 2\frac{2}{6}$

Example: $3\frac{1}{7} = \frac{22}{7}$ $(7 \times 3) + 1 = \frac{22}{7}$

To change a mixed number into a fraction, multiply the denominator by the whole number, add the numerator and write it on top of the denominator.

Directions: Write each fraction as a mixed number. Write each mixed number as a fraction.

$\frac{21}{6} = 3\frac{3}{6}$ $\frac{24}{5} = 4\frac{4}{5}$ $\frac{10}{3} = 3\frac{1}{3}$ $\frac{21}{4} = 5\frac{1}{4}$

$\frac{11}{6} = 1\frac{5}{6}$ $\frac{13}{4} = 3\frac{1}{4}$ $\frac{12}{5} = 2\frac{2}{5}$ $\frac{10}{9} = 1\frac{1}{9}$

$4\frac{3}{8} = \frac{35}{8}$ $2\frac{1}{3} = \frac{7}{3}$ $4\frac{3}{5} = \frac{23}{5}$ $3\frac{4}{6} = \frac{22}{6}$

$7\frac{1}{4} = \frac{29}{4}$ $2\frac{3}{5} = \frac{13}{5}$ $7\frac{1}{2} = \frac{15}{2}$ $6\frac{5}{7} = \frac{47}{7}$

$\frac{11}{8} = 1\frac{3}{8}$ $\frac{21}{4} = 5\frac{1}{4}$ $\frac{33}{5} = 6\frac{3}{5}$ $\frac{13}{6} = 2\frac{1}{6}$

177 — Mix and Match

When adding mixed numbers, add the fractions first, then the whole numbers.

Examples:
$9\frac{1}{3}$
$+3\frac{1}{3}$
$12\frac{2}{3}$

$2\frac{3}{6}$
$+1\frac{1}{6}$
$3\frac{4}{6}$

Directions: Add the number in the center to the number in each surrounding section.

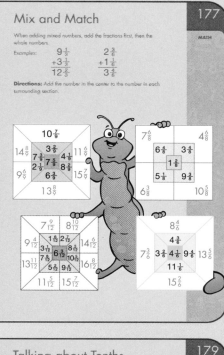

178 — Mixed Up Math

When subtracting mixed numbers, subtract the fractions first, then the whole numbers.

Directions: Subtract the mixed numbers. The first one is done for you.

$7\frac{3}{8}$ $4\frac{5}{6}$ $4\frac{1}{2}$ $7\frac{5}{8}$ $6\frac{6}{8}$
$-4\frac{2}{8}$ $-3\frac{1}{6}$ -3 $-6\frac{3}{8}$ $-1\frac{1}{8}$
$3\frac{1}{8}$ $1\frac{4}{6}$ $1\frac{1}{2}$ $1\frac{2}{8}$ $5\frac{5}{8}$

$5\frac{2}{3}$ $4\frac{8}{10}$ $9\frac{8}{9}$ $7\frac{2}{3}$ $7\frac{2}{3}$
$-3\frac{1}{3}$ $-3\frac{3}{10}$ $-4\frac{3}{9}$ $-6\frac{1}{3}$ -5
$2\frac{1}{3}$ $1\frac{5}{10}$ $5\frac{5}{9}$ $1\frac{1}{3}$ $2\frac{2}{3}$

$4\frac{7}{9}$ $6\frac{7}{8}$ $6\frac{3}{4}$ $5\frac{6}{7}$ $7\frac{6}{7}$
-2 $-5\frac{3}{8}$ $-3\frac{1}{4}$ $-3\frac{1}{7}$ $-2\frac{4}{7}$
$2\frac{7}{9}$ $1\frac{4}{8}$ $3\frac{2}{4}$ $2\frac{5}{7}$ $5\frac{2}{7}$

Tessa needs $1\frac{6}{8}$ yards of cloth to make a dress. She has $4\frac{8}{8}$ yards. How much cloth will be left over? $3\frac{2}{8}$

179 — Talking about Tenths

When a figure is divided into 10 equal parts, the parts are called tenths. Tenths can be written two ways—as a fraction or a decimal. A decimal is a number with one or more places to the right of a decimal point, such as 6.5 or 2.25. A decimal point is the dot between the ones place and the tenths place.

Examples:

ones	tenths
0	3

$\frac{3}{10}$ or 0.3 of the square is shaded. $\frac{6}{10}$ 0.6

Directions: Write the decimal and fraction for the shaded parts of the following figures.

$\frac{3}{10}$ 0.3 $\frac{9}{10}$ 0.9

$\frac{4}{10}$ 0.4 $1\frac{5}{10}$ 1.5

$1\frac{8}{10}$ 1.8 $\frac{8}{10}$ 0.8

180 — Fill It Up!

Directions: Add or subtract. Remember to include the decimal point in your answers.

Example: $1\frac{3}{10} = 1.3$
$1\frac{6}{10} = 1.6$

1.3
$+1.6$
2.9

8.1 4.1 0.5 7.6 7.2
$+1.7$ $+6.2$ -6.5 -2.6 -2.6
9.8 10.3 2.1 1.1 4.6

        7.8 16.5 6.4
        -6.8 -7.3 $+5.3$
        1.0 9.2 11.7

        0.42 0.98 0.78
        $+0.35$ -0.87 -0.13
        0.77 0.11 0.65

        0.95 3.23 4.68
        -0.14 $+2.48$ -2.65
        0.81 5.71 2.03

        6.98 3.27 4.65
        $+1.40$ $+1.82$ -1.32
        8.38 5.09 3.33

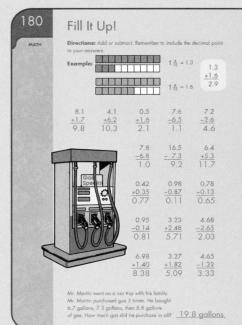

Mr. Martin went on a car trip with his family. Mr. Martin purchased gas 3 times. He bought 6.7 gallons, 7.3 gallons, then 5.8 gallons of gas. How much gas did he purchase in all?   19.8 gallons

181 — Get on Track

Directions: Add or subtract the problems. Then, fill in the circle next to the correct answer.

Example: 2.4 ○ 2.5
$+1.7$ ○ 3.1
● 4.1

2.8	○ 5.2	5.7	● 1.9
+3.4	○ 7.4	−3.8	○ 2.5
6.2	● 6.2	1.9	○ 2.9
7.6	○ 15.9	16.3	○ 25.11
+8.9	● 16.5	+ 9.8	● 26.1
16.5	○ 17.3	26.1	○ 26.01
28.6	○ 73.6	43.9	● 100.4
+43.9	● 72.5	+56.5	○ 107.4
72.5	○ 71.9	100.4	○ 101.4
12.87	○ 16.32	47.56	● 13.61
− 3.45	○ 10.31	−33.95	○ 80.41
9.42	● 9.42	13.61	○ 14.61
93.6	○ 14.8	11.57	● 22.21
−79.8	○ 15.3	+10.64	○ 1.93
13.8	● 13.8	22.21	○ 21.12
27.83	○ 14.09	106.935	○ 111.1
−14.94	● 12.89	− 95.824	○ 111.11
12.89	○ 11.97	11.111	● 11.111

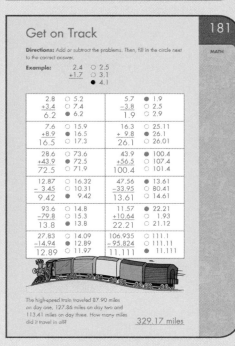

The high-speed train traveled 87.90 miles on day one, 127.86 miles on day two and 113.41 miles on day three. How many miles did it travel in all?   329.17 miles

---

182 — Inching Along
MATH

An **inch** is a unit of length in the standard system equal to $\frac{1}{12}$ of a foot. A ruler is used to measure inches.

This illustration shows a ruler measuring a 4-inch pencil, which can be written as 4" or 4 in.

MATH RULES

inch

Directions: Use a ruler to measure each object to the nearest inch.

1. The length of your foot _____
2. The width of your hand _____
3. The length of this page _____
4. **Answers will vary**
5. The length of a large paper clip _____
6. The length of your toothbrush _____
7. The length of a comb _____
8. The height of a juice glass _____

---

183 — Rulers Rule
MATH

An inch is divided into smaller units, or fractions of an inch.

Example: This stick of gum is $2\frac{1}{2}$ inches long.

Chewing Gum

Directions: Use a ruler to measure each line to the nearest quarter of an inch. The first one is done for you.

1. $\frac{3}{4}$ inch ____
2. $1\frac{1}{2}$ inches _____
3. $2\frac{1}{4}$ inches _____
4. $3\frac{3}{4}$ inches _____
5. $3\frac{1}{2}$ inches _____
6. $1\frac{3}{4}$ inches _____
7. $2\frac{1}{2}$ inches _____

---

184 — How Do You Measure Up?
MATH

Directions: Choose the measure of distance you would use for each object.

1 foot = 12 inches
1 yard = 3 feet
1 mile = 1,760 yards or 5,280 feet

inches

miles

yards

inches

yards

yards

miles

---

185 — Make It Metric
MATH

In the metric system, there are three units of linear measurement: centimeter (cm), meter (m), and kilometer (km).

Centimeters (cm) are used to measure the lengths of small to medium-sized objects. **Meters (m)** measure the lengths of larger objects, such as the width of a swimming pool or height of a tree (100 cm = 1 meter). **Kilometers (km)** measure long distances, such as the distance from Cleveland to Cincinnati or the width of the Atlantic Ocean (1,000 m = 1 km).

Directions: Write whether you would use cm, m, or km to measure each object.

km
Chicago
New York City

cm   m

cm

m   km

cm   m   m

---

186 — Figure It Out
MATH

Perimeter is the distance around a figure. It is found by adding the lengths of the sides. **Area** is the number of square units needed to cover a region. The area is found by adding the number of square units. A unit can be any unit of measure. Most often, inches, feet, or yards are used.

Directions: Find the perimeter and area for each figure. The first one is done for you.

☐ = 1 square unit

Perimeter = **18** units
Area = **17** sq. units

Perimeter = **36** units
Area = **40** sq. units

Perimeter = **24** units
Area = **14** sq. units

Perimeter = **42** units
Area = **46** sq. units

Perimeter = **28** units
Area = **32** sq. units

Perimeter = **42** units
Area = **65** sq. units

---

187 — Inside, Outside, All Around
MATH

Area is also calculated by multiplying the length times the width of a square or rectangular figure. Use the formula: $A = l \times w$.

Directions: Calculate the perimeter of each figure.

2 ft.
2 ft.   2 ft.
2 ft.   2 ft.
2 ft.
12 ft.

1"   1"
1"   1"
1"
5 in.

1 ft.   1 ft.
1 ft.   1 ft.
1 ft.   1 ft.
1 ft.   1 ft.
8 ft.

Directions: Calculate the area of each figure.

5 ft.
3 ft.
15 square ft.

1 yd.
4 yd.
4 square yd.

24 ft.
20 ft.
480 square ft.

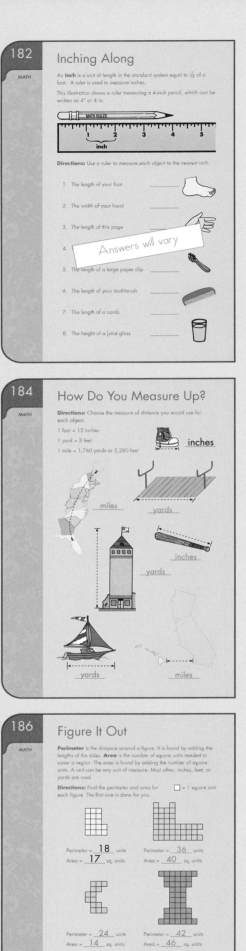

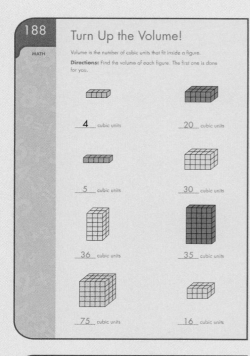

188

MATH

Turn Up the Volume!

Volume is the number of cubic units that fit inside a figure.

Directions: Find the volume of each figure. The first one is done for you.

4 cubic units

20 cubic units

5 cubic units

30 cubic units

36 cubic units

35 cubic units

75 cubic units

16 cubic units

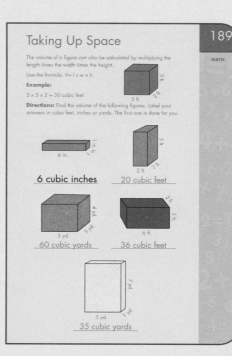

189

MATH

Taking Up Space

The volume of a figure can also be calculated by multiplying the length times the width times the height.

Use the formula: V = l x w x h.

Example:

$3 \times 5 \times 2 = 30$ cubic feet.

Directions: Find the volume of the following figures. Label your answers in cubic feet, inches or yards. The first one is done for you.

6 cubic inches

20 cubic feet

60 cubic yards

36 cubic feet

35 cubic yards

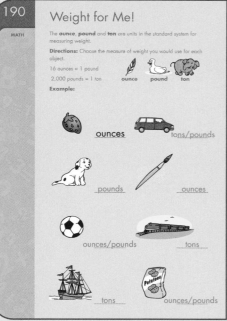

190

MATH

Weight for Me!

The **ounce**, **pound** and **ton** are units in the standard system for measuring weight.

Directions: Choose the measure of weight you would use for each object.

16 ounces = 1 pound

2,000 pounds = 1 ton   **ounce   pound   ton**

Example:

ounces   **tons/pounds**

pounds   **ounces**

ounces/pounds   **tons**

tons   **ounces/pounds**

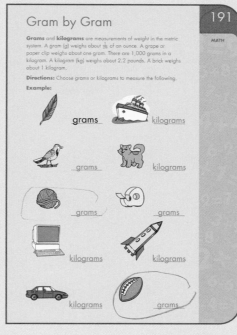

191

MATH

Gram by Gram

Grams and **kilograms** are measurements of weight in the metric system. A gram (g) weighs about $\frac{1}{28}$ of an ounce. A grape or paper clip weighs about one gram. There are 1,000 grams in a kilogram. A kilogram (kg) weighs about 2.2 pounds. A brick weighs about 1 kilogram.

Directions: Choose grams or kilograms to measure the following.

Example:

grams   **kilograms**

grams   **kilograms**

grams   **grams**

kilograms   **kilograms**

kilograms   **grams**

192

MATH

Counting Quarts

The **cup**, **pint**, **quart** and **gallon** are units in the standard system for measuring liquids.

Directions: Gather the following materials: 2 dish tubs, one filled with water, sand or rice; measuring cups; pint container; quart container; gallon container. Then, answer the questions and complete the chart.

1. Use the cup measure to pour water, sand or rice into the pint container. How many cups did it take?

   2 cups = 1 pint

2. Use the cup measure to find out how many cups are in a quart and a gallon.

   4 cups = 1 quart

   16 cups = 1 gallon

3. Use the pint container to pour water, sand or rice into the quart container. How many pints are in a quart?

   2 pints = 1 quart

4. How many pints does it take to fill a gallon?

   8 pints = 1 gallon

5. Use the quart measure to find out how many quarts are in a gallon.

   4 quarts = 1 gallon

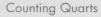

Measurement Chart

2 cups = 1 pint

4 cups = 1 quart

16 cups = 1 gallon

2 pints = 1 quart

8 pints = 1 gallon

4 quarts = 1 gallon

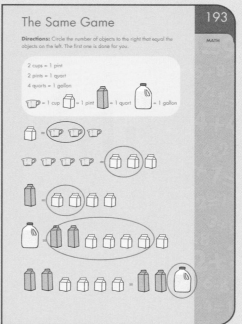

193

MATH

The Same Game

Directions: Circle the number of objects to the right that equal the objects on the left. The first one is done for you.

2 cups = 1 pint
2 pints = 1 quart
4 quarts = 1 gallon

= 1 cup   = 1 pint   = 1 quart   = 1 gallon

194 Liter Reader

Liters and **milliliters** are measurements of liquid in the metric system. A milliliter (mL) equals 0.001 liter or 0.03 fluid ounces. A drop of water equals about 1 milliliter. Liters (L) measure large amounts of liquid. There are 1,000 milliliters in a liter. One liter measures 1.06 quarts. Soft drinks are often sold in 2-liter bottles.

Directions: Choose milliliters or liters to measure these liquids.

Example:

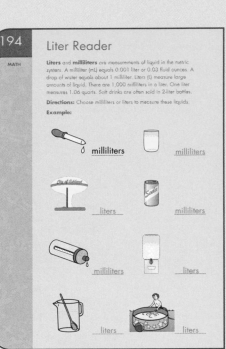

milliliters — milliliters
liters — milliliters
milliliters — liters
liters — liters

195 Weigh In

Directions: Choose grams (g) or kilograms (kg) to weigh the following objects. The first one is done for you.

rhinoceros **kg** — person **kg**
dime **g** — airplane **kg**
bucket of wet sand **kg** — spider **g**
eyeglasses **g** — pair of scissors **g**

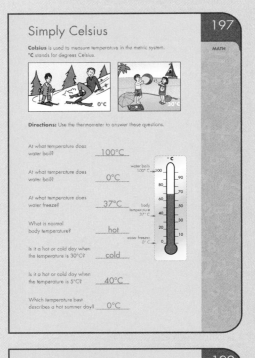

Directions: Choose milliliters (mL) or liters (L) to measure the liquids in the following containers. The first one is done for you.

swimming pool **L** — baby bottle **mL**
small juice glass **mL** — teapot **mL**
gasoline tank **L** — outdoor fountain **L**
test tube **mL** — ink pen **mL**

196 Focus on Fahrenheit

Fahrenheit is used to measure temperature in the standard system. °F stands for degrees Fahrenheit.

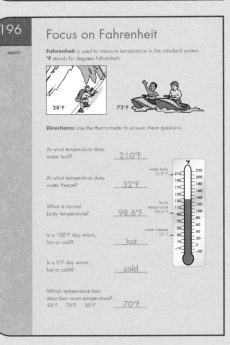

28°F — 72°F

Directions: Use the thermometer to answer these questions.

At what temperature does water boil? **210°F**
At what temperature does water freeze? **32°F**
What is normal body temperature? **98.6°F**
Is a 100°F day warm, hot or cold? **hot**
Is a 0°F day warm, hot or cold? **cold**
Which temperature best describes room temperature? 58°F 70°F 80°F **70°F**

197 Simply Celsius

Celsius is used to measure temperature in the metric system. °C stands for degrees Celsius.

0°C

Directions: Use the thermometer to answer these questions.

At what temperature does water boil? **100°C**
At what temperature does water boil? **0°C**
At what temperature does water freeze? **37°C**
What is normal body temperature? **hot**
Is it a hot or cold day when the temperature is 30°C? **cold**
Is it a hot or cold day when the temperature is 5°C? **40°C**
Which temperature best describes a hot summer day? **0°C**

198 Get Organized!

A **graph** is a drawing that shows information about changes in numbers.
Directions: Answer the questions by reading the graphs.

Bar Graph

Video Rentals by Month

How many videos did the store rent in June? **80 videos**
In which month did the store rent the fewest videos? **May**
How many videos did the store rent for all 4 months? **190 videos**

Line Graph

CD's Sold by Days of Week

On which days did the store sell the fewest CD's? **Tuesday and Sunday**
How many CD's did the store sell in 1 week? **180 CD's**

199 A Dot Marks the Spot

An **ordered pair** is a pair of numbers used to locate a point.
Example: (8, 3)

Step 1: Count across to line 8 on the graph.
Step 2: Count up to line 3 on the graph.
Step 3: Draw a dot to mark the spot.

Directions: Map the following spots on the grid using ordered pairs.

(4, 7) (9, 10) (2, 1) (5, 6) (2, 2) (1, 5) (7, 4) (3, 8)

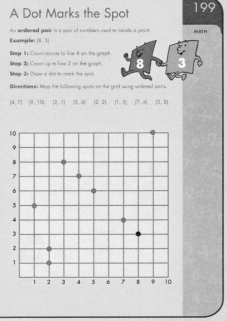

200 — Picture a Polygon

MATH

A **polygon** is a closed figure with three or more sides.

Examples:

triangle — 3 sides
square — 4 equal sides
rectangle — 4 sides

pentagon — 5 sides
hexagon — 6 sides
octagon — 8 sides

Directions: Identify the polygons.

octagon   rectangle

square   hexagon

pentagon   triangle

201 — Get in Line!

MATH

A **line segment** has two end points.

A ——— B   Write: $\overrightarrow{AB}$

A **line** has no end points and goes on in both directions.

C ——— D   Write: $\overleftrightarrow{CD}$

A **ray** is part of a line and goes on in one direction. It has one end point.

E ——— F   Write: $\overrightarrow{EF}$

Directions: Identify each of the following as a line, line segment, or ray.

line segment   ray

line   ray

line   line

202 — Angle Wrangler

MATH

The point at which two line segments meet is called an **angle**. There are three types of angles — right, acute and obtuse.

A **right angle** is formed when the two lines meet at 90°.

An **acute angle** is formed when the two lines meet at less than 90°.

An **obtuse angle** is formed when the two lines meet at greater than 90°.

Angles can be measured with a protractor or index card. With a protractor, align the bottom edge of the angle with the bottom of the protractor, with the angle point at the circle of the protractor. Note the direction of the other ray and the number of degrees of the angle.

right   acute   obtuse

Place the corner of an index card in the corner of the angle. If the edges line up with the card, it is a right angle. If not, the angle is acute or obtuse.

right   acute   obtuse

Directions: Use a protractor or index card to identify the following angles as right, obtuse or acute.

acute   right   acute

obtuse   right   acute

203 — Send in the Circles

MATH

A **circle** is a round figure. It is named by its center. A **radius** is a line segment from the center of a circle to any point on the circle. A **diameter** is a line segment with both end points on the circle. The diameter always passes through the center of the circle.

Directions: Name the radius, diameter and circle.

Example:

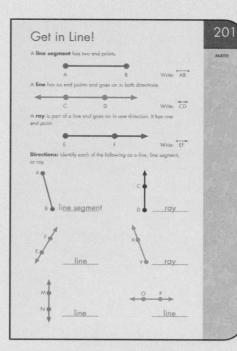

Circle — A
Radius — AB
Diameter — DC

Circle — X
Radius — XY
Diameter — ZW

Circle — B
Radius — BA
Diameter — DC

204 — Heads or Tails

MATH

One thinking skill to get your brain in gear is figuring probability. **Probability** is the likelihood or chance that something will happen. Probability is expressed and written as a ratio.

The probability of tossing heads or tails on a coin is one in two (1:2).

The probability of rolling any number on a die is one in six (1:6).

The probability of getting a red on this spinner is two in four (2:4).

The probability of drawing an ace from a deck of cards is four in fifty-two (4:52).

Directions: Write the probability ratios to answer these questions.

1. There are 26 letters in the alphabet. What is the probability of drawing any letter from a set of alphabet cards?   **1:26**

2. Five of the 26 alphabet letters are vowels. What is the probability of drawing a vowel from the alphabet cards?   **5:26**

3. Matt takes 10 shots at the basketball hoop. Six of his shots are baskets. What is the probability of Matt's next shot being a basket?   **6:10**

4. A box contains 10 marbles: 2 white, 3 green, 1 red, 2 orange and 2 blue. What is the probability of pulling a green marble from the box?   **3:10**
   A red marble?   **1:10**

5. What is the probability of pulling a marble that is not blue?   **8:10**

205 — How Does Your Garden Grow?

MATH

Grace is planting a garden. The garden will be a semi-circle in shape and have two rows. The first row will have three sections and the back row will have six sections. Grace needs to decide how many plants she can put in each section of her garden.

She wants the total number of plants in the back row to be double the total number of plants in front.

Directions: Help Grace finish her garden plan by using the numbers 1, 2, 3, 4, 5, 6, 7, 8, and 9. Each number may only be used once. Three numbers have been written in place for you.

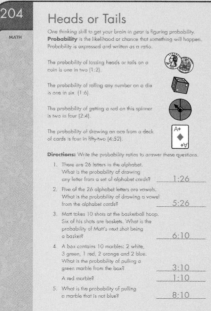

4 plants   6 plants
2 plants   8 plants
7 plants
1 plants   3 plants   5 plants   9 plants

Directions: Arrange the digits 1 through 9 in the circles on the triangle so the numbers on each of the sides add up to 17.

3
5   4
7   9
2 — 8 — 6 — 1

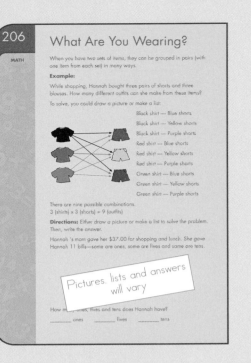

What Are You Wearing?

206

MATH

When you have two sets of items, they can be grouped in pairs (with one item from each set) in many ways.

Example:

While shopping, Hannah bought three pairs of shorts and three blouses. How many different outfits can she make from these items?

To solve, you could draw a picture or make a list:

Black shirt — Blue shorts
Black shirt — Yellow shorts
Black shirt — Purple shorts
Red shirt — Blue shorts
Red shirt — Yellow shorts
Red shirt — Purple shorts
Green shirt — Blue shorts
Green shirt — Yellow shorts
Green shirt — Purple shorts

There are nine possible combinations.
3 (shirts) x 3 (shorts) = 9 (outfits)

Directions: Either draw a picture or make a list to solve the problem. Then, write the answer.

Hannah 's mom gave her $37.00 for shopping and lunch. She gave Hannah 11 bills—some are ones, some are fives and some are tens.

Pictures, lists and answers will vary

How many ones, fives and tens does Hannah have?

_____ ones   _____ fives   _____ tens

I just want to do
a quick review
with you on

decimal place
~~new~~ value. OK?